Pathways to Thinking: Strategies for Developing Independent Learners K–8

Expanded Professional Version

Pathways to Thinking: Strategies for Developing Independent Learners K–8

Expanded Professional Version

by Elinor Parry Ross

Christopher-Gordon Publishers, Inc.
Norwood, MA

Credits

Every effort has been made to contact copyright holders for permission to reproduce borrowed material where necessary. We apologize for any oversights and would be happy to rectify them in future printings.

Christopher-Gordon Publishers, Inc.
1502 Providence Highway, Suite 12
Norwood, MA 02062
Tel: 781-762-5577

10 9 8 7 6 5 4 3 2 1   02 01 00 99 98 97

ISBN: 0-926842-69-2

Contents

Introduction

As you begin your journey along the pathways to thinking, recall the familiar views of Jean Piaget and Lev Vygotsky on the ways in which children learn language and thought. While still in familiar territory, take another look at Benjamin Bloom's levels of cognition, as well as the views of others noted for their contributions to thinking. Now consider ideas about diverse students whose ways of knowing differ, and move into less familiar territory to look at Howard Gardner's theory of multiple intelligences. As you do so, take with you your prior knowledge about thinking and an awareness of the differences among the students you teach.

As you head out, make sure that you have the necessary equipment and that you become comfortable with your fellow travelers. Learn to cooperate, trust, and take risks as you deepen your relationships with them. In order to learn all you can, ask questions and encourage others to question you so that you may appreciate each other and learn together. In the evenings as you rest, reflect on what the day has brought, write your thoughts in a journal, and find something good to read before falling asleep.

You will find that there are many pathways that lead to your destination, and you may want to try them all. Being naturally curious, you will want to check out your route by sharing the information you already have and by reading to find out more. Along one pathway, you discover that books not only give you information but also cause you to appreciate and enjoy life. Along another pathway, you organize and analyze your journey with charts, maps, and graphs of the remaining pathways and their distances. Technology leads you down yet another pathway, opening new possibilities for using your mind. Near the journey's end, take time to consider your travels—what you have learned from them and what they may mean to you in the future.

As you reach your destination, you realize that your pathways have helped you discover useful strategies for coping with the problems and issues that you face. Your luggage contains not only what you brought with you but also many souvenirs to remind you of the pathways you traveled.

The above analogy parallels the organization of this book on creating a thinking classroom. Learning how to think is essential for children to grow into responsible citizens and contribute to society. Many students, however, learn only to memorize and repeat back what teachers say; they cannot think for themselves. Schools need curricula that support a variety of thinking strategies as students read, write, study content-area subjects, and learn to evaluate and manage what they do.

Most thinking situations should arise from the curiosity and wonder of the children themselves—in response to their ideas and their needs to investigate, explore, and discover. Situations occur naturally that require the use of thinking processes as students develop story maps from reading, investigate topics for theme studies, verbalize math problems in order to find solutions, work through the writing process, and deal with interpersonal situations.

In most cases teachers do not have to teach these processes directly, but can integrate them naturally as the need and opportunities arise. Direct teaching of certain strategies, however, helps children understand how to use them for themselves. For instance, children learn how to read and think metacognitively by observing a teacher's demonstration of thinking aloud while reading a short selection.

Most thinking strategies are not subject-specific. Reflection, for example, can be used across the curriculum as children learn to think back on the significance of their experiences. Problem solving may occur in any situation, in or out of school, but the procedure may vary somewhat in different situations. Metaphor, on the other hand, is most likely taught when children observe its use in literature, watch for other examples, and then weave it into their own writing.

May your journey through this book be a rewarding one, and may you find ideas that will help your children become eager, proficient thinkers.

Acknowledgements

I appreciate the cooperation of the people at Christopher-Gordon, particularly Sue Canavan, Laurie Maker, and Jacob Schulz, who have worked with me on writing this book. The suggestions from the reviewers, Dr. Bill Harp, Polly Tafrate, Cynthia Jones, Elizabeth Fielding, and Patty Norman were helpful as I developed the manuscript, made revisions, and added finishing touches.

Both children and teachers have contributed to this book by responding to my questions and submitting samples of work. Early on, I went into classrooms and asked children in grades three through six to react to questions about thinking. Most children thoughtfully considered the questions and wrote honest responses, even though many had not thought about such things before. I selected a sampling of their views and placed them at the beginning of each section of this book. The teachers who responded to my questions about thinking were in my graduate class, and I appreciate their taking the time to consider appropriate answers. Selected answers to their questions appear at the beginning of each chapter.

As is frequently the case when writing a book about how children learn, nothing clarifies a point as well as samples of children's own work. Teachers designed lessons to meet my requests, helped me collect samples, and sometimes asked children to copy work over to make it more legible.

Many ideas and work samples are taken from schools I visited in Australia, where I spent a month of noninstructional leave. Many thanks go to family members there for helping me arrange school visits: Karen and Neil in Wollongong, Lois and Brent in Melbourne, and Sharon and Rob in Sale. Also, many special friends whom I have visited on more than one occasion proved to be excellent resources: Marie Emmitt, Lesley and Ken Wing Jan, and Debbie Sukarno.

To my husband, Jim, I offer thanks for putting up with my seclusion and for being a ready resource of information and common sense about things in general.

Special thanks go to Ann Peterson, who explained how she and other teachers use computer technology, and to the following students who agreed to have their work included in this book: Rebecca Boucher, Melody Caroline Boze, Rachel Fox, Angelina Frankhanel, Julie Gibbons, Corey Hinton, Jonathan Justice, Katie Mahan, Elizabeth Branch McGhee, and Felicia Shoulta.

I

Introduction to
Thinking in the Classroom

I asked the children,

"Why is it important to learn how to think?"

and the children said:

> Why is it important to learn how to think? So you can make your own desisions, and not let other people make them for you.

> To now what you want to do in the future, and kniow weather to do a right or a wrong thing.

> Because there are many problems in life you must solve. Also you must think to get anywhere in life!

> I think it is important to think so you do the right things.

It is important to learn how because you will need to have that information on thinking in the future.

It's important beacouse if you Amanda don't think about the cause and effect of things you'll never know what the result will be.

It is important to learn to think so you know how to comprehend and analyse problems you need to solve.

It will help you understand what kind of information is important and what kind is not, and it will also help you comprehend facts quicker and clearer,

So you know to make the right choices.

The children's responses give us many reasons why thinking is important: to make your own decisions, to do a right thing instead of a wrong thing, to know what to do in the future, to analyze problems, and to get anywhere in life. Yet, teachers often neglect instruction in thinking strategies because their attention is consumed by other curricular obligations.

Many educators and psychologists have contributed to our knowledge of how children learn and think, particularly Jean Piaget and Lev Vygotsky, and to our understanding of various thinking skills (e.g., John Dewey and Benjamin Bloom). Their theories have provided teachers with a conceptual framework for guiding children in the development of their thinking processes.

The great diversity among learners compels us to consider the different ways in which children think and learn. We have long been aware of student preferences in learning styles and modalities, and Howard Gardner, with his theory of multiple intelligences, has helped us understand more about nontraditional learners. When we teach, we should give students opportunities to think and respond in a variety of ways.

The chapters in this section lay the groundwork for the rest of the book. In them you will find some ideas about children's growing ability to use thought, the beliefs of a few well-known theorists, ways that thinking processes can be applied to classroom experiences, ways to begin integrating thinking strategies across the curriculum, and types of intelligence that students display.

CHAPTER 1

Overview of Thinking Strategies

When I asked the teachers,

"Why is it important for children to learn to think?"

the teachers said:

- Learning to think helps us solve problems and make decisons that we face in life.
- Many children do well in the classroom but have difficulty applying what they have learned to real life.
- Thinking children are able to figure things out on their own and make their own decisions, which creates responsible individuals.
- It enables children to be self-regulators by making their own decisions.
- It enables them to develop easier or better ways of doing things and to understand concepts and ideas.
- They will understand themselves and the world around them better.
- Adults, as well as students, must be able to make sound decisions. The foundation for that is thinking critically.
- Everything is changing so fast that just learning facts is of little use unless you are a history teacher. Children must be able to respond to an environment that is changing every day.
- Those who think can function on their own and tackle situations, get ahead, and create new ideas because they are not waiting for someone to tell them what to do.

How would you answer this question?

Concepts to watch for

- The importance of thinking strategies
- Contributions of Piaget and Vygotsky to understanding the ways in which children think and learn
- The scope of thinking skills in Bloom's taxonomy
- Views about thinking from leading theorists
- Some types of thinking strategies

Near the beginning of the year when I was teaching first grade, my students were eagerly dictating sentences for me to record on language experience charts. We read and reread the charts, and some of the children were beginning to develop sight word vocabularies.

One morning, Diana burst into the room and excitedly said, "Guess what! My daddy's newspaper has the same words that we have on our charts!" Diana had discovered a real-world application for the words we were learning together in class.

The Importance of Developing Thinking Strategies

Enabling children to think, to see connections, and to make discoveries for themselves should be a priority for teachers today. We value authentic learning situations in which children understand why learning something is important and are aware of its useful applications. We understand that children, driven by natural curiosity, become actively involved in learning by exploring and discovering what interests them. We are also coming to realize that students need a variety of thinking strategies to process information, solve problems, and make sense of what they are learning.

Knowledge is expanding so rapidly that no one can learn everything there is to know. Thus, we must not only help children acquire information; we must also help them know how and where to find it and then what to do with it. Much teaching, therefore, now emphasizes the process of learning and the use of thinking strategies rather than the mastery of discrete facts. Although we can easily forget memorized facts, thinking strategies and learning procedures become part of us.

Unfortunately, some teachers expect students to cover the material and acquire information, but they provide few opportunities for students to reflect and respond. Also, students, accustomed to finding a single correct answer, may not readily explore options to open-ended questions or find multiple solutions to problems. Thinking can be hard work!

Nevertheless, thinking strategies are well worth the time and effort to develop because of their long-term benefits. By learning various ways of thinking, students will be able to do the following:

- Make valid judgments
- Analyze situations
- Transfer learning from one area to another
- Solve problems
- Make reasonable decisions
- Create ideas
- Clarify values
- Reason intelligently
- Understand relationships
- Set and realize goals

All these processes are useful not only in school but also in life beyond the classroom.

Figure 1-1 shows some shifts in instructional practices that have occurred in recent years. Because of these new directions, instruction and practice in the use of thinking strategies is essential. Knowledge of facts and skills is still important, but students can learn them best when they are embedded in higher-order tasks and problems. When teachers use dull, irrelevant teaching strategies, students often resist learning skills. Even low-performing students, however, are likely to gain knowledge when it is presented in a vital, challenging context (Schmoker, 1996).

Thinking strategies do not exist in isolation; they cannot proceed without a base of knowledge and experience. Thinking and knowledge go hand in hand. We must have something to think about! The more we know about something, the better we are able to critique, analyze, or evaluate it. Thus, teachers should present thinking strategies within the context of imparting knowledge. Both are essential for learning.

Figure 1-1. Trends in Instructional Practice

Traditional	**Emerging**
Teacher-directed learning	Student-centered learning
Prescribed curriculum	Inquiry-based curriculum
Finding the one correct answer	Valuing different viewpoints
Mostly facts and skills	Higher-order thinking
Acquiring facts	Analyzing and interpreting facts
Extrinsic motivation	Intrinsic motivation
Accepting without question	Seeking supporting evidence
Working individually	Working collaboratively
Skill-based instruction	Discovery learning

Robert Siegler and Eric Jenkins (1989, p. 9) proposed an analogy that helps us understand the balance between thought, or learning processes, and knowledge.

A child's mind is like a workshop. This workshop contains a remarkable collection of materials (knowledge) and tools (learning processes) that can be used to make new products (rules, strategies, hypotheses, schema, causal networks, etc.) Some of the tools and materials are useful for a great many tasks. Many others are specialized for a particular purpose, but are invaluable when they are needed.

Siegler and Jenkins extend the analogy by saying that orders for products arrive constantly at the workshop. Familiar products are easy to make because they have been made before, but new products challenge the workshop by calling for different tools and materials. They add, ". . . the broader the range of products the workshop has produced in the past, the greater its potential for meeting future demands" (p. 1). As teachers, therefore, we need to make sure that children have both the tools and the materials they need to accomplish their tasks, and we need to provide them with a wide range of opportunities to use them so that they will be successful in future tasks.

What is the school's role in teaching thinking? John Goodlad (1994, p. 103) says that schools should assume only those social purposes that can readily become educational goals. "The schools should take on . . . the attributes of thought—understanding, relating, judging, integrating, reflecting, and the like—that require deliberate, systematic, and sustained attention." School should be a place, therefore, that helps children not only acquire essential information but also learn thinking strategies that will serve them well throughout their lives.

Development of Thinking Within the Child

Two highly respected psychologists, Jean Piaget and Lev Vygotsky, studied the growth of language and thought in children. They found young children to be egocentric; that is, they think about things only from their own limited perspectives. Both researchers found that as children interact with others, they move beyond egocentricity and begin to consider the views of others. Both also believed that children need to participate actively in their own learning, much of which occurs in social ▮▮▮▮▮ with peers and adults (Campbell, 1976; Dixon-Krauss, 1996).

Piaget believed that children move through four stages of cognitive development, beginning with concrete learning and continuing toward formal, abstract learning, which begins at about age twelve (Piaget, 1973). In classes where a community of inquiry exists, however, students are able to deal with abstractions long before they reach the formal stage (Wilks, 1995). Early stages satisfy children's needs at the time and create a base for the more complex strategies they will use later. Piaget found that children structure their thinking as they observe and manipulate things in their environment, before they ever learn to use language.

On the other hand, Vygotsky believed that children's use of language stimulates their cognitive development. By talking to themselves, children begin to think things through and achieve their goals. At first, children's speech is social, but it soon becomes their most important psychological tool for structuring thought (Dixon-Krauss, 1996; Vygotsky, 1986).

We shouldn't underestimate the thought processes of young children. Siegler (1991) claims that the thinking processes of young children and adults are not as different as we once believed. Infants and young children are capable of quite logical, complex thoughts at times, and adults may not always think so rationally and scientifically! Thus, there is no single age when children acquire the ability to think in certain ways, but thought processes grow increasingly complex over a long period of time.

In a similar vein, Geoff Bull (1989) believes that individuals of all ages have a desire to make sense of the world and bring it under control. Even a young child finds ways to do this. When this child enters school, however, teachers may not encourage problem solving and discovery, believing that these are suitable only for older, more mature children.

Actually, children amaze us with how quickly they learn to think for themselves. They learn how to get what they want, how to solve problems, and how to put words together to make meaning. An infant learns that crying gets attention, that banging the table with a spoon makes noise, that pushing aside an obstacle makes a toy accessible, and that attempts to say "mama" or "dada" bring warm responses from adults. In a sense, this is the beginning of cause-and-effect reasoning.

From age two onward, the development of the symbolic function leads to rapid progress in learning language. It also brings about better problem-solving procedures and more mental imagery, pretend play, stories, dreams, and fantasies. Memory improves, largely because of increased conceptual ability and expanding knowledge. Children seem able to think rationally and to choose from a variety of alternatives to solve problems. They can usually reason logically about familiar events and settings, but they have difficulty thinking about unfamiliar situations. As yet they are unaware of their own thought processes; thus, they are lacking in metacognition.

Two-year-old Sara climbs onto the chair in front of the computer, turns it on, and uses the mouse to create images. She carefully watches her mother tend the baby, then role plays the part of the mother with her doll. When asked if she wants to go to the park, she asks a series of questions: "Will baby go to the park?"; "Will Mum go to the park?"; "Will Dad go to the park?" She listens carefully to each answer and then thinks for a moment before giving her answer. Much of Sara's problem solving, however, still relies on force (fitting a puzzle piece into a space) and trial and error.

Thought-Provoking Question

Think of some young children you know. How do they demonstrate the use of thinking strategies? What limitations do they still have?

By the time that children reach the age of five or six, they can use such higher-order thinking skills as analysis, synthesis, application, and evaluation. Rapidly increasing verbal facility enables them to express their knowledge, ask questions, and think about ideas in large, meaningful contexts. They are eager to discover how and why things work as they do, and an increased attention span enables them to focus on complex tasks. For example, when building a tower of blocks, a kindergartner considers various types of construction, evaluates the result, analyzes why the tower falls over, and begins again with a plan to construct a more stable tower.

Young children are already capable of developing strategies for thinking. Some strategies take only a few minutes to learn, but others take weeks, months, or even years (Siegler and Jenkins, 1989). Strategy construction can be divided into two periods: strategy discovery and strategy generalization. The *discovery* period leads up to and includes the initial use of the new strategy; this first use is a sudden, startling awareness that brings immediate insight. When Diana realized the application of her school words to her dad's newspaper in the opening vignette, she had such an "aha" experience. *Generalization* is the transfer of this new strategy from its first use to a wide range of applicable situations. It is often a slow, gradual process that may never, in fact, fully occur.

Many students find higher-order thinking strategies too demanding to learn on their own, so teachers need to offer support, or *scaffolding*. This is a technique that helps students bridge the gap between their present knowledge and their intended goals (Rosenshine and Meister, 1992). Scaffolds may be in the form of modeling, prompts, or cue cards that help students move to higher levels of understanding. The teacher gradually withdraws the scaffolding as students become more proficient and no longer need support.

Scaffolding works well within Vygotsky's "zone of proximal development," which is the range between what a learner can do independently and what he or she can do with assistance. The teacher who operates as a facilitator within this zone can help a child advance to a higher level of thinking and learning.

Models of Thinking

Many individuals have contributed to what we know about thinking strategies. To name them all is not possible within this chapter, but we will consider a few outstanding theorists to provide background information for the remainder of the book.

Of all the models of thinking skills, perhaps the best known is Benjamin Bloom's Taxonomy of Educational Objectives (Hunkins, 1995). It provides a framework for enabling students to think about an issue at different levels of cognition (Fig. 1-2).

Figure 1-2. Bloom's Taxonomy of Educational Objectives

Knowledge: Literal recall.

Comprehension: Knowledge with understanding.

Application: Making sense of information and putting it to use.

Analysis: Breaking down a whole into its parts and examining the parts in terms of their functions and relationships.

Synthesis: Combining elements in a new way to form a whole.

Evaluation: Making a judgment based on specific criteria.

In a theme study on saving the whales, Bloom's taxonomy would provide a framework for investigating whales from a number of perspectives instead of just acquiring facts about them. Figure 1-3 shows how students might perceive the theme at each level of Bloom's taxonomy.

Figure 1-3. Bloom's Taxonomy for "Saving the Whales"

Knowledge: Ability to recall information about whales.

Comprehension: Awareness and understanding of the plight of whales.

Application: Determining ways to save the whales.

Analysis: Identifying issues related to saving the whales; weighing the pros and cons.

Synthesis: Creating an innovative response, such as developing a public awareness program.

Evaluation: Making judgments about the need to save whales and the most effective procedures to use.

Writing during the era of progressive education, John Dewey proposed ideas that are still widely held today. He emphasized democratic ways of interacting and believed that the curriculum should center on the interests of the child. Learning, Dewey believed, should deal with authentic, true-to-life situations and should be an active, not a passive, process. "Doing," however, must be accompanied by reflective thinking during and after an experience.

Dewey viewed learning as problem solving. In fact, he proposed an early model for problem solving, which included the following steps (Gowan et al., 1967):

- Awareness of a difficulty
- Analysis of the problem to understand its nature
- Generation of possible solutions
- Testing the solutions
- Accepting or rejecting them

This series of procedures can vary slightly but has remained essentially the same over the years.

In addition to these well-known theorists, others have contributed significantly to the field of thinking. Hilda Taba, an investigator of children's thinking, proposed three stages in her inductive thinking model (Hunkins, 1995). She relied on questioning strategies to cause students to think about what was happening. *Concept formation*, the first stage, deals with identifying relevant information, developing clusters of information with common attributes, and labeling each cluster. During this stage, the teacher asks:

- What did you observe?
- What belongs together?
- What can we call these groups?

The second stage is *interpretation of data,* in which Taba encourages children to see and explore relationships, from which they make inferences and generalizations. At this stage, the teacher asks:

- What did you find?
- Why did this happen?
- What does this mean?

The final stage, *application of principles,* invites students to relate new information to their prior knowledge and experiences in order to predict consequences and then verify their predictions. Questions appropriate for this stage are the following:

- What would happen if . . . ?
- Why might this happen?
- How could this be generally true?

Thought-Provoking Question

How could you apply Taba's inductive questioning technique to a lesson or theme that you teach? How would her questions cause students to think about what they are learning?

Brian Cambourne (1988) devised a model of natural conditions for learning (Fig. 1-4). Nearly all of these conditions relate to creating an environment in which thinking can occur (see Chapter 3), and some relate to the freedom to think without fear of consequences, particularly engagement and approximation.

Another way to look at thinking strategies is Edward deBono's "thinking hats" (1991) (Fig. 1-5). DeBono's model helps children become aware of different ways to view ideas. Each color of hat represents one kind of thinking, and the student must use only the type of thinking that is appropriate for the color of hat being worn.

Figure 1-4. Brian Cambourne's Model of Natural Conditions for Learning

---

Immersion: Involving learners in all kinds of texts.

Demonstration: Showing learners how texts are constructed and used.

Engagement: Convincing the learner that the task is doable, worthwhile, and safe to "have a go."

Expectation: Maintaining high standards for students with whom one has bonded.

Responsibility: Empowering learners to make their own decisions about learning tasks.

Use: Providing time and opportunities for learners to use their developing control in authentic ways.

Approximation: Allowing students to take risks and make educated guesses, realizing that mistakes are necessary for learning to occur.

Response: Providing timely, relevant, nonthreatening feedback.

Figure 1-5. deBono's Six Thinking Hats

Red hat: Feelings, emotions, intuition. How do I feel about this?

Yellow hat: Strengths, benefits. What are some good points?

Black hat: Weaknesses, caution. What could be wrong with this?

Green hat: New ideas, creativity. What are some possibilities and alternatives?

White hat: Information, questions. What facts do we have and what information do we need to get?

Blue hat: Organization of thinking. How far have we come and what should we do next?

Types of Thinking Strategies

From the models presented here, you can see that many thinking strategies have been identified. You will find many of these, as well as others, listed in the glossary. Knowing individual thinking strategies and teaching them directly is not what counts, however; what really matters is that you believe in the value of creating a thinking classroom and find ways to weave thinking into your class activities throughout the day. Thinking becomes second nature as you and the children share in exploring, investigating, and discovering. Figures 1-6 through 1-11 define some thinking strategies and show some ways to integrate them with daily activities and lesson themes.

Thought-Provoking Question

Do you have a curious nature? As a child, did you wonder about things? How do you respond when a child asks you a lot of questions that are difficult to answer?

Figure 1-6. Decision Making

The following steps are used in decision making:
1. Identifying the goal
2. Collecting relevant information
3. Recognizing potential problems
4. Finding alternatives
5. Evaluating the alternatives

Lesson: Mrs. Watson's class wanted to have an end-of-the-year picnic, so the children brainstormed possible locations. Different groups investigated the availability, cost, distance, and facilities of each location. Information in hand, the children then considered potential problems. These included time available for the trip, cost of taking the school bus, availability of a shelter in case of bad weather, and desirability of the location.

Hailey pointed out that the class could ask the principal to reserve a special area on the playground for their picnic during lunch time; Dylan thought the class could walk two blocks to a park for lunch; Darby held out for a picnic by the lake. On further investigation, the children found that the principal would agree to reserve a special area on the playground; the park would not reserve any space, but the class was welcome to come; the bus trip to the lake would cost more money than the class had available, but the children could try to raise the money. Mrs. Watson then listed the options on the board and the class voted. The trip to the lake got the highest number of votes, and the children agreed to find a way to raise the money (another opportunity for decision making).

Figure 1-7. Predicting

Predicting is anticipating or foretelling possible consequences.

Lesson: During reading class, Mrs. Nixon consistently asked the children to predict what the story would be about. As a result, they comprehended well because they were able to anticipate what was likely to happen. Mrs. Nixon would typically ask the following questions before the children began to read a new story:

- From the title, what do you think the story will be about?
- Look at the pictures in this story. Can you anticipate what might happen from the picture clues?
- Why do you think that?

She would remind them to readjust their predictions as they read in case something unexpected happened. She suggested that they ask themselves these questions as they continued reading:

- Do I still think _____ will happen?
- What's happening to change my original predictions?
- What do I think might happen now?

Figure 1-8. Problem Solving

Steps in problem solving vary, but the following procedure is often used:

1. Identifying a problem
2. Obtaining information about the problem
3. Forming hypotheses
4. Testing the hypotheses and reaching a conclusion
5. Applying the solution and evaluating it

Although not included here, problem *finding* is sometimes considered part of the process and may be the most difficult step of all.

Lesson: The students in Mr. Ferraro's class complained that his six-week tests make them so nervous that they can't remember the answers. Their minds go blank and they can't think straight. They wondered what to do about this. Mr. Ferraro agreed that they had a problem and asked them to consider some possible solutions.

Figure 1-8 continued on next page

Figure 1-8 continued from previous page

The students decided to ask the guidance counselor and school nurse to suggest ways to reduce anxiety before a test, and they also searched for information on stress in the school library. After learning about test anxiety, they decided that it was caused by two things: the test itself and their fear of taking it.

Regarding the test, the students asked Mr. Ferraro to give more frequent, shorter tests so that one test wouldn't count so much and to give them a study guide that would them prepare for each test. He agreed to both suggestions. The students thought that they would be less nervous if they had time to study with partners during class and if they took deep breaths before the test began. When it was time for the next test, the students tested their hypotheses and found that the changes they recommended did cause them to be much less nervous.

Figure 1-9. Inductive Reasoning

Inductive reasoning means examining specific examples to find a common characteristic that leads to the formation of a rule or generalization. It is the opposite of *deductive reasoning,* in which students consider the rule or generalization first and then apply it to specific examples or situations.

Lesson: During a spelling lesson, Miss Teeple wrote two lists of word pairs on the board as follows:

city	cities	valley	valleys
story	stories	play	plays
party	parties	toy	toys

She told the children that she had formed plurals for each word and asked them to tell her why she sometimes changed the *y* to *i* and added *es,* whereas at other times she simply added *s* to the word.

Some of the children began guessing the reason, and Jason suddenly called out, "I know! If there's a consonant in front of the *y*, you have to change the *y* to *i* and add *es*, but if a vowel is right in front of the *y*, all you have to do is add *s*." By reasoning inductively, Jason had looked for the similarities and differences that helped him discover the rule. Miss Teeple wrote Jason's rule on the board and asked the children to think of other examples that fit it.

Figure 1-10. Comparing and Contrasting

Comparing and *contrasting* consist of examining objects or bodies of information to identify similarities and differences among them. This activity can be done with very young children as they manipulate objects, and it can be done with older students as they examine issues and complex topics.

Lesson: Mr. Cho's class was studying amphibians, and he had brought a toad and a frog to school. He asked the students to observe similarities and differences between the two and to read to find other ways to compare and contrast them. He began to make lists of similarities and differences as the children gave him information, which looked like this:

Similarities
Both amphibians
Cold-blooded
Have poisons in or on their bodies

Differences		
	Frog	**Toad**
Color	Green	Brown
Skin	Smooth, moist	Rough, warty
Movement	Fast hopper	Clumsy

Mr. Cho then showed the children how to compare and contrast the animals' features by using a Venn diagram (see Chapter 9).

Figure 1-11. Classifying

Classifying is arranging items in groups according to common characteristics and labeling each group by its commonalities.

Lesson: Early in the year Mrs. Fernandez brought sealable plastic bags containing pictures she had cut from catalogs. She divided her class into groups and gave each group a bag. When the children had removed the pictures and spread them on their tables, she asked them to put the pictures together that belonged together. She told them that they could discuss their reasons for grouping certain pictures together, but they had to find a name, or a label, for each group. The children tried various arrangements before they were satisfied, and Mrs. Fernandez stopped by each group to see how the children had classified their pictures. She listened to their reasons and then asked them to see if they could think of other ways to group the pictures. Sometimes the children combined two groups, sometimes they separated each group into two categories, and sometimes they scattered the pictures and completely reorganized them into fresh categories. As the children explained their reasons to each other and to Mrs. Fernandez, they began to understand different ways to classify items logically.

Incorporating thinking strategies into your lessons will take time, but students need time to really understand the material they are learning. Because of curricular demands and standardized tests, many teachers think that they must rush through the material in order to cover it. This superficial treatment may enable students to score well, but it fails to leave them with the understanding that comes from in-depth exploration and opportunities for discovery.

Summary

In order to prepare students for the responsibilities they will face in life, teachers need to provide authentic situations that require higher-order thinking and problem-solving strategies. As children and later as adults, students must be able to think clearly and critically in order to make wise decisions.

Even an infant has rudimentary thinking abilities, and the young child quickly finds effective ways to interact with others and with the environment. Piaget and Vygotsky helped us understand how children learn and think, and they both believed in the social nature of learning. Other prominent educators and psychologists have provided a conceptual framework for thinking strategies: Dewey, with his learning-by-doing and problem-solving strategies; Bloom, with his taxonomy of six levels of thinking; Taba, with her inductive learning based on thoughtful questioning; Cambourne, who proposed a model for creating natural conditions for learning; and deBono, who suggested using six different-colored hats to represent six ways of thinking.

With so many types of thinking strategies, how does the teacher begin to incorporate them all? It is not as important to cover a large number of discrete thinking skills as it is to adopt an inquisitive, curious nature that lures children into investigation and discovery. In a classroom where the teacher encourages critical and creative thinking, specific strategies can become a natural part of theme studies and daily activities. Some thinking processes that can be implemented readily are decision making, predicting, problem solving, inductive reasoning, comparing and contrasting, and classifying. Taking time for investigation and discovery promotes understanding rather than superficial knowledge of facts that may quickly be forgotten.

References

Beyer, B. (1995). *Critical thinking.* Bloomington, IN: Phi Delta Kappa.

Brandt, R. (1993). On teaching for understanding: A conversation with Howard Gardner. *Educational Leadership 50* (7): 4–7.

Bull, G. (1989). *Reflective teaching.* Carlton South, Victoria: Australian Reading Association.

Cambourne, B. (1988). *The whole story*. Gosford, New South Wales, Australia: Ashton Scholastic.

Campbell, S. (Ed.). (1976). *Piaget sampler*. New York: John Wiley.

Church, E.B. (1996). Planning curriculum together. *Scholastic Early Childhood Today, 10*(6): 16, 19.

Chuska, K. (1986). *Teaching the process of thinking*. Bloomington, IN: Phi Delta Kappa.

deBono, E. (1991). *Six thinking hats*. Logan, IA: Perfection Learning.

Dixon-Krauss, L. (1996). *Vygotsky in the classroom*. White Plains, NY: Longman.

Fisher, B. (1995). *Thinking and learning together*. Portsmouth, NH: Heinemann.

Garbarino, J., and Stott, F. (1989). *What children can tell us*. San Francisco: Jossey-Bass.

Glover, J., Ronning, R., and Reynolds, C., (Eds.). (1989). *Handbook of creativity*. New York: Plenum.

Goodlad, J. (1994). *What schools are for.* Bloomington, IN: Phi Delta Kappa.

Goodman, K., Smith, E. B., Meredith, R., and Goodman, Y. (1987). *Language and thinking in school* (3rd ed.). New York: Richard C. Owen.

Gowan, J., Demos, G., Torrance, E.P. (1967). *Creativity: Its educational implications*. New York: John Wiley.

Hunkins, F. (1995). *Teaching thinking through effective questioning* (2nd ed.). Norwood, MA: Christopher-Gordon.

Piaget, J. (1973). *The child and reality*. Translated by A. Rosin. New York: Grossman.

Rosenshine, B. and Meister, C. (1992). The use of scaffolds for teaching higher-level cognitive strategies. *Educational Leadership, 49*(7): 26–33.

Schmoker, M. (1996). *Results: The key to continuous school improvement*. Alexandria, VA: Association for Supervision and Curriculum Development.

Siegler, R. (1991). *Children's thinking* (2nd ed.). Englewood Cliffs, NJ: Prentice-Hall.

Siegler, R. and Jenkins, E. (1989). *How children discover new strategies*. Hillsdale, NJ: Lawrence Erlbaum.

Thompson, G. (1991). *Teaching through themes*. New York: Scholastic.

Vygotsky, L. (1986). *Thought and language*. Translated and edited by A. Kozulin. Cambridge, MA: MIT Press.

Wilks, S. (1995). *Critical & creative thinking*. Portsmouth, NH: Heinemann.

CHAPTER 2

Addressing the Needs of Diverse Learners

When I asked the teachers,

"How can we best meet the needs of students who learn in different ways?"

the teachers said:

- Try to recognize their learning styles and make lesson variations to fit those styles.
- First, we need to be aware that students are different and don't learn in the same ways or at the same pace. Then we need to apply what we have learned about them to our teaching.
- Allow time for self-discovery or self-directed learning.
- Provide different types of activities and teaching methods.
- Keep checking yourself until it becomes second nature to include different ways that students learn.
- Identify the way in which a student learns best, and teach him or her in that way.
- Provide students with a variety of materials that they can choose from to best help them learn.

How would you answer this question?

> **Concepts to watch for**
>
> - The extent of diversity among learners
> - Preferences for learning: modalities and learning styles
> - The theory of multiple intelligences
> - What "different ways of knowing" means for teachers

When I was an undergraduate majoring in teacher education, I knew a student who brought music into all her teaching. All the elementary education majors admired Marilyn's ability to integrate music because it enhanced each of her lessons. She used her own love of music to teach the children to sing folk songs related to historical periods, story songs in reading, and even rhythmic tunes to remember math facts.

Marilyn's students responded enthusiastically to her lessons. By using one of her own strengths, she tapped the musical aptitudes of her students and gave them another way of knowing.

Diversity Among Students

Diversity among students in our classrooms appears to increase each year, and we wonder how we can meet each child's needs. The policy of inclusion means that we are likely to have children with physical, emotional, or mental disabilities. These children may require the aid of an assistant teacher or, at the very least, our understanding of their special needs and how to meet them. As we continue to integrate students from different cultural backgrounds, we need to be aware of potential language difficulties. Also, some cultures have ways of communicating and interacting that differ from traditional school practice.

In some cases, differences among students are obvious, but often they are so subtle that we are unaware of them. Students have many ways of knowing, but we tend to teach them in the ways that we ourselves learn best. Thus, if we prefer to learn by reading and writing, we are probably neglecting the kinesthetic or auditory learner. Unfortunately, teachers often interpret mismatches in learning styles between themselves and the students as a lack of ability on the part of the students.

If we want our students to be able to think and understand, we need to address their strengths and offer them different ways of knowing. By including music, art, movement, and cooperative learning activities in our teaching repertoires, we are likely to reach students who would otherwise remain untouched by our lessons.

To become aware of the diversity among students in your classroom, complete the checklist in Figure 2-1. You might want to insert students' names or initials beside some items to remind you later of those who match certain behavioral characteristics. Your responses will give you clues to help you identify the types of learners you have. Then, as you read this chapter, look for ways to help these students think in ways that match their strengths.

Figure 2-1. Observed Behaviors

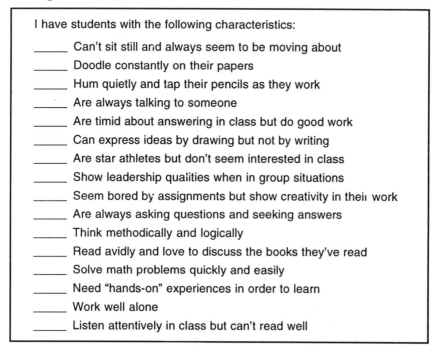

I have students with the following characteristics:

_____ Can't sit still and always seem to be moving about

_____ Doodle constantly on their papers

_____ Hum quietly and tap their pencils as they work

_____ Are always talking to someone

_____ Are timid about answering in class but do good work

_____ Can express ideas by drawing but not by writing

_____ Are star athletes but don't seem interested in class

_____ Show leadership qualities when in group situations

_____ Seem bored by assignments but show creativity in their work

_____ Are always asking questions and seeking answers

_____ Think methodically and logically

_____ Read avidly and love to discuss the books they've read

_____ Solve math problems quickly and easily

_____ Need "hands-on" experiences in order to learn

_____ Work well alone

_____ Listen attentively in class but can't read well

Modalities and Learning Styles

For many decades researchers have proposed theories about preferred ways of learning. Controversy surrounds such theories; some research supports the need to teach to learners' strengths, whereas other research disputes the value of such practice. Naysayers argue that children do not fit neatly into one category or another, that they use different styles for learning in different disciplines, that they are influenced by the type of instruction and the materials, and that preferred styles change over time. Nevertheless, most of us realize that we learn better in some ways than in others, so we will briefly consider theories about modalities and learning styles.

A *modality* is any of the sensory systems through which a learner receives, processes, and responds to sensations. In education, the three primary systems are auditory (listening), visual (reading), and kinesthetic (movement and touch). Although teachers readily teach to auditory and visual learners, they often neglect kinesthetic learners.

Basing his work on that of Jerome Bruner, Bob Samples (1992) classified modalities as shown in Figure 2-2.

Figure 2-2. Learning Modalities

Symbolic abstract: Representing experiences in symbols, as in reading, writing, and using numbers and codes (3 Rs–based).

Visual-spatial: Reasoning and expressing experiences through visual and spatial media (arts-based).

Kinesthetic: Expressing experiences through movement and dance (movement-based).

Auditory: Sensing and reasoning through sound and music (sound-based).

Synergic: Combining previous modes of learning (combination).

Teachers who infused these learning modalities into their teaching, according to Samples, turned reluctant learners into stars and helped students improve their test performance on concepts they learned through preferred modalities.

A *learning style* is a preferred way to learn something. Kenneth and Rita Dunn (1986) view learning styles as children's preferences for conditions such as the following:

- Working in bright or dim light
- Wanting structured or flexible learning environments
- Learning alone or with others
- Learning by doing, listening, viewing, or touching
- Working in quiet or working with background noise
- Moving about while learning or sitting still

They suggest creating a room environment that supports different learning styles so that each child feels comfortable while engaged in learning.

Robert Sternberg (1994, p. 39) says this about learning styles: "Teachers must accommodate an array of thinking and learning styles, systematically varying teaching and assessment methods to reach every student." Teachers need not abandon familiar ways of teaching, but need only to expand their strategies so that they reach children with different learning styles. By doing so, the teacher becomes more flexible in teaching approaches and the students expand their styles of thinking and learning.

Thought-Provoking Idea

Identifying individual learning styles is not as important as the following:

1. Recognizing that children learn in many ways
2. Providing opportunities for all children to learn in their preferred styles at some time during the day
3. Helping children discover other ways to learn
4. Expanding your own learning preferences so that you can teach all students

---

Theory of Multiple Intelligences

For a variety of reasons, educators have regarded intelligence (I.Q.) test scores with suspicion. Some claim that the tests are culturally biased, that motivation to perform well influences results, or that the types of questions do not let children show what they know and can do. Entire areas are excluded, such as music, art, athletics, and social interactions. The inadequacy of I.Q. tests to measure general intelligence, along with evidence of other types of intelligence, led Howard Gardner to develop a theory of multiple intelligences (Siegler, 1991). Figure 2-3 lists these intelligences.

Figure 2-3. Howard Gardner's Multiple Intelligences

Verbal/Linguistic: Words and language, both written and spoken.

Logical/Mathematical: Scientific thinking, number systems, deductive reasoning, awareness of abstract patterns.

Visual/Spatial: Visualization, creation of mental images.

Bodily/Kinesthetic: Physical movement, wisdom of the body.

Musical/Rhythmic: Recognition of pitch, tone, and rhythm; awareness of sounds in the environment.

Interpersonal: Person-to-person relationships and communication.

Intrapersonal: Self-reflection, metacognition, spiritual awareness.

Each intelligence relates to a separate domain with a distinct symbol system, but some intelligences overlap and appear to be related.

Typically, school curriculum is organized around verbal/linguistic and logical/mathematical intelligences. To enable each child to reach full potential, however, teachers should teach to the strengths of all students. This means that at some time during the day, students whose dominant intelligence is bodily/kinesthetic can learn by movement, those who are predominantly musical/rhythmic have a chance to learn through sound or rhythm, and so forth. Figure 2-4 shows how learning activities centered on a weather theme can support each of the intelligences.

Not every lesson has to include all seven ways of learning, of course, nor do the intelligences need to be represented equally in the curriculum. In fact, as children reach fifth and sixth grades, teachers often find it difficult to use intelligences other than linguistic and mathematical to ensure mastery of content (Hoerr, 1994). The following lesson shows how one teacher, Ann Burns, used several intelligences when teaching math to her first graders.

Lesson: Problem Solving in Math

With the children seated in a circle around her on the floor, Ann begins her lesson by reading one of the chart stories she has created to get her class to think in certain ways about math. Encouraging the children to read along, Ann begins reading "The Hungry Monster Problem." The story tells us that the hungry monster ate the wheels off two pairs of skates (four wheels on each skate) and a wagon (four wheels). Ann asked the children to use manipulatives to find out how many wheels the hungry monster ate. Before leaving the circle, each child found a partner. One of each pair chose a set of manipulatives to use for solving the problem, and the children began to work.

Each pair found a space on the floor and began talking about how to figure out the number of wheels eaten by the monster. The children referred back to the chart story and began laying out objects that represented the wheels. After a great deal of discussion and realignment, most children believed that they had found the correct answer. They then got their math notebooks and drew sets of circles representing wheels for their answers. Some children added words to go along with the circles, and some showed their work as an addition problem. They could choose any form of answer they thought was appropriate.

Back in the circle, Ann asked the children to explain how they had solved the problem. She asked for the different ways that they had found to work it out and gave all the children credit for their attempts.

Proponents of the theory of multiple intelligences argue that it gives all children opportunities to learn instead of favoring those with linguistic and mathematical preferences. Also, exposure to other intelligences

Figure 2-4. Using Seven Intelligences to Teach a Weather Theme

WEATHER

Verbal/Linguistic

Make a semantic map (see Chapter 9).

Find weather idioms (e.g., "on cloud nine").

Read weather books (e.g., *Time of Wonder*).

Learn vocabulary and spelling words (e.g., *precipitation*).

Logical/Mathematical

Do experiments on forming a cloud or evaporation.

Graph temperatures and rainfall for a month.

Figure how long it takes a weather system to move.

Visual/Spatial

Create different kinds of clouds from cotton and construction paper.

Make a mural of the water cycle.

Interpret weather maps.

Bodily/Kinesthetic

Simulate an approaching and receding storm with creative movement.

Go outside to observe clouds and run with the wind.

Make and mount a windsock.

Musical/Rhythmic

Simulate an approaching and receding storm with rhythmic finger snapping and clapping.

Listen to environmental tapes.

Sing weather songs.

Interpersonal

Form groups to research weather systems.

Debate global warming: Does it exist?

Intrapersonal

Write an essay on how the weather makes you feel.

Keep a journal to record how weather affects your moods.

Thought-Provoking Question

What modalities, styles, and intelligences did Ann Burns address in this lesson?

---

offers children different perspectives, such as feeling and expressing through art, moving to music and rhythm, and sharing ideas with others. Engagement in multiple ways of knowing makes a person fully literate and able to move easily from one form of expression or understanding to another (Leland and Harste, 1994).

Similarly, students should be able to use multiple communication systems, including art, music, dance, movement, and mathematics, to express meaning and understanding of the same text (Silver and Kucer, 1997). In particular, second language learners benefit from using alternatives to the written word as they discover meaning and communicate ideas in a variety of ways.

It isn't always easy, however, for teachers to find ways to adapt lessons to different ways of knowing and communicating. How does one use bodily/kinesthetic intelligence for teaching state capitals or use musical/rhythmic intelligence for teaching the multiplication tables? The following sections, which treat each intelligence separately, may be helpful for understanding the range of possibilities for each.

Verbal/Linguistic Intelligence

Methods and materials for teaching: Lectures, discussions, books, writing activities, storytelling, debates, tape recordings, word games, work sheets, choral reading.

Classroom application: Junior Great Books program (Criscuola, 1994).

A great deal of class activity—speaking, listening, reading, and writing—centers around verbal/linguistic learning, so here we will focus on a specific program that deals with language and thinking. Lessons from the Junior Great Books program provide a framework for interpretive discussion of books and for making inferences and forming opinions about reading. In the shared inquiry method of discussion, teachers link four esssential features.

1. Interpretation of text. Students discuss their opinions about the meaning of the text.

2. Literature that is rich in meaning. Books selected for the program must be worthy of interpretation and discussion.

3. Teacher as director of discussion. Teachers stimulate discussion by asking questions related to the text that have two or more text-supported answers.

4. Student opinions. As students respond to open questions, they explain their thinking, comment on others' remarks, and find evidence to support their interpretations.

Sample student activities

1. Writing a new ending for a story
2. Learning new, interesting words and finding ways to use them in conversation
3. Participating in book discussion groups
4. Solving and making up riddles and word puzzles
5. Giving a talk or participating in a debate

Career options: Teacher, religious leader, salesperson, journalist, editor, politician, attorney, author.

Logical/Mathematical Intelligence

Methods and materials for teaching: Math problems, scientific demonstrations, problem solving, logic puzzles, codes.

Classroom application: Math and science

Although used primarily in math and science, logical/mathematical intelligence can extend into every area of the curriculum in the form of critical thinking. It deals with seeing patterns and relationships, reasoning and classifying, calculating and estimating, and, of course, answering questions in math books. Students construct their own understandings of math concepts by using manipulatives to explore relationships and hypothesize about concepts. According to Armstrong (1994a), teachers can apply logical/mathematical intelligence to all school subjects in the following ways:

1. Calculations and quantifications. Teachers can find ways to integrate math in social studies (How far would General Sherman's march be in kilometers?), literature (discussing the math problems in Jon Scieszka's *Math Curse*), health (rate of heartbeat), and so forth.
2. Classification and categorization. As children place items in categories or classify them according to some system, they are displaying logical/mathematical intelligence. In early years they may group their toys, and later they can classify things according to gas, liquid, or solid.
3. Socratic questioning. Based on the way Socrates questioned his students, teachers engage children in critical thinking activities. They ask probing questions that encourage students to examine their beliefs and defend their opinions.
4. Heuristics. Students learn by following guidelines, strategies, and suggestions for logical problem solving. They may make analogies

to the problem to be solved, find a similar problem and solve it, or separate various parts of the problem.

5. Scientific thinking. By thinking like a scientist, students learn to apply scientific principles to all areas of the curriculum. For instance, they can apply their knowledge of science to global issues (e.g., overpopulation) and to science fiction books to see if the ideas presented are feasible.

Sample student activities

1. Defending your stand on an issue
2. Categorizing a large group of objects by certain characteristics
3. Creating a code according to some system
4. Using the problem-solving process to find a solution
5. Solving number problems

Career options: Inventor, accountant, banker, scientist, doctor, computer programmer, engineer, economist.

Visual/Spatial Intelligence

Methods and materials for teaching: Charts, graphs, maps, diagrams, videos, movies, visualization activities, visual arts.

Classroom application: Art and visualization

The visual/spatial learner is creative and imaginative, especially in the area of art. The visual arts are expressions of thoughts and feelings; they represent pictorially what words describe. Children communicate through art, and painting is visual thinking (Christoplos and Valletutti, 1990). Simple drawings can be the basis for powerful ideas, and communicating with rough sketches gives visual/spatial students a way to demonstrate their understanding of subject matter (Armstrong, 1994a).

This intelligence also enables children to visualize—to make mental pictures of the story they are reading or the period of history that they are living through vicariously. They can turn these images into drawings if they wish. Using guided imagery, teachers can enourage children to make pictures in their minds before and during the reading of a new story in order to help them appreciate and remember it.

Sample student activities

1. Constructing a collage to explain who you are
2. Making or following a map for a treasure hunt
3. Creating metaphors by using one idea to refer to another
4. Drawing your interpretation of a story
5. Visualizing what it was like to live in a pioneer village

Career options: Commercial artist, graphic designer, engineer, production editor, painter, architect.

Bodily/Kinesthetic Intelligence

Methods and materials for teaching: Creative drama, charades, simulations, games, manipulatives, role playing, sports, dance.

Classroom application: Creative movement

It is natural for young children to express themselves through movement—running and jumping, pushing and pulling, throwing and swinging, and gesturing as they tell stories. This natural inclination to move continues into the school years, where teachers can convert it into simulations of science concepts and dramatizations in social studies. Math concepts take on new meanings as children use their bodies to explore geometric shapes and act out story problems.

Griss (1994) points out that creative movement has the following advantages:

- Helps children internalize abstract information
- Is expressive, analytical, and informative
- Turns disruptive energy into creative activity
- Enables ESL (English as a second language) children to find an alternate mode of expression
- Lets children explore themes and feelings in stories
- Builds trust, cooperation, discipline, creativity, problem solving, and discipline

Sample student activities

1. Acting out a story (e.g., *Caps for Sale*)
2. Simulating science concepts (such as simple machines and light waves)
3. Rotating and orbiting as planets in the solar system
4. Making letter shapes with your body
5. Playing charades of stories to review a literature unit

Career options: Actor, dancer, athlete, coach, physical therapist, circus performer, farmer.

Musical/Rhythmic Intelligence

Methods and materials for teaching: Rhythmic patterns, singing, environmental sounds, musical instruments, music tapes.

Classroom application: Integrating music

This chapter's opening vignette about Marilyn illustrates ways that a teacher can integrate music with any area of the curriculum. Jingles lodge facts in the brain, and students can use them to remember addition facts, spelling rules, names of continents, and so forth. Children can create musical rhymes of their own, which make facts even more memorable.

Mood music (often classical selections) provides a quiet time for relaxing between active learning sessions, as do recordings of environmental sounds, such as waves lapping on the shore or a gurgling stream. Using both musical and kinesthetic intelligences, folk songs and dances enrich social studies by letting children experience part of history. The music of marching bands heightens a sense of patriotism, and background music for reading a story aloud evokes emotional response.

Sample student activities

1. Responding to music in terms of feelings, images, and memories
2. Making a musical jingle out of something to be memorized
3. Relaxing to mood music or environmental sounds
4. Providing sound effects for a mock radio show
5. Composing new words for a familiar melody

Career options: Disc jockey, singer, sound engineer, musician, music therapist, choral director, music teacher, conductor.

Interpersonal Intelligence

Methods and materials for teaching: Cooperative learning, group projects, reading and writing conferences, feedback, board games.

Classroom application: Cooperative learning and partnerships

Years ago teachers admonished their students to sit in their seats and not talk to their neighbors. New strategies today, particularly cooperative learning, recognize how much students can learn from and with each other. Typically, students in cooperative learning groups represent different abilities and talents, so each one can contribute to the group's endeavors.

Getting a second opinion or bouncing an idea off someone is reassuring, so working with a partner or a buddy helps students affirm or rethink their ideas. Opportunities for peers to work as partners occur throughout the day and across the curriculum, as in the following examples:

- Studying spelling words with a partner
- Peer conferencing to decide how to revise a story
- Sharing responses to a story
- Reviewing for a test by going over a study guide
- Creating a joint project related to a theme study
- Tutoring of a weaker student by a stronger one

Sample student activities

1. Participating as a member of a club or committee
2. Planning a group culminating activity for a theme study
3. Playing a board game with others
4. Listening carefully to someone and asking relevant questions
5. Being part of a team effort

Career options: Administrator, psychologist, guidance counselor, salesperson, travel agent, sociologist, personnel worker.

Intrapersonal Intelligence

Methods and materials for teaching: Metacognition and self-evaluation, higher-order reasoning, writing, research, journals.

Classroom application: Self-awareness

Individuals with highly developed intrapersonal intelligence need time to reflect and meditate during the school day. In most classrooms, however, students spend their time working on teacher-directed tasks or with other students, and there is little personal time. Given the opportunity, these students are often capable of higher-order thinking, deep concentration, thoughtful analysis of problems and issues, and self-directed goal setting.

In order to help these learners maximize their strength and enable others to cultivate self-awareness, teachers can use the following strategies:

- Give occasional short periods of time for students to reflect.
- Ask students to write on a card one thing they learned from a lesson and one thing they still want to know.
- Give students choices about their learning experiences.
- Find opportunities that encourage students to express feelings, such as joy, amazement, and excitement.
- Let students set personal goals.
- Don't require students to share; let them volunteer.
- Relate new material to students' prior experiences and individual needs.

Sample student activities

1. Writing personal reflections in journals
2. Taking time to think about things
3. Keeping personal records of books read, information learned, and ideas for writing
4. Considering appropriate career choices
5. Evaluating work and considering what to do to improve it

Career options: Theologian, clergy member, author, researcher, explorer, philosopher.

We can teach children to be intelligent in many ways and on many levels, and we can teach anything using any of the intelligences. These two assumptions underlie David Lazear's thinking on multiple intelligences (1992). Lazear contends that teaching with multiple intelligences falls into the following four stages.

Stage 1: Awakening the intelligences. We can awaken intelligences that have lain dormant by stimulating the brain and activating the senses. For example, distributing crayons, paints, or clay can activate visual/spatial abilities, and opportunities for creative movement can unleash bodily/kinesthetic capacities. This stage makes us aware that we can learn in many ways and that we can find strategies for awakening different intelligences.

Stage 2: Amplifying the intelligences. This stage enables us to strengthen areas in which we are weak or uncomfortable. As with any ability, the more we use it, the better it becomes. Examples are improving interpersonal intelligence by encouraging others and reaching consensus, and developing musical/rhythmic abilities by recognizing different sounds and expressing emotions through sound. In this stage we can learn how the intelligences work and how to improve our use of them.

Stage 3: Teaching with the intelligences. The goal of this stage is to teach lessons that use different intelligences for mastering academic material. For example, ask students to act out unfamiliar words (bodily/kinesthetic) or create a song for remembering geography facts (musical/rhythmic).

Stage 4: Transferring the intelligences. Once students have learned to use multiple intelligences, they need to transfer them to their lives outside school. Students should be able to use a variety of techniques to solve problems, make decisions, and evaluate situations. They can adapt cooperative learning strategies to family situations (interpersonal) and transfer their journal writing skills to reflective accounts of important events in their lives (intrapersonal).

Thought-Provoking Idea

You can help children transfer their capacity for using multiple ways of knowing from school to life outside school by the following:

1. Asking them to answer a question by drawing, composing a song, or acting it out instead of writing the answer
2. Posing a problem and asking them to think like an inventor or think like a mathematician (Leland and Harste, 1994)
3. Letting students role play situations in which they use different intelligences to solve problems that they face outside school

Summary

In classrooms across the country, children differ in physical, emotional, and mental capacities; language and cultural backgrounds; and ways of knowing. Researchers have studied variations among children, and some conclude that students favor different modalities—auditory, visual, or kinesthetic—and have different learning styles.

In addition, Howard Gardner proposed a theory of multiple intelligences that credits learners with having strengths or preferences for learning in different ways. The intelligences include verbal/linguistic, logical/mathematical, visual/spatial, bodily/kinesthetic, musical/rhythmic, interpersonal, and intrapersonal. Teaching through strengths enables children who do not learn well through traditional instruction, typically linguistic and mathematical intelligences, to approach learning in more viable ways.

Awareness of students' needs to learn and think in multiple ways enables teachers to provide a variety of instructional strategies that accommodate individual strengths. It also exposes many children to new ways of knowing. Applications of Gardner's theory can be found in all content areas. For example, hands-on science, capitalizing on bodily/kinesthetic intelligence, is meaningful for students and piques their curiosity. They learn by touching, measuring, manipulating, making charts, and recording data. Teaching to various intelligences consists of four stages: awakening each intelligence, amplifying it, teaching with it, and transferring it to out-of-school situations.

References

Armstrong, T. (1994a). *Multiple intelligences in the classroom.* Alexandria, Va: Association for Supervision and Curriculum Development.

Armstrong, T. (1994b). Multiple intelligences: Seven ways to approach curriculum. *Educational Leadership, 52*(3), 26–28.

Barbe, W., and Swassing, R. (1988). *Teaching through modality strengths: Concepts and practices.* Columbus, Ohio: Zaner-Bloser.

Brandt, R. (1993). On teaching for understanding: A conversation with Howard Gardner. *Educational Leadership, 50*(7), 4–7.

Bull, G. (1989). *Reflective teaching.* Carlton South, Victoria: Australian Reading Association.

Christoplos, F. and Valletutti, P. (1990). *Developing children's creative thinking through the arts.* Bloomington, IN.: Phi Delta Kappa.

Criscuola, M. (1994). Read, discuss, reread: Insights from the Junior Great Books Program. *Educational Leadership, 51*(5), 58–61.

Dunn, K. and Dunn, R. (1986). The look of learning styles. *Early Years, 16* (7), 49–53.

Dunn, R. (1995). *Strategies for educating diverse learners.* Bloomington, IN: Phi Delta Kappa.

Ellison, L. (1992). Using multiple intelligences to set goals. *Educational Leadership, 50*(2), 69–72.

Fielding, E.N. (1995). Teaching to the strengths. *Reading Today, 13*(1), 29.

Gardner, H. (1983). *Frames of mind.* New York: Basic Books.

Gardner, H., and Boix-Mansilla, V. (1994). Teaching for understanding: Within and across the disciplines. *Educational Leadership, 51*(5), 14–18.

Goodman, K., Smith, E.B., Meredith, R., and Goodman, Y. (1987). Language and thinking in school (3rd ed.). New York: Richard C. Owen.

Griss, S. (1994). Creative movement: A language for learning. *Educational Leadership, 51*(5), 78–80.

Gwiazda, C. (1995). *Improving classroom instruction through multiple intelligences.* Presentation at National Council of Teachers of English Annual Convention, San Diego.

Hoerr, T. (1992). How our school applied multiple intelligences theory. *Educational Leadership, 50*(2), 67–68.

Hoerr, T. (1994). How the New City School applies the multiple intelligences. *Educational Leadership, 52*(3), 29–33.

Howard Gardner on multiple intelligences. (1995). *Scholastic Early Childhood Education Today, 10*(1), 30–32.

Jasmine, J. (1995). *Addressing diversity in the classroom.* Westminster, CA: Teacher Created Materials.

Lange, J., and Lange, M. (1996). *Fostering critical and creative thinking in Title I classrooms.* Presentation at the International Reading Association Convention, New Orleans.

Lazear, D. (1992). *Teaching for multiple intelligences.* Bloomington, IN: Phi Delta Kappa.

LeBuffe, J. (1994). *Hands-on science in the elementary school.* Bloomington, IN: Phi Delta Kappa.

Leland, C., and Harste, J. (1994). Multiple ways of knowing: Curriculum in a new key. *Language Arts, 71*(5), 337–345.

Murray, W. (1996). Intelligent? *Instructor, 105*(8), 53–57.

Nelson, K. (1995). Nurturing kids' seven ways of being smart. *Instructor, 105*(1), 26–31.

Samples, B. (1992). Using learning modalities to celebrate intelligence. *Educational Leadership, 50*(2), 62–66.

Siegler, R. (1991). *Children's thinking* (2nd ed.). Englewood Cliffs, NJ: Prentice-Hall.

Silver, C., and Kucer, S. (1997). Expanding curricular conversations through unification, diversity, and access. *Language Arts, 74*(1), 26–32.

Sternberg, R.J. (1994). Allowing for thinking styles. *Educational Leadership, 52*(3), 36–40.

Tobias, C.U. (1993). *The way they learn.* Colorado Springs: Focus on the Family.

II

Building Thinking Strategies

I asked the children,

"What helps you to think?"

and the children said:

> I prttey shure that is your Brain.

> To know that you are smart.

> Talking with friends and getting their opinion helps me to think.

> I like classical music in the back ground. I think it gets my brain working.

> to drol apitcher

> Some times my friends help me think. By telling me some thing and I half to think about my answer.

If I'm alone I can think better.

It helps me to think if I write it down on paper and apply myself.

For serious thinking I sometimes go off by myself or listen to some music. But I do most of my problem-solving thinking when I'm asleep.

To talk with somewon.

A lot of times I like to just go outside and think by myself. whenever I'm really nervous I visualize what I'm going to do.

to really consintrate and think of the problem

To ask somebody about there ideas.

The children's responses remind us of the diversity among learners discussed in Chapter 2. Their answers included drawing a picture, writing an idea down on paper, talking with friends and getting their opinions, going outside to think alone, visualizing what they want to do, planning things out on paper, using their imaginations, knowing that they are smart, and listening to music. In order to accommodate these preferences, we need to offer a variety of approaches, room arrangements, and materials.

Chapters 3 and 4, which are closely related, consider optimal conditions for creating a classroom of thinkers. Setting up a stimulating physical environment is a starting point, but even more important is establishing a classroom climate that enables children to feel free to learn in a variety of ways without fear of failure. The classroom should become a democratic community of learners in which teacher and children share an attitude of inquiry. Recognizing the social nature of learning, teachers should provide opportunities for cooperative learning, working in group situations, and valuing children's talk.

Reading and writing present us with many opportunities for facilitating critical, creative, and logical thinking. These include constructing meaning from the text, clarifying thinking by writing, and using metacognitive strategies or think alouds while reading. Closely related to an attitude of inquiry are the authentic questions that teachers and students generate in the process of learning content—not questions with one-word, predetermined answers, but questions that cause us to ponder and lead us to discover.

CHAPTER 3

Creating a Supportive Classroom Environment

When I asked the teachers,

"How can you create an environment for thinking?"

the teachers said:

- Allow children the opportunity for testing, experimenting, and decision making rather than structuring every moment of their day. Use blank pages instead of coloring books; be open to and accepting of ideas so that children are not afraid of rejection, ridicule, or correction.

- Show children that it's okay to make mistakes.

- Provide interesting things to think about. Make time for discussion. Accept all answers. Children will be willing to express ideas if they know that you are interested in what they have to say.

- Let them know that there are no right or wrong answers to some questions.

- Model the desired behavior. Let students see you thinking and expressing ideas.

- Give feedback that lets children feel accepted and know that their thoughts are important.

- Value each child's opinion. Encourage effort and creativity.

How would you answer this question?

Concepts to watch for

Ways to create a stimulating physical environment
- How to establish a nonthreatening climate that frees children to make approximations and take risks
- Procedures for building self-esteem and self-discipline
- Ways to establish a democratic community of learners
- How to create an inquiry-based classroom

If you don't have a go, you'll never know.

It's OK if you make a mistake.

Team up for a great year.

Things That Make Our Room Happy (followed by a student-dictated list)

Signs and posters such as these invite children to discover, investigate, and find innovative ways to solve problems. Not bound by emphasis on the one correct answer or procedure for doing something, children are free to make choices and explore a wide range of possibilities. Knowing that it's acceptable to make a mistake and try again, they don't fear failure.

Physical Environment of the Classroom

Desks in clusters, a nearly invisible teacher's desk, walls filled with colorful displays of children's work, pillows on the floor by a library corner, nooks and crannies, a prominently located author's chair, a computer center, and a message board cluttered with children's notes—such are the trappings of today's elementary classroom. No longer teacher dominated, the classroom reflects children's interests and fosters social interaction.

In the past, teachers gave little thought to room arrangement. Desks were in straight rows with the teacher's desk at front and center. Bulletin boards displayed perfect papers, or a selection of a dozen or so neatly colored dittoes of squirrels holding nuts. Decorations consisted primarily of commercially prepared seasonal or holiday displays.

Though not as neat and well-ordered, classrooms today are second homes for the children. In organizing furniture, teachers consider comfort, ease of traffic flow, and areas where children can work alone, in pairs, in small groups, and as a whole class. They consult the children about how their room should look, and they accept each child's best work for display.

Planning for a Thinking Classroom

If you want to create a thinking classroom, what should you consider in planning its physical design? Much about the flexibility and child-centeredness of today's classroom applies, and Figure 3-1 lists some special areas for challenging children to think, or for showing evidence of thinking that has already occurred.

Figure 3-1. Special Areas for a Thinking Classroom

Areas where children can talk over and jot down their ideas (a conference corner or a small table with a chair on either side)

Displays created by the children (three-dimensional table displays or themed bulletin boards)

Centers where children can learn through different intelligences (more about this later in the chapter)

Bins of supplies that allow children to experiment and create (old clocks, discarded jewelry, puppets, costumes, magnets, magnifying glasses, and measuring spoons)

Many forms of children's work that inform visitors about what the class has been studying (models, art, videos, written work, and original songs)

An area where children can collaborate to deal with school and community issues (local newspapers dealing with the issue, related materials, paper and pencils for recording ideas)

A few private areas for working alone (behind a bookcase, under a loft, at a carrel)

A classroom library for getting information (nonfiction materials, biographies, atlases, almanacs, reference books, etc.)

A puzzle center where children can create and solve puzzles (math games, crossword puzzles, word searches, analogies, riddles, puns)

Shelves for math and science resources (Cuisenaire Rods, color cubes, calculators, Unifix Cubes, thermometer, balance scale, seeds, and measuring cups)

Thought-Provoking Question

How many of the areas in Figure 3-1 have you tried, or would you like to try, in your classroom? Can you think of other areas that would encourage children to think?

In addition to displays and special areas, you may want to include a message board and an author's chair in your room. A *message board* is a place for children to post messages and receive them (Harste et al., 1988). It may be a bulletin board or simply a large piece of corrugated cardboard propped against a wall. This is one way for children to communicate with each other. An *author's chair* is a special chair where a child may read an original story and ask for constructive criticism. As classmates respond, the author considers each suggestion and decides how to revise the writing.

Establishing a Theme-Related Environment

The environment reflects the theme when theme studies are well underway. Evidence of children's creative energies appears in their writing, self-constructed three-dimensional models, and dictated charts. Theme-related books are available for perusal, and exhibits are prominently displayed. In some cases, items hang suspended from the ceiling, swaying gently with the air currents.

One school carried out a schoolwide theme by transforming its hallways into different habitats. One hallway became a rain forest with vines overhead and tropical trees all around, whereas another represented a treeless, frozen Arctic tundra. The effect was so realistic that a visitor walking from one hallway into another seems to experience a drop in temperature, even though it actually remains constant. Such environmental transformations can be schoolwide, as in this example, or can simply occur within individual classrooms. In the following examples, we see how Gail Tate's and Ann Beck's rooms assumed the characteristics of the themes being investigated.

In Gail Tate's second grade class, the children had been learning about toys. They had interviewed teachers about their favorite toys at age seven and written up their findings, read books about toys, and brought old-fashioned toys to school to see how toys had changed. A glance around the room quickly informed the observer of the focus on toys, and Gail's next theme-centered lesson gave children opportunities to add their own creations to the existing displays. Gail's lesson shows how children can create new products when supplied with a box of scrap materials and time to experiment with them.

Lesson: Making Toys With Movable Parts

Gail asked her children to brainstorm ways that toys move. They mentioned cogs, wind, batteries, motors, wheels, levers, and linkages. Giving each group of four children a box of scrap materials, Gail challenged each child to make a toy with movable parts. The boxes contained such items as empty cracker boxes, bottle caps,

Lesson continued on next page

> Lesson continued from previous page
>
> sheets of clear plastic, brads, spools, and scraps of poster board. Before long, Thomas proudly handed Gail his toy: a construction-paper crab with moving claws that were linked with brads. The teacher's praise for Thomas's clever invention encouraged other children to try even harder to find ways to create their own movable toys.

In another class, Ann Beck's theme study shows how children can use a variety of learning styles and intelligences to investigate and report on information related to a theme. The room environment reflects the work that students have been doing.

Theme Study: Outer Space

As I entered Ann's third-grade class, I had no doubt what her children had been studying. Models of planets hung from the ceiling and rested on display tables; wall charts listed questions the children had asked about space, whereas other charts gave facts they had discovered; and illustrated information sheets revealed the children's prior knowledge about space. On another wall were story maps that children had made from books they had read about space, and beside the story maps was a list of spelling words, including *astronaut, comet, universe,* and *orbit.*

Ann told me that she began the theme study by asking the children to put on their thinking caps (deBono, 1991) and consider what it would be like to be an astronaut. As the theme progressed, the children investigated various subtopics about space and decided how they would present their findings. In group or individual projects, they conducted interviews, made posters, put on small plays, or wrote big books. Although the theme study was nearing completion, Ann still wanted each child to choose a planet and write a letter home explaining what it was like to live there. She also planned to invite someone who had trained as an astronaut to visit the class, to connect with NASA through the Internet, to visit a nearby planetarium, and to have the children act as astronauts themselves by wearing space suits and eating space food.

In addition to creating stimulating room environments, teachers can facilitate thinking and learning by the way they arrange the room and organize supplies. Some guidelines for making your classroom user-friendly follow.

- Make supplies (scissors, glue, folders, paper, etc.) readily accessible. Try to keep them in the same places so that children can find them easily, and don't run out of frequently needed materials.
- Build enough free time into your day to allow children time to work on special projects.

- Have places where children can display the graphs, charts, reports, and other items that they have created.
- Change centers, displays, and supply bins often enough to stimulate curiosity and maintain interest.
- Play different kinds of background music if the whole class responds favorably. If some children object, you may want to supply headphones for children who enjoy the music.
- Observe your children and provide activities that build on their natural curiosity.
- Arrange furniture for easy traffic flow and consider needs of special learners.

Creating Centers

Traditional learning centers where children go to complete learning tasks independently have been around for a long time. Typically, centers relate to units, and each center meets the skills and objectives of a different subject area.

With the recent emphasis on child-centered, integrated, authentic learning, centers have taken on a new look (Staab, 1991). The children's curiosity and ideas are the stimulus for a center, and the teacher facilitates investigation by providing materials and guiding children's thinking. Questions, generated by the children and recorded by the teacher, appear on large charts above centers. Such centers allow children to discover new information about what they really want to know. Children choose the centers they want; decide to work alone, in pairs, or in groups; evaluate their choices; and set goals for future work. Staab (1991, p. 113) says that "centers can foster a child's natural curiosity to learn as materials and resources are gathered and assembled to help a child discover what is known and to push beyond to what is unknown."

Centers can be permanent or temporary, and open-ended or topic-specific (Armstrong, 1994). By focusing on different types of intelligences, they can appeal to different kinds of learners. Figure 3-2 shows some typical kinds of center materials and/or activities related to each intelligence discussed in Chapter 2 (Armstrong, 1994).

Emotional Climate

Beginning With the Child

Setting a positive emotional climate and developing positive attitudes toward learning are priorities for teachers who wish to create thinking classrooms. In order for children to feel free to participate fully as members of the class community, they must be able to do the following:

- Feel confident
- Feel safe enough to take risks
- Regulate their own behavior
- Establish trusting relationships with teacher and peers
- Realize that school work is worth doing
- Handle personal problems effectively

Figure 3-2. Centers Organized by Intelligences

Verbal/Linguistic Centers
- Publishing center (materials for making student books)
- Library corner (books, posters, and cushions)
- Language lab (earphones, story audiotapes)
- Computer center (computerized, interactive stories)

Logical/Mathematical Centers
- Discovery and nature centers for science
- Manipulative, problem-solving centers for math
- Mathematical puzzles and games

Visual/Spatial Centers
- Painting center (easel, paints, brushes, large paper)
- Creativity area with manipulatives (beads, pasta shells, string, screening, pictures for collage)
- Geography center with local maps, atlases, and globes
- Audiovisuals (videotapes, filmstrips, slides)

Bodily/Kinesthetic Centers
- Creative dramatics (puppets, costumes, simple props)
- Tactile learning (relief maps, textured fabrics, blocks with raised alphabet letters)
- Hands-on materials (clay, colored tissue paper for tearing into shapes, magnetic letters for making words)

Musical/Rhythmic Centers
- Listening center (music audiotapes, rhythmic poetry, sounds of nature)
- Instruments for rhythm band (tambourines, bells, blocks)

Interpersonal Centers
- Group or partner games and activities for free time
- Areas for groups to work together on special projects

Intrapersonal Centers
- Nooks and crannies for independent work
- Study carrels
- Journal writing for recording thoughts and ideas

By creating an atmosphere where children feel comfortable, the teacher is enabling them to reach their full potential.

Building self-esteem is important for increasing confidence, and teachers can do this in a variety of ways (Fig. 3-3).

Figure 3-3. Building Self-Esteem

Provide positive feedback when deserved.

Allow children to make choices whenever possible.

Listen to children when they want to share something.

Help children become aware of their progress.

Reward children's best efforts.

Accept approximations as part of the learning process.

Avoid ridiculing or embarrassing a child.

Respect children's decisions when they are reasonable.

Be careful, however, not to build self-esteem falsely. Praise and recognition should be earned, not given freely for little or no effort. Children who receive undeserved praise may feel no need to work up to capacity or may harbor inflated ideas of their own abilities. Respond honestly and treat your students with respect in order to build realistic self-esteem.

One teacher found a way to get to know her children, to help them become acquainted with each other, and to make them feel special. The children introduced themselves with pictures and stories, as described in the following observation.

Observation: A Class of Special Children

As I entered a third-grade classroom near the beginning of the school year, I saw a wall covered with children's pictures and stories on large pieces of construction paper. Each student had written his or her name on the top left side of the paper, then drawn a self-portrait under the name. On the other side the children had written brief biographies. Each story ended with a preprinted statement: "I am special because I am me."

From the beginning of the school year, strive to build trust between you and the students and among the students themselves. Help them to reach their potential, and show them that their thoughts and ideas are important to you.

Thought-Provoking Question

How do we show children that we value their thinking?

1. Listen to a child's ideas.
2. Give time and encouragement for developing ideas.
3. Suggest additional resources for investigation (books, props, people) if the child is unable to find them.
4. Provide opportunities for sharing.

The ideas given here show some specific strategies that help children to develop trust and a sense of self-worth.

Taking a Personal Interest in Each Child

Learn children's names quickly and call them by name as soon as you can. You may wish to greet them at the door as they arrive or shake their hands as they leave to make sure that you have spoken with each child every day. Observe and listen to find out what is important to the children, and inquire about special interests or activities (a motocross event, a hospitalized family member, or a new puppy). Make eye contact with students, give them a smile or a touch on the shoulder, and find other ways to show that you care. Don't discriminate against students for any reason, and avoid having teacher's pets.

Acting in a Trustworthy Manner

Be fair and consistent to the best of your ability. Keep promises and avoid making threats, particularly those you may not be able to carry out. Prepare lessons well, make them interesting, include different types of intelligences, be enthusiastic about your subject, and give appropriate feedback. Return papers promptly and keep grades confidential. Never embarrass or humiliate a child, and don't betray a confidence unless it's a matter that should be reported to authorities.

Establishing Class Rules

You and the children need to know what behavior is acceptable and what is not, as well as what the penalties are for unacceptable behavior. If children have a voice in establishing class rules, they are more likely to follow them than if you set them up without their input. Rules should be posted so that everyone can see them, and they may be modified during the year if changes are needed.

Helping Students Gain Acceptance From Their Peers

Children often have difficulty being accepted by their classmates and don't know why. Acceptance is important for their personal well-being and for becoming a respected member of the class community.

Thought-Provoking Question

How can you help your students be accepted?

1. Make tactful, constructive suggestions about their behavior.
2. Refer them to a guidance counselor if social maladjustment is serious.
3. Suggest books that deal with particular problems they are experiencing.
4. Ask sympathetic classmates to help them win approval.
5. Help them to realize that it is more important to be *interested* than to be *interesting* (Marzano et al., 1992a).

Assigning Interesting, Worthwhile Tasks

Make sure that your students understand why their work is useful and worth knowing. Relate it to themes that connect different areas of the curriculum, and help them select authentic activities that they can easily connect to real-life needs. Create tasks that challenge them to think creatively and critically, and give them time and resources to do so. Encourage students to generate their own investigations and initiate their own activities.

Helping Students Set Goals

Students need to feel a sense of purpose, and many of the goals set for the whole class apply to most students. Each student is an individual, however, and has a personal agenda. Help students set their own goals by having them evaluate what they know and can do and by asking them to look ahead to what they want to do or become. By guiding their goal setting, you are helping students realize their own personal objectives. Whenever possible, link your instruction to their goals.

Enabling Students to Assume Responsibility for Their Behavior

Students must eventually be responsible for their own actions. Many teachers find that they are gradually able to relinquish control and turn much of the decision making over to the students, once the students are used to the classroom routines and expectations. Children can also learn to handle their own problems, as in the following observation.

Observation: Responsibility for Handling One's Own Problems

As the children play on the equipment during recess, they often find reasons to tell tales or complain about accidental injuries. A teacher who wants children to settle their own disputes might respond in the following manner.

observation continued on next page

---

observation continued from previous page

Child: Jeremy kicked me when I was on the monkey bars.

Teacher: Did I kick you?

Child: No.

Teacher: Well, who did?

Child: Jeremy.

Teacher: Then you need to talk to Jeremy about it.

Exchanges such as these mean that children learn to resolve problems themselves by dealing with them directly instead of involving the teacher.

Creating a Community of Learners

Once you have created a supportive physical environment and set conditions for building trust, your class is likely to become a community of learners. A sense of community takes time to develop, and it evolves as you and the children come to know and care about each other. As the teacher, your behavior and attitudes set the tone for the class because the children imitate the way you interact and react. When you show respect and express concern, they are likely to do the same. Figure 3-4 identifies some features of classroom communities.

Figure 3-4. Features of Classroom Communities

Students and teacher know each other well.

The teacher learns along with the children.

The children and their teacher can take risks and make approximations without fear of embarrassment.

Children have a say in making class rules and planning the curriculum.

Trade books in the classroom library have worthy themes that show respect and kindness.

Students gradually assume more responsibility for their own behavior and the smooth operation of their class.

All students take part in making decisions and solving problems that arise.

Each class member listens respectfully when someone is speaking.

Students understand and respect established routines and procedures but know that they are free to suggest modifications.

Community members are valued for their strengths, for what they *can* do.

Students often take the lead in investigating topics of their choice, with the teacher acting as facilitator.

Some class meetings operate as communities. At these meetings children take part in creating their own communities, perhaps by contributing their ideas about ways to operate their classroom. They listen to each other's points of view and reflect on what transpired during the meeting (Letts, 1994). Children in Bobbi Fisher's class (1995) hold weekly meetings to discuss ways to maintain a positive classroom community and deal with any problems. Some of their topics are criteria for being a good leader,ways to listen well, and rules that are negotiable or nonnegotiable.

Negotiated curriculum is often a feature of classroom communities; that is, the teacher and children create the curriculum together (Davenport et al., 1995, 1996/1997). On one hand, teachers must consider curricular guides and grade-level expectations because there are certain concepts and skills they must cover. In fact, in some school systems, teachers are bound by strictly controlled state curricular standards, budgets, and assessment guidelines. On the other hand, teachers and children seek ways to pursue their own special interests within existing curricular frameworks. Where teachers have some flexibility in designing the curriculum, they should consider the following criteria when they negotiate it (Davenport et al., 1995, 1996/1997):

- Goals for learning
- District and statewide curricular mandates
- Students' interests and areas of expertise
- Schoolwide themes
- A context rich with possibilities for learning
- Parental concerns
- Meaningful activity in a variety of disciplines

The following theme study resulted from a negotiated curriculum (Davenport et al., 1996/1997).

Theme Study: Arising From a Negotiated Curriculum

Immersed in a unit on an Arctic expedition, students in a multiage classroom became deeply involved in inquiry and exploration. Based on inquiries generated by the whole class, each group of students investigated a different aspect of the expedition for their culminating activities. Addressing the intelligences of different learners, the students conveyed information through music, mathematics, dance, technology, and various art forms. For example, students demonstrated map making, ship building, cooking, singing, writing, speaking, and clay sculpting.

theme study continued on next page

theme study continued from previous page

To facilitate the students' efforts during their Arctic expedition, the teacher had negotiated the curriculum with them and assisted in planning explorations, collecting materials, and adjusting the schedule to permit them to pursue their questions. Because they had a voice in developing their curriculum, the students had a commitment to learning and a sense of pride in what they did. "In a negotiated curriculum, the students generate enthusiasm from their need to know and the pursuit of their own burning questions" (Davenport et al., 1996/1997, p. 353).

Thought-Provoking Question

If the fifth-grade curriculum requires a study of United States history, what can you negotiate with your students?

1. Events to emphasize (wars, inventions, industrial revolution)
2. Resources to use (trade books, textbooks, reference materials, resource people, videos)
3. Ways to learn (group work, projects, independent study)
4. Ways to report (art, written booklets, reenactments of events, panel discussions)

Parents, projects, and portfolios are the three cornerstones for building a community of learners in Ruth Nathan's classroom (1995). Parental involvement is critical for developing positive family attitudes toward school and getting cooperation. Big, long-term projects get children working and talking together about common goals, and portfolios are reflections of who the students are and what they can do. As children talk about their portfolios, they are creating a sense of community.

Although many principles for forming classroom communities remain the same, they operate in different ways. The next examples are two ways of building community that involve special learners.

Community of Learners: Inclusion

First graders in a Georgia school system bonded as they supported their classmate, Katie, who had multiple disabilities (Logan et al., 1994/1995). The children helped Katie through cooperative learning activities and buddy programs, but they also went beyond the classroom to write letters to the newspaper editor and the President of the United States. As advocates of inclusion, the children explained how they had been able to help Katie and how she had also helped them by showing them that people can be different.

Community of Learners: Bilingual Classroom

Children from dissimilar backgrounds—Mexican-American and nonminority—became a community of learners through the guidance of their teacher (Whitmore and Crowell, 1994). Caryl Crowell encouraged her children to take responsibility for their learning, ask their own questions, use bilingual materials, and follow research procedures. The students planned a thematic curriculum and immersed themselves in meaningful reading and writing activities. Various factors enabled this diverse class to act as a community, including high expectations, trusting relationships, authentic literacy events, and bilingualism.

Creating a community of learners raises the issue of control. Many teachers are uncomfortable turning over so many of the management and curricular decisions to the children. In the past, teachers directed instruction; now they join the children in establishing a democratic community where each participant has a part to play. The solution appears to be in the early establishment of positive attitudes and sensible routines, with the teacher gradually relinquishing control as the children grow in their ability to manage themselves.

Thought-Provoking Question

Have you been able to establish a community in your class? If so, how did you do it? Share your ideas with others.

Creating a Generative or an Inquiry Curriculum

Much like the negotiated curriculum, the generative curriculum builds on the interests of the children and the teacher, as well as the curriculum prescribed by the school district (Fisher and Cordeiro, 1994). Students have a say in what and how they learn, and they follow their individual pursuits and avenues of inquiry within the mandated curricular framework. A generative curriculum is created collaboratively, with teachers and students becoming learners together. Although the curriculum is creative and spontaneous, it has boundaries and goals that evolve as teacher and children collaborate.

Also valuing children's interests and curiosity, Jerome Harste (Monson and Monson, 1994) proposes building the curriculum around children's inquiry questions instead of the disciplines. Children in an inquiry curriculum become researchers who ask questions and seek answers in undetermined ways. Harste (1993) contends that three sources of knowledge are necessary for creating an inquiry curriculum: the disciplines, the sign systems, and personal knowing.

In an inquiry curriculum, disciplines (math, science, social studies, and so on) become the tools for seeking answers to questions that stem from children's natural curiosity. The disciplines offer different perspectives on questions children ask, such as how a historian or a biologist would respond differently to environmental issues.

Sign systems, such as speech, music, art, mathematics, and dance, give us other ways to think about our world. As with multiple intelligences, sign systems offer children alternative ways of learning. Each sign system has its own symbols that represent meaning. Sign systems open up new ways of knowing and perceiving, for viewing a sunset as a scientist is quite different from viewing it as an artist. To fully understand and appreciate a concept, we need to be able to envision it in different sign systems. By moving from one sign system to another, we gain new insights and perspectives.

We must base instruction on what children already know, for they cannot learn new information if they lack essential background experience and knowledge. In planning an inquiry curriculum, teachers must find ways that children can relate to the topic being discussed.

The need to pursue their inquiries motivates students to perform up to their potential (Wray and Lewis, 1996). During inquiry investigations, children use talk to support, argue, defend, explore, and share.

Much of the value of an inquiry curriculum lies in its attention to underlying processes. The breadth, depth, and changing nature of the disciplines makes it impossible for us to teach everything, and how can we anticipate what children will need to know in the future? Giving them the strategies to work through their own questions prepares them for learning in the years ahead.

Within a community of learners, children can collaborate on seeking answers to their inquiries. In groups or with partners, students learn to value diversity and respect each individual's unique perspective (Short and Burke, 1991). Working together, student researchers begin with what they want to know, use whatever methods seem effective, and often continue with a new round of inquiry. As teachers, we, too, should share an interest in the topic of inquiry, for it is difficult to teach what does not interest us.

Research, the essence of an inquiry curriculum, is "systematic inquiry which develops from being interested in the world, asking questions about aspects of the world that are puzzling, and investigating those questions and possible solutions" (Short and Burke, 1991, p. 55). The following classroom examples show ways that teachers use inquiry and research to stimulate critical thinking.

Inquiry Lesson: Estimation

Quite unintentionally, Debbie Peterman's sixth graders became involved in finding out how much a million is. After a math lesson on quantity and estimation, several students raised the following questions:

- "How much is a million, really?"
- "How long would it take to count to a million?"
- "Has anyone in this class ever seen a million of something?"

Since the students really wanted to know, Debbie asked them to brainstorm items that they could bring to class and count. They decided on grains of rice and then estimated the size of the container that would be needed to hold the rice and the number of packages they would need.

To get started, Debbie brought a one-pound bag of rice, which she distributed among the students. They found that there were approximately 15,000 grains of rice in one pound and then calculated that they would need 33 two-pound bags of rice in order to have a million grains. As the students continued to bring in bags over the next few weeks, they revised their estimates of the size of container necessary to hold a million grains. Many who had estimated containers such as bathtubs and dump trucks soon found their estimations to be humorous, as the class eventually realized that a 10-gallon container would hold a million grains of rice. Debbie followed this extended inquiry lesson with selections from children's literature, including David Schwartz's *How Much Is a Million?* and *If You Made a Million* and Rod Clement's *Counting on Frank.*

Inquiry- or Research-Based Classroom: Authentic Research

In her sixth-grade class, Gina Schack (1993) encourages her children to develop their questions into research projects. If a topic doesn't emerge naturally, she asks students to brainstorm ideas related to their current interests. She helps them focus their problems, find suitable research designs, gather and interpret their data, and share research findings. These are some topics her students investigated.

- Gathering information on the use of playground equipment by observing peers
- Surveying children's fears of nuclear war
- Conducting studies of pollution in a nearby stream
- Interviewing students to determine what conditions would cause classmates to cheat
- Designing and analyzing a survey about students' transitions to middle school
- Conducting experimental research to determine how rye seeds grow best

Inquiry- or Research-Based Classroom: Discovery Club

In one fifth-grade classroom, children participate in a Discovery Club in order to ask and find answers to their own "wonderful questions" (Leland and Harste, 1994; Monson and Monson, 1994). Held during the last period of the day three days a week, Discovery Club lets students select and explore topics that interest them. When students share interests, they collaborate to investigate their topics. The focus is on conversation, collaboration, inquiry, and research.

Inquiry- or Research-Based Classroom: Shared Inquiry

Using a slightly different approach, Thomas and Oldfather (1995) describe an inquiry program that focuses on literacy events. As partners with their teachers in shared inquiry, 10- and 11-year-olds evaluate their learning experiences and actively paricipate in planning and implementing classroom literacy activities. The form of inquiry may be literature discussion groups, self-selected writing activities, or reading to investigate topics in science or social studies. Primarily through interactive journals, students reflect on their purposes for reading, criteria for quality books, and goals for self-selected reading. From these journals teachers learn about students' thinking, understanding, questions, and problems.

These classroom examples show us that there is no single way to implement an inquiry classroom; it evolves from interactions between teachers and students. An inquiry classroom has a certain ambiance, a distinctive atmosphere that allows children to pursue answers to genuine questions. As such, it frees children to think about what really matters to them.

Summary

The physical environment of the classroom should be stimulating; it should reflect students' interests and offer opportunities for discovery, exploration, and invention. Movable furniture that allows for flexible room arrangements enables students to work independently, as partners, in groups, or with the entire class. A wide variety of materials and useful supplies should be available for students. Using themes and questions generated by students, teachers can design centers that represent a variety of intelligences.

In order to learn and think as well as they can, children must feel good about themselves. Teachers should take time to create a positive emotional environment by building self-esteem, taking a personal interest in each child, being trustworthy and consistent, and helping children to be accepted by their peers. Students should feel safe enough to share their thoughts and ideas without fear of ridicule.

When a classroom community exists, the children and teacher accept joint responsibility for classroom management and learning opportunities. They negotiate curriculum, and children become full participants in a democratic community. In such a community of learners, an inquiry-based classroom thrives. A generative, or an inquiry-based, classroom is a collaborative effort between teacher and students, with students seeking answers to real questions and teachers facilitating their efforts.

References

Armstrong, T. (1994). *Multiple intelligences.* Alexandria, VA: Association for Supervision and Curriculum Development.

Bull, G. (1989). *Reflective teaching.* Carlton South, Victoria: Australian Reading Association.

Cambourne, B. (1988). *The whole story.* Gosford, Australia: Ashton Scholastic.

Carroll, J., and Christenson, C. (1995). Teaching and learning about student goal setting in a fifth-grade classroom. *Language Arts, 72*(1), 42–49.

Cecil, N.L. (1993). *Teaching to the heart.* Salem, WI: Sheffield.

Cecil, N. (1995). *The art of inquiry.* Winnipeg, MB, Canada: Peguis.

Church, E.B. (1996a). "Let's figure it out!" *Scholastic Early Childhood Today, 10*(5), 20–21.

Church, E.B. (1996b). Planning curriculum together. *Scholastic Early Childhood Today, 10*(6), 16–19.

Clement, R. (1990). *Counting on Frank.* North Ryde, New South Wales, Australia: Collins/Angus & Robertson.

Davenport, M.R., Jaeger, M., and Lauritzen, C. (1995). Negotiating curriculum. *The Reading Teacher, 49*(1), 60–62.

Davenport, M.R., Jaeger, M., and Lauritzen, C. (1996/1997). A curriculum of caring. *The Reading Teacher, 50*(4), 352–353.

deBono, E. (1991). *Six thinking hats.* Logan, IA: Perfection Learning.

DeStephen, T. (1995). Making connections: A teacher and her rural at-risk students. In J. Bertrand and C. Stice (Eds.), *Empowering children at risk of school failure: A better way.* Norwood, MA: Christopher-Gordon.

Establishing patterns of communities through language. (1996). *Primary Voices, 4*(2).

Fisher, B. (1989). The environment reflects the program. *Teaching K–8, 20*(1), 82–87.

Fisher, B. (1995). *Thinking and learning together.* Portsmouth, NH: Heinemann.

Fisher, B., and Cordeiro, P. (1994). Generating curriculum: Building a shared curriculum. *Primary Voices, 2*(3), 2–7.

Garan, E. (1994). Who's in control? Is there enough "empowerment" to go around? *Language Arts, 71*(3), 192–199.

Gwiazda, C. (1995). *Improving classroom instruction through multiple intelligences.* Presentation at National Council of Teachers of English Annual Convention, San Diego.

Harste, J. (1993). Curriculum for the millennium: Putting an edge on learning through inquiry. *The Australian Journal of Language and Literacy, 16*(1), 7–23.

Harste, J., Short, K., and Burke, C. (1988). *Creating classrooms for authors.* Portsmouth, NH: Heinemann.

Howell, M. (1991). Choreography of the language arts class. *Language Arts, 68*(8), 650–651.

Leland, C., and Harste, J. (1994). Multiple ways of knowing: Curriculum in a new key. *Language Arts, 71*(5), 337–345.

Letts, N. (1994). Building classroom unity. *Teaching K–8, 25*(1), 106–107.

Logan, K., Diaz, E., Piperno, M., Rankin, D., MacFarland, A.D., and Bargamian, K. (1994/1995). How inclusion built a community of learners. *Educational Leadership, 52*(4), 42–44.

Marzano, R., Pickering, D., Arredondo, D., Blackburn, G., Brandt, R., and Moffett, C. (1992a). *Dimensions of learning,* teacher's manual. Alexandria, VA: Association for Supervision and Curriculum Development.

Marzano, R., Pickering, D., Arredondo, D., Blackburn, G., Brandt, R., and Moffett, C. (1992b). *Dimensions of learning,* trainer's manual. Alexandria, VA: Association for Supervision and Curriculum Development.

Monson, R., and Monson, J. (1994). Literacy as inquiry: An interview with Jerome C. Harste. *The Reading Teacher, 47*(7), 518–522.

Nathan, R. (1995). Parents, projects, and portfolios: 'Round and about community building in room 14. *Language Arts, 72*(2), 82–87.

Play to learn. (1996). *Scholastic Early Childhood Today, 10*(8), 23.

Pogrow, S. (1994). Helping students who "just don't understand." *Educational Leadership, 52*(3), 62–66.

Prawat, R. (1992). From individual differences to learning communities— Our changing focus. *Educational Leadership, 49*(7), 9–13.

Schack, G. (1993). Involving students in authentic research. *Educational Leadership, 50*(7), 29–31.

Scheu, J., Blake, K., Pai, N., and Wong-Kam, J.A. (1995). Looking in and out: Rethinking classroom dynamics. *Language Arts, 72*(6), 449–456.

Schwartz, D. (1985). *How much is a million?* New York: Lothrop, Lee & Shepard.

Schwartz, D. (1989). *If you made a million.* New York: Scholastic.

Short, K. and Burke, C. (1991). *Creating curriculum.* Portsmouth, NH: Heinemann.

Short, K., Schroeder, J., Laird, J., Kauffman, G., Ferguson, M., and Crawford, K. (1996). *Learning together through inquiry.* York, ME: Stenhouse.

Siu-Runyan, Y. (1991). Learning from students: An important aspect of classroom organization. *Language Arts, 68*(2), 100–107.

Staab, C. (1991). Classroom organization: Thematic centers revisited. *Language Arts, 68*(2), 108–113.

Thomas, S., and Oldfather, P. (1995). Enhancing student and teacher engagement in literacy learning. *The Reading Teacher, 49*(3), 192–202.

Whitmore, K., and Crowell, C. (1994). *Inventing a classroom: Life in a bilingual, whole language learning community.* York, ME: Stenhouse.

Wilson, J., and Wing Jan, L. (1993). *Thinking for themselves.* Portsmouth, NH: Heinemann.

Wing Jan, L. (1991). *Write ways.* Melbourne, Victoria, Australia: Oxford.

Wray, D., and Lewis, M. (1996). "But bonsai trees don't grow in baskets": Young children's talk during authentic inquiries. In L. Gambrell and J. Almasi (Eds.), *Lively discussions!* Newark, DE: International Reading Association.

CHAPTER 4

Valuing the Social Nature of Learning

When I asked the teachers:

"How can children learn with and from each other?"

the teachers said:

- By working in groups; in a noncompetitive atmosphere children can help each other.
- By getting the opportunity to learn with and from each other.
- By teaching each other; children sometimes do this better than the teacher because they are on the same level and can understand each other.
- Through discussion, playing, and interacting with each other.
- By allowing children to work together in cooperative learning groups, in large group discussions with the teacher, and at learning centers.
- By having partners with whom to share ideas, discuss stories, and tell experiences.
- By trying to teach, which is the best way to learn something. Through peer teaching both the student teaching and the student being taught benefit. A person who has recently learned something is more familiar with the thought processes required to learn it than someone who learned it 20 years ago.

How would you answer this question?

Concepts to watch for

- Learning as a social process
- The role of talk in thinking
- Different forms of talk
- Use of partnerships and cooperative learning activities to promote thinking

---

Always a traditional teacher, Debra made sure that her class was quiet and orderly. One day, after attending a workshop where she heard that children could learn by talking, Debra decided to begin letting her students talk to each other about their reading and writing. She noticed that the children seemed more interested in their work and were actually sharing some surprisingly perceptive insights.

Still finding it hard to let go of control and allow the murmur of children's voices, Debra asked Tracy, a neighboring teacher, to step into her room. Seeking reassurance, Debra asked Tracy, "Is it okay if they're talking?" Listening in for a moment, Tracy convinced Debra that not only was it okay, but the children were getting much more from their work by talking it over than by working alone.

Thinking and Learning as Social Processes

In Chapter 3 we considered ways to create physical and emotional environments that encourage children to become members of a community of learners. In such a community, they feel comfortable and secure, yet stimulated by opportunities to pursue special interests. This chapter continues in much the same vein, with children learning together as they think through and talk over their ideas.

As noted in Chapter 1, Vygotsky believed that social interaction is vital for a person's cognitive growth. He said that children are forced to think and communicate about their thinking as they interact with others (Dixon-Krauss, 1996). Believing that all learning is centered in social interaction, Vygotsky supported the idea of collaboration and cooperation, a well-accepted concept in many of today's classrooms.

Vygotsky also believed that children's thinking is shaped by the sociocultural setting of the classroom. In other words, where a community of learners exists, children will be empowered to think and exchange ideas. On the other hand, in classrooms where rules are rigid and the teacher dominates, children will be constrained in their thinking.

Thought-Provoking Question

Will children be empowered to think and exchange ideas in your classroom, according to Vygotsky's belief? Why or why not?

Addressing the connection between thought and language, Vygotsky (1986) claimed that language is at first *social,* when used for contact with others, then *egocentric,* when the child talks out loud to herself. Speech soon becomes *intellectual* as well when the child learns to use *inner speech,* or soundless language, for internal thought. Thinking arises from the child's ability to use speech.

When children enter school, they use spoken language as the primary means of cognitive development. After all, they have been using speech to communicate and express ideas since they first began listening and speaking, so it is natural for them to continue to do so. Therefore, we need to allow them to continue learning through talk, even as they acquire concepts about printed language. In the following vignette, we see how children are able to negotiate and solve problems by talking through a situation.

Team Collaboration: Problem Solving

Filling in for the gym teacher, Denise divided her first graders into teams to run relay races. Each team was to do its best, and winning was not a priority. The children enjoyed running, but one team had a problem finishing with the other teams because Charlie was a really slow runner. The team offered Charlie encouragement, but he just couldn't run any faster.

Talking over the problem, members of Charlie's team considered their options. They decided to put Charlie first and their fastest runners at the end. By doing so, Charlie's team was able to finish close to the other teams. In the spirit of community, the team resolved its problem.

The Significance of Talk for Thinking

Talking and thinking "are interdependent and complementary" (Bull, 1989, p. 51). Talk enables children to acquire new ideas and concepts; reflect on and clarify existing concepts, values, and ideas; and formulate and develop higher-order thinking strategies.

Benefits of Classroom Talk

As the incident with Debra at the beginning of the chapter illustrates, teachers are beginning to realize that children's talk helps them learn.

Classes in which children discuss their ideas and collaborate on projects are gradually replacing quiet classes in which children work in isolation. Talk offers many advantages as a way of thinking and learning (Barnes, 1995).

- Talk is flexible, allowing us to change direction, modify our first thoughts, and discover new connections.
- Talk is easily shared with others.
- Most children come to school already knowing how to talk.
- Talk lets children think aloud about new ideas and information.

Here are some additional benefits of allowing children to talk in school.

Talk clarifies thinking. Putting thoughts into words in order to convey ideas to someone else forces the speaker to choose words carefully. First, the speaker must clarify his or her thinking by asking, "What is it that I really want to say?" Instead of groping for words and ending with, "Oh—you know what I mean," the speaker must articulate thoughts in clear language that the listener can understand. The listener, in turn, may ask for clarification, thus causing the speaker to reconsider what was said and seek a better way to communicate ideas.

Talk helps students expand their understanding. Whether discussing a theme from literature or an issue in social studies, children are exposed to a wide variety of viewpoints. They realize that they can approach matters from many perspectives, and they discover that others may have valid opinions that differ from their own. Narrow views broaden and deepen as students modify their thinking by absorbing some ideas and rejecting others. Talk becomes the foundation for adding new information to existing ideas and knowledge (Wollman-Bonilla, 1993).

Talk develops acceptable social behaviors. Through committees, town meetings, or simply class discussions, children learn socially acceptable ways to interact. They learn to listen respectfully, take turns talking, and not to interrupt. When they take the lead in discussions, they learn how to treat participants fairly. They become aware of undesirable behaviors, such as monopolizing the discussion and making rude comments, and take measures to correct such situations.

Talk is useful in each area of the curriculum. Instead of being restricted to show-and-tell time or formal speech making, talk permeates each area of the curriculum. Children talk through the steps in solving word problems in math. If they need help, they ask a peer to explain how to work the problem, which helps both students understand the process. When given the responsibility for conducting science experiments, children demonstrate the steps and then explain the concepts that are illustrated by the experiment. In reading, children discuss books in literature circles, and in writing, children confer with each other about their drafts.

Social studies is rich in opportunities for talk; it allows children to debate issues, present reports, interview resource people, and engage in panel discussions.

Talk is rehearsal. Talking over ideas with someone helps students prepare to write a piece, tell a story, solve a problem, plan or complete a project, and so on. Reflecting on what happened during the school day by letting each child share something significant is rehearsal for answering a parent's proverbial question, "What did you do in school today?" (Fraser and Skolnick, 1994).

Talk provides teachers with insights. As teachers listen to students talk, they discover what students know, what misconceptions they hold, and what they still need to learn. This knowledge serves as an assessment tool, a means for planning further instruction, and a way of understanding how children might benefit from scaffolding.

Talk offers ESL students a natural way to learn language. The emphasis on oral language that occurs in inquiry classrooms gives ESL children opportunities to use the types of language skills they need to grow socially and academically. Through meaningful class discussions, they gain confidence in using English by listening to their peers and beginning to share their own ideas (Wilks, 1995).

The Teacher's Role in Guiding Discussion

The teacher plays an important part in setting the tone for open class discussion. A positive mindset toward classroom talk is more important than including specific activities for talking during the day (Staab, 1996). Teachers who believe in the benefits of classroom talk make it a natural part of daily activities across the curriculum, without having to set aside special times for talk. Negative feedback during discussion can stifle children's thinking and cause them to withdraw, whereas positive feedback nudges them to expand their thoughts and pursue additional ideas. Moreover, verbal exchanges can profoundly affect children's understanding of themselves and their concepts of the world in which they live (Booth, 1994).

Teachers who value classroom talk model effective discussion techniques so that they can gradually turn over much of the responsibility for classroom talk to the students. Many opportunities exist for children to talk during the day, including student-to-teacher, student-to-student, student-to–small group, and student-to–whole class interactions (Staab, 1996). Examples of each type of interaction follow.

Student-to-teacher interactions. Traditionally, in one-to-one conferences the teacher directs the interaction by asking questions and expecting students to respond. In student-to-teacher meetings, however, the student usually takes the lead in sharing information with the teacher and asking for help. This kind of interaction occurs frequently during reading and writing conferences.

Student-to-student interactions. Conversations between students occur naturally on the playground, in the lunchroom, and during free times, but they also take place when students are on-task. Meaningful exchanges occur as children offer constructive criticism during writing conferences or help each other work through math problems. Once suspicious of children's talk during class, teachers are finding that children are likely to use talk for worthwhile purposes if they have interesting, meaningful work.

Student-to–small group interactions. Students have many opportunities to participate in groups, such as cooperative learning, literature circles, and science experiments. Teacher modeling of appropriate group interactions and patience in helping groups establish behavior patterns are necessary for small discussion groups to function well. Sometimes groups meet without the teacher's presence, and sometimes the teacher is present as a participant, not a director.

Thought-Provoking Question

How can you encourage small groups to consider you as a participant rather than a group leader?

Student-to–whole class interactions. Students speak before the whole class when they share during show-and-tell or morning talk, report on a project, lead opening exercises, or present news items related to a topic of special interest. Such activities should be purposeful and authentic so that children can learn the importance of communicating effectively with a large group.

In a community of learners, a teacher usually acts as a mediator or facilitator instead of a director of instruction. As a group participant, the teacher can guide thoughtful discussion, as shown in Figure 4-1.

In a community of learners, all children have a right to be heard—children at risk, who speak English as a second language, who are "included," and who march to a different drummer (Gilles, 1995). By providing a variety of speech opportunities, the teacher should enable each child to find a niche where talk is comfortable and respected. Children who are too shy to talk before the whole class may speak individually to the teacher or converse with a supportive peer, and those who have difficulty speaking English may work with proficient speakers in small-group settings in order to gain confidence.

Figure 4-1. Ways That Teachers Can Guide Thoughtful Discussion

Encouraging children to think and reflect

Showing appreciation for children's contributions to the discussion

Expanding on students' comments in order to extend the discussion to deeper levels

Joining a group informally and modeling thoughtful verbal exchanges

Casually offering alternative wording in standard English

Seeking clarification of the speaker's intent

Listening intently with appropriate nonverbal responses (nodding to affirm, raising an eyebrow to question)

Refocusing discussion when children get off track

Changing the mood or tone of discussion if advisable

Asking authentic questions out of sincere interest instead of teacher-type questions

Being nonjudgmental

Respecting the ideas of others

Thinking aloud when offering an idea

Forms of Talk

Talk covers a wide range of oral expression, from the babbling of an infant to the sophisticated speech making of a politician. This section will focus on the forms of speech that stimulate thinking.

Exploratory Talk

Children engage in exploratory talk as they make initial attempts to communicate new ideas. They do this by thinking out loud and grasping for the right words to express their ideas. Typical of exploratory talk are frequent hesitations, false starts, rephrasing, and changes in direction (Booth, 1994). Such talk helps children clarify, rehearse, and internalize ideas by thinking aloud in small, nonjudgmental groups (Coelho, 1994).

Children working in groups use exploratory talk to investigate inquiries that arise from their experiences. Literature studies offer opportunities for children to use exploratory talk to discover new perspectives and move their thinking to deeper levels of understanding (Pierce, 1995). When attempting to solve unfamiliar problems, students often use exploratory talk to try out their ideas within their group. This sort of talk leads to higher-level thinking as children analyze their thoughts, evaluate situations, apply new information, and create original ideas.

Thought-Provoking Question

Recall the last time that you had difficulty expressing a thought. What did you do to communicate your meaning?

Brainstorming

Brainstorming is one of the easiest ways to get children to think divergently. They are usually full of ideas and only need opportunities to be heard. The purpose of brainstorming is to get children to think of as many ideas as possible that address the issue at hand. The quality of ideas doesn't matter, and children are encouraged to "piggyback" on each other's ideas. No judgment is to be made, and no one is allowed to criticize another's ideas. In the lesson that follows, Stacy Ross is asking her students to brainstorm.

Lesson: Brainstorming

Near the end of the year, Stacy gathered her kindergartners on the rug and asked them what changes they would like to make. Suggestions tumbled from them, with one idea often leading to another. This is what they said: (*T* is for teacher; *S* is for student.)

 T: I'm wondering how we could make our kindergarten a better place. Think about it, and then tell me your ideas.

 S: We could have a talent show in our room.

 S: Let's get more games for the computer.

 S: We could do some things at different times.

 T: Can you tell me what you mean by that?

 S: We could have lunch after playground.

 S: Yes, and we could do journals after work folders.

 T: Any other ideas?

 S: We could watch a movie every day.

 S: Let's put up more decorations.

 T: What kind of decorations would you like?

 S: Things that the kids make.

 S: I know. Let's move the American flag so you can see it as soon as you come in the room.

 S: You could buy us more stickers.

 T: Why would you want me to do that?

 S: So we wouldn't ever run out.

Lesson continued on next page

Lesson continued from previous page

T: What if we could do some really wild and crazy things? What would you like to do then?

S: We could have monkeys on the ceiling. To play with.

S: A lion.

S: Elephants. We could ride a baby elephant.

T: What would we do with all those animals in here?

S: We'd make a cage to keep them in.

S: We could have real fish in a big fish tank. We could feed them.

S: Yes, and we could paint our walls blue to look like the ocean.

S: I know. Let's have a swimming pool!

T: Would you put it in here?

S: No, outside.

T: Then, who would use it? Would the whole school use it?

S: It could have a little part and a big part. You know, like a part for the little kids—for us.

S: We'd need a ladder to jump off.

S: And a water slide.

S: And a diving board.

S: We'd need life jackets, too.

S: We could have air that blows the water to make waves.

S: Let's have an ant farm.

T: Tell me about the ant farm.

S: We could put it in the center of the room.

S: We'd watch the ants and feed them.

S: Let's have a hamster farm.

T: Think what you would like to have most of all. We'll vote.

The children voted almost unanimously for the pool, with one holdout for the ant farm. The teacher then had to help the children realize that it would be unlikely for them to actually get a pool, even though it is fun sometimes to imagine what could be. Jason, however, persisted and asked her to speak with the principal about it after the children went home.

Interviews

Conducting interviews offers opportunities for children to use talk for a specific purpose, such as gathering information for a school newspaper. Students should prepare questions in advance but allow for spontaneity if surprising answers lead in new directions. After information is collected, students should compile it and analyze the results.

Lesson: Interview

In a second-grade class, children were deeply engrossed in a theme study on toys. One activity involved interviewing the teachers in their school to find out what their favorite toys were when they were children. The purpose of the interview was to learn how toys have changed over the years.

Working in pairs and carrying clipboards, students went from room to room asking questions and recording information. First they wrote the teacher's name, then checked the appropriate age bracket (20–30, 30–40, etc.). Of each teacher they asked the following questions:

1. What was your favorite toy when you were seven years old?

2. What was it made of?

Taking their findings back to the classroom, the children then analyzed the results. There were opportunities to identify preferred toys, organize them by teachers' age categories, find out which materials were used to make the toys, and compare this information with children's favorite toys today.

Discussion

Discussion takes place throughout the school day in a variety of situations. As opposed to recitation, in which teachers ask students factual questions, discussion allows participants to exchange views on a variety of topics. A comment by one student may trigger new ideas, and the direction of the discussion may take a different turn. Although the leader may try to hold the class to the topic, there is no predetermined agenda for a discussion.

Discussion stimulates thinking as students listen carefully to what others say and then modify or extend their own thinking. They find themselves reevaluating their opinions, formulating new ideas, drawing conclusions, thinking logically and critically, and considering different points of view. Discussions in class communities center around genuine inquiries, and students often take the lead with little or no teacher intervention.

The content and nature of peer-group discussions differ from discussions in which the teacher is present. Even though the teacher acts as a participant, children may be somewhat inhibited about what they say, or they may expect the teacher to take the lead.

Both types of discussion offer advantages. The teacher as participant can facilitate thinking and model procedures for group interactions. Without the teacher, however, children are likely to assume leadership roles themselves and explore issues more openly and honestly. Students participating in peer discussions instead of teacher-led discussions engage in higher-level thought processes, according to a research study conducted by Janice Almasi (1995). Student-led discussions also result in wider participation by group members and richer inquiry.

Thought-Provoking Question

What opportunities do you provide for students to discuss issues without your presence? How do you evaluate the effectiveness of these discussions?

Dialogue

Much like discussion, dialogue is a conversation between two or more people. Whereas lecture and listening are solitary activities, partners in dialogue actively construct meaning in the natural give-and-take of exchanging ideas (Peterson and Eeds, 1990). Dialogue is built on knowledge of facts, but it extends well beyond the factual level as students draw on their experiences, weigh their values, and react to the views of their peers.

Meaningful dialogue is difficult because it requires participants to take initiative, engage in critical thinking, and pursue avenues of inquiry. In fact, dialogue ceases to be effective unless students put forth a great deal of energy and imagination. When it results in new insights and original ideas, dialogue becomes exciting and rewarding.

Debate

As we consider what happens during discussion and dialogue, we realize that children can articulate different opinions on many issues. Jill Ramsey (1996) writes about ways that she uses the technique of point-counterpoint, an informal type of debate, in her classroom to encourage students to look at an issue from different points of view.

> In my third grade classroom, we sometimes discuss issues using point/counterpoint. For example, one issue we discussed was if girls should get to play little league baseball with boys. The point side said they should, and the reasons they gave were:
>
> 1. Girls at that age can run as fast and play ball as well as boys. (One boy said, "The girls on my team are better than the boys!")
> 2. Girls should be treated as equals to boys.
>
> The counterpoint side (which consisted only of three boys) only gave one reason and that was that girls have their own teams that boys aren't allowed to play on. I was very surprised at how vocal and opinionated the children are at this age. They had definite views and attitudes about the issues we discussed.

Another issue we discussed was the location of the capital of the United States. We discussed the options and arguments that our founding fathers faced. Did they make a good choice? Why did they choose Washington, D.C.? In the end they agreed with the choice that was made. Good points were brought out though about whether the location of the capital would affect representation of the regions of the United States.

I think point/counterpoint is an excellent way to discuss issues and encourage children to really think about important issues. Another advantage is that children learn to respect and listen to other people's views and often change their opinions.

More structured than point-counterpoint is debate, a formal presentation before an audience with one side supporting an issue and the other side opposing it. Topics for debate may grow out of class discussions that generate strong controversy. In addition to two teams of debaters, you will need a moderator, a timekeeper, and judges to determine the side with the stronger arguments. While preparing to debate and during the actual debate, children get involved in the following processes:

- Conducting research to find information to support their views
- Anticipating what the opposition will say so that they can defend their position
- Presenting clear, logical, persuasive arguments grounded in fact
- Thinking through issues so that they can be prepared to speak spontaneously on whatever aspect of the issue the opposition introduces
- Forming summations to convince the audience of the validity of the team's position

Collaboration

Students collaborate when they work together in small groups to learn information, create a product, or reach a common goal. Collaboration occurs throughout the day in a number of ways as opportunities arise. When collaborating, children encourage each other to continue working, discuss information, work together to understand difficult material, try different techniques for finding information, and ask each other for help or advice (Wray and Lewis, 1996).

In some collaborations, partners work together in either tutorial or buddy relationships. At other times, teachers may use cooperative learning, a highly structured form of group work, as a framework for helping children learn. The next sections focus on these two types of collaboration.

Partnerships

As the teachers interviewed at the beginning of this chapter admitted, children can often teach other children more effectively than adult teachers can. Since children have just recently learned the information or procedures, they easily recall what they have learned and are able to communicate ideas in "kids' talk."

Many teachers use cross-age pairings to establish tutorial and buddy relationships between students at different grade levels. Usually, the older partners guide the younger ones in reading, writing, or math activities, and the younger children are eager to learn from their new mentors. Such interaction benefits both partners, with the upper-grade students developing a sense of responsibility for guiding the learning and development of their young partners, and the lower-grade students working hard to please their new teachers.

Lesson: Cross-Age Mentoring

As an observer during a library class, I listened to the librarian read two of Alison Lester's books, *Clive Eats Alligators* and *Imagine*, to a mixed kindergarten and first-grade class. Following the story, the librarian handed out copies of a double-page spread from *Imagine,* showing an illustration of Australian animals with the names of the animals printed around the outer edge of the two pages.

While the librarian called three children at a time to check out books, the other children worked in cross-grade pairs to match each animal with its name. When they found a match, they colored the word and the picture the same color. I listened to the first-grade students help the kindergartners identify the words. One conversation went like this: (*K* represents kindergartner; *1* represents first-grade student.)

1: Let's find a picture of a kangaroo.

K: Look, there's one.

1: Right! Now we need to find a word that says *kangaroo.* What letter do you think *kangaroo* starts with?

K: K?

1: Yes. Is it going to be a long word or a short word? Listen while I say it: *kan—ga—roo.*

K: It sounds long.

1: Yes, it's a long word because it has three parts. Can you find a long word that begins with *k*?

K: This one?

Lesson continued on next page

Lesson continued from previous page

1: That's a good guess, but I think that word is *kookaburra* because it starts with *kook.*

K: How about this one?

1: Let's see. I think that's *kangaroo* because it starts with *kang* and ends with *roo.* Now, what color shall we make the word and the picture?

The first-grade student was obviously doing a lot of teaching while trying to help the kindergartner find the right word, and the kindergartner was picking up useful clues for word identification.

I've seen children in many classrooms helping each other learn, often by imitating what the teacher would say in a similar situation. I've also seen children learning—and having fun doing so—by sharing and discussing books together, collaborating on a class project, studying individualized lists of spelling words, working with math manipulatives, and so on. Working with partners provides instant feedback and gives children a sense of security as they attempt new tasks.

Thought-Provoking Question

How would partnerships work in your classroom?

Cooperative Learning

Cooperative learning enables students to work in small, heterogeneous groups for specific purposes. A major concept behind cooperative learning is that group members are linked together so that everyone must succeed if anyone succeeds; that is, they sink or swim together. It thrives in a class environment where there is acceptance, safety, and a sense of belonging.

The highly structured nature of cooperative learning and the various strategies within its framework mean that teachers generally need training and practice before they can implement it successfully. In this brief overview, we can only view its basic structure and its possibilities for stimulating thinking. Cooperative learning consists of five basic elements (Johnson, Johnson, and Holubec, 1990):

1. Positive interdependence: Mutual goals, joint rewards, shared materials and information, assigned roles (such as summarizer, encourager of participation, and elaborator).

2. Face-to-face interaction: Oral summarizing, giving and receiving explanations, elaborating.

3. Individual accountability: Group support for individual learning, an individual test for each student.

4. Interpersonal and small-group skills: Acquisition of social interaction skills, including communication, leadership, trust, decision making, and conflict management.

5. Group processing: Time and procedures for analyzing effectiveness of group functioning and social skills.

Figure 4-2 lists some of the thinking strategies students use when they participate in cooperative learning.

Figure 4-2. Thinking Strategies Used in Cooperative Learning

Asking probing questions	Appreciating others' ideas
Reflecting on the group's	Summarizing major concepts
effectiveness	Reaching consensus
Elaborating on ideas	Justifying reasons
Supporting others	Defending opinions
Offering constructive	Checking accuracy
criticism	Thinking creatively
Evaluating ideas	Analyzing results

A cooperative learning environment that offers peer assistance provides a more culturally appropriate learning environment for minority groups than do traditional, competitive classrooms. Minority students and low achievers perform better academically in classrooms that support interaction and democratic principles. In addition, interracial cooperation is likely to improve racial attitudes and behaviors and result in long-term improvement in race relations (Coelho, 1994).

Summary

The social nature of learning recognizes the importance of talk in the classroom. Students learn by interacting with the teacher and other students, by sharing ideas and getting responses, and by reflecting on the feedback.

Student talk has many benefits: clarifying thinking, expanding understanding, acquiring acceptable social behaviors, enhancing each curriculum area, providing rehearsal time, and giving teachers insights into students' thinking. The teacher's role in guiding discussion is important; the teacher should act as facilitator, not director, of the discussion and turn much of the responsibility for leading discussion over to the students.

Classroom talk can take many forms, including exploratory talk, for articulating roughly formed ideas; brainstorming, for generating many ideas on a subject; interviewing, for examining what others think; discussion, for exchanging views on a variety of subjects; dialogue, for constructing meaning; and debate, for analyzing opposing points of view. All these forms can enhance thinking strategies.

Partnerships and cooperative learning are two forms of small group work. In partnerships students work in tutorial and/or buddy relationships, and cooperative learning offers ways for all students to benefit by working in heterogeneous groups. Cooperative learning activities are especially effective for minority students and low achievers.

References

Almasi, J. (1995). Who says conflict can't be good? *Reading Today, 13* (1), 26.

Alvermann, D., Dillon, D., and O'Brien, D. (1987). *Using discussion to promote reading comprehension.* Newark, DE: International Reading Association.

Baloche, L., and Platt, T. (1993). Sprouting magic beans: Exploring literature through creative questioning and cooperative learning. *Language Arts, 70*(4), 264–271.

Barnes, D. (1995). Talking and learning in classrooms: An introduction. *Primary Voices K–6, 3*(1): 2–7.

Bellanca, J. (1991). *Building a caring, cooperative classroom: A social skills primer.* Palatine, IL: Skylight.

Booth, D. (1994). *Classroom voices.* Toronto, ON, Canada: Harcourt Brace.

Bull, G. (1989). *Reflective teaching.* Carlton South, Victoria: Australian Reading Association.

Burpo, D., and Wheeler, P. (1994). Cooperative learning centers in an inner city classroom. *Teaching K–8, 25*(1): 76–78.

Coelho, E. (1994). *Learning together in the multicultural classroom.* Markham, Ont., Canada: Pippin.

Cullinan, B. (1993). Introduction. In B. Cullinan (Ed.), *Children's voices: Talk in the classroom.* Newark, DE: International Reading Association.

Dixon-Krauss, L. (1996). *Vygotsky in the classroom.* White Plains, NY: Longman.

Ellis, S., and Whalen, S. (1990). *Cooperative learning: Getting started.* New York: Scholastic.

Emmitt, M., and Pollock, J. (1991). *Language and learning.* South Melbourne, Victoria, Australia: Oxford.

Fisher, B. (1995). *Thinking and learning together.* Portsmouth, NH: Heinemann.

Fraser, J., and Skolnick, D. (1994). *On their way.* Portsmouth, NH: Heinemann.

Gambrell, L. (1996). What research reveals about discussion. In L. Gambrell & J. Almasi (Eds.), *Lively discussions!* Newark, DE: International Reading Association.

Gilles, C. (1995). Reflections. *Primary Voices K–6, 3*(1), 39–43.

Johnson, D., Johnson, R., and Holubec, E. (1990). *Cooperation in the classroom.* Edina, MN: Interaction.

Neff, R., and Lengel, A. (1990). That's debatable. *Teaching K–8, 20*(6), 34–35.

Peterson, R., and Eeds, M. (1990). *Grand conversations.* Richmond Hill, ON, Canada: Scholastic.

Pierce, K. (1995). A plan for learning: Creating a place for exploratory talk. *Primary Voices K–6, 3*(1), 16–24.

Ramsey, J. (1996). Point-Counterpoint. Cookeville, TN. Unpublished.

Routman, R. (1994). *Invitations* (2nd ed.). Portsmouth, NH: Heinemann.

Short, K., and Klassen, C. (1993). Literature circles: Hearing children's voices. In B. Cullinan (Ed.), *Children's voices: Talk in the classroom* (pp. 66–86). Newark, DE: International Reading Association..

Staab, C. (1996). Talk in the whole-language classroom. In V. Froese (Ed.) *Whole-language: Practice and theory* (2nd ed.). Boston: Allyn & Bacon.

Vygotsky, L. (1986). *Thought and language.* Translated and edited by A. Kozulin. Cambridge, MA: MIT Press.

Wollman-Bonilla, J. (1993). "It's really special because you get to think": Talking about literature. In B. Cullinan (Ed.), *Children's voices: Talk in the classroom.* Newark, DE: International Reading Association.

West, J. and Oldfather, P. (1993). On working together: An imaginary dialogue among real children. *Language Arts, 70*(5): 373–384.

Wilks, S. (1995). *Critical & creative thinking.* Portsmouth, NH: Heinemann.

Wray, D. and Lewis, M. (1996). "But bonsai trees don't grow in baskets": Young children's talk during authentic inquiries. In L. Gambrell and J. Almasi, (Eds.), *Lively discussions!* Newark, DE: International Reading Association.

CHAPTER 5

Connecting Thinking to Reading and Writing

When I asked the teachers,

"What strategies do (or might) you use to stimulate thinking?"

the teachers said:

- Provide opportunities for problem solving, experimentation, and analysis.
- Have students relate things to their own lives or personal experiences.
- Use creative writing and learning centers.
- Have students invent new ways to solve problems.
- Provide opportunities for self-discovery.
- Use journal writing to help students express their ideas and think about several subjects.
- Have students imagine themselves in situations where they have to solve problems similar to real-life experiences.
- Ask students to rewrite stories from a different perspective or put themselves in the character's place.

How would you answer this question?

Concepts to watch for

- The significance of metacognition in learning and thinking processes
- Ways to teach children to think about their thinking
- Specific reading and thinking strategies
- Some ways that thinking is part of writing

As I observed a third-grade class, I noticed that the children seemed engaged in a variety of self-selected tasks. Most of them seemed to be working with math, but they were reading and writing as well.

Catching up with Karen McKinnon, the teacher, I asked her what lesson she was teaching. She thought for a moment, then said that she wasn't sure if it was reading, writing, or math because the lesson involved all three. The children were using their knowledge of math to create stories for other children to read.

Thinking About Thinking

In order for students to become strategic learners, they need to know how they learn—what helps them understand, what interferes with learning, and what strategies they can use. They should be aware of the thought processes that help them acquire knowledge and expand concepts as they approach new learning tasks.

Thought-Provoking Idea

Ask students to help you create charts on "What Helps My Learning" and "What Hinders My Learning" (Wilson and Wing Jan, 1993).

Defining Metacognition

A long and somewhat intimidating term, *metacognition* simply refers to thinking about our own thinking. It is the awareness of our thought processes and the ability to monitor and control them. In other words:

1. We are conscious of our own thought processes and know what thinking strategies we can use to unlock meaning.
2. We are aware of what we understand or do not understand.
3. We know how to help ourselves understand when we are confused.

In a sense, we temporarily step out of the role of learner and assume the role of an outsider in order to consider our thinking from an objective point of view.

Metacognition can be used to enhance learning in any subject area. For example, in science students can learn to think consciously about their thinking by participating in experiments and then explaining what they did and why they did it. In math they can reflect on successful strategies they have used in the past in order to explore possible solutions for similar problems.

A variation of metacognition is *metatextual awareness,* or the conscious awareness of the functions of reading and writing and ways to deal with reading and writing problems (Cambourne, 1988). Students possessing this awareness would be able to do the following:

- Explain how reading and writing are connected
- Show how reading and writing help them learn to punctuate and spell
- Articulate where and how they get ideas for writing
- Know what strategies to use for getting through trouble spots
- Make decisions about their writing in terms of purpose, audience, and other variables

The Value of Using Metacognition

A student's ability to use metacognitive processes is more powerful than any other type of influence on a student's learning, according to an analysis of research (Wang et al., 1993/1994). These processes include the ability to *plan* what strategies to use in order to gain understanding, to *evaluate* the effectiveness of using them, and to *revise* or *replan* if so indicated. Art Costa (1986) claims that considerable evidence indicates that metacognitive learners persist in problem solving; think insightfully, critically, and flexibly; and know how to apply their intellectual abilities to various situations.

Students who know how to manage their thinking have an advantage over students who are unaware of their thought processes. Poor readers and young readers often lack metacognitive abilities. Figure 5-1 shows the characteristics of students possessing or lacking metacognition.

The Development of Metacognition

In most cases, children under six or seven lack the ability to think metacognitively because they are unaware of their own thinking strategies (Gabarino and Stott, 1989). This means that they may have difficulty distinguishing fact from fantasy and the rational from the irrational.

Between the ages of six and twelve, however, children become increasingly aware of their thought processes, especially if the teacher encourages them. They become able to reflect on and take control of such thinking strategies as planning, rehearsing, checking, reviewing, reasoning, problem solving, monitoring, and predicting. They begin to consider a wide range of alternatives and possibilities for solving problems systematically and flexibly.

Figure 5-1. Characteristics of Metacognitive Learners

Student Possessing Metacognitive Processes	Student Lacking in Metacognitive Processes
Carefully monitors performance	Cannot monitor performance well
Tries to fill in gaps of knowledge	Allows gaps of knowledge to continue
Can use different strategies to solve problems	Is limited in use of strategies to solve problems
Makes strategic plans	Seldom plans
Can identify sources of difficulty	Cannot recognize sources of difficulty
Can draw on prior knowledge	Makes little use of prior knowledge
Uses text features (concept maps, summaries, graphics, etc.) to determine meaning	Skips over graphics and helpful text features
Adjusts reading rate to difficulty and purpose	Reads everything at the same rate
Rereads selected portions for clarification	Reads everything only once
Focuses on what is important	Considers all material to be of equal importance
Can generate appropriate hypotheses	Has little idea of what to expect
Is aware of limitations and capabilities	Is unaware of limitations

In her studies of first graders, Julianne Turner (1997) found that these children tend to focus on decoding instead of getting meaning when they read. They know little about monitoring, managing, and regulating their reading, and they may not recognize inconsistencies in the text and be able to self-correct. Turner found that children gained in their ability to use metacognitive strategies, however, when teachers gave explicit reminders about planning, monitoring, and evaluating their activities. Teachers guided children's thinking by asking such questions as the following:

- What do you already know about . . . ?
- What do you do when you come to the hard parts?
- Who can tell what to do?
- Is there another way to do it?
- Are you focused?
- What strategies did you use?

- Were they successful?

As children considered answers to such questions, they became more thoughtful and proficient readers.

Modeling Metacognition

Modeling is an effective way to teach children how to think about their thinking. By modeling, the teacher demonstrates how to apply strategies and explains why they work. In Figure 5-2, the teacher puts a sample of text on a transparency, projects it, and reads it aloud to the class. After reading it, the teacher makes comments about thinking processes that help to clarify the meaning of the passage.

When modeling, choose a short passage so that you can focus attention on specific ways of thinking about text. Read it through first without interruption; then reread it and make comments about your thinking as you move through it. After you have modeled ways of thinking, point out the strategies you used. It's a good idea to make a list of these strategies so that children can refer to them as they read. In the beginning, you may want to use only one or two strategies, but later you can use several, as in Figure 5-2.

Thought-Provoking Question

How can you help children feel a sense of ownership or responsibility for thinking about their thinking?

After the children understand what you are doing, invite them to help you notice clues that uncover meaning as you model. Ask the following questions:

- What might be confusing in this sentence?
- What are some ways to help you make sense of this?
- Can you find any other places that might cause difficulties?
- What strategies could you use to clarify meanings?

Discovering points of confusion and brainstorming useful strategies help students understand how to read metacognitively for themselves.

To further increase students' understanding of how metacognition works, let them practice modeling procedures with partners and in small groups. Listen as they share their thoughts, and slip into the modeling role yourself if you feel that some students in the partnership or group don't yet understand. Eventually, you should be able to trust most of them to think about their thinking while they are reading independently.

Figure 5-2. Modeling Metacognition

Bats

Bats are nocturnal animals, flying at night and sleeping during the day. Although they fly, they are not birds but small, furry mammals. Their membranous wings connect their armlike limbs to their legs. There are several hundred species (kinds) of bats, and most of them are useful because they eat large quantities of insects.

Modeling

Text: Bats

Thought 1: I've seen bats. They fly above our house when it begins to get dark. They look like birds.

Text: Bats are nocturnal animals . . .

Thought 2: Nocturnal. I wonder what that means. Maybe if I read more, I'll find out.

Text: . . . flying at night and sleeping during the day.

Thought 3: Oh, now I see. *Nocturnal* must mean that bats are awake at night and sleep in the daytime—just the opposite of me.

Text: Although they fly, they are not birds but small, furry mammals.

Thought 4: There are two signal words here, *although* and *but,* which make me think that there is going to be something different from what I might expect to find.

Thought 5: Bats may fly like birds, but they're really mammals, and I know what a mammal is because we studied those already.

Text: Their membranous wings . . .

Thought 6: The author isn't telling me what *membranous* means, but it looks like *membrane*, which I think is like a thin piece of skin.

Text: . . . connect their armlike limbs to their legs.

Thought 7: Limbs makes me think of a tree, but I think that here it means the bat's arms. It must be one of those words that has more than one meaning.

Text: There are several hundred species (kinds) of bats . . .

Thought 8: That word *species* could be hard to figure out, but seeing *(kinds)* after it helps me know what it means.

Text: . . . and most of them are useful because they eat large quantities of insects.

Thought 9: There's another signal word, *because,* which tells me that a reason will follow.

Thought 10: Interesting. I never knew that bats help us by eating lots of insects. I'll try to remember that.

Figure 5-2 continued on next page

Figure 5-2 continued from previous page
Strategies Used

Thought 1: Relating topic to previous experiences.

Thought 2: Reading ahead to get information or clarification.

Thought 3: Making use of author's explanation.

Thought 4: Observing signal words, which indicate a change or extension of meaning.

Thought 5: Using prior knowledge (about mammals) to relate to the text.

Thought 6: Looking for the base word of a long word to figure out the meaning.

Thought 7: Being aware that words can have more than one meaning and selecting the meaning that is appropriate for the context.

Thought 8: Using clues or synonyms provided by the author to understand word meanings.

Thought 9: Realizing that signal words help the reader anticipate what will come next.

Thought 10: Incorporating new ideas or knowledge into what is already known and understood.

Using Think Alouds

One classroom application of metacognition is *think alouds,* or talking about thinking processes while reading orally. In this activity, students select a passage of text, begin reading orally, and stop occasionally to report on what they are doing and thinking. The teacher may give prompts and ask probing questions from time to time to encourage students to think more deeply or use other strategies. During this activity, the focus is on comprehension strategies; learning the content of the text is not important.

Identifying questions that lead to comprehension helps students know what to do during think alouds. The teacher may model appropriate questions, or the class may generate a list of useful questions. Figure 5-3 shows some questions that students may ask themselves. The first question is the most important and should be repeated periodically as reading continues.

Working with fourth graders, James Baumann and his colleagues (1993) found that collaboration among students may have been the most powerful component in helping students internalize the process of thinking aloud. Students in pairs or small groups applied various comprehension-monitoring strategies. In one procedure, students thought aloud in a group

Figure 5-3. Questions for Think Alouds

Does this make sense?

If it doesn't make sense, what can I do?

What hints provide me with information about what might happen next?

How can I relate what I already know to what I am reading?

Can I visualize what's happening?

What seems to be most important here?

Does this text fit with what I already know?

What, if anything, makes me think that the author may be biased?

If I come to a word I don't know, what can I do?

Am I able to follow the author's development of this text? Is it logical and sequential?

What do I think or believe about this text?

Do I need to change my mind about my first thoughts?

Would it be helpful to reread any portion of the text?

setting and then worked in pairs, reading alternately from short sections of text. After each section, one student tried to think aloud and the other student asked if it was making sense. The students then reversed roles and continued reading. During this time, the teacher offered guidance and encouragement while listening to student exchanges.

As a result of their research, Baumann and his colleagues (1993) identified the following advantages of using think alouds:

- To help students learn to monitor their reading comprehension
- To enable students to use fix-up strategies when they discover difficulties in comprehension
- To help students learn a variety of comprehension strategies
- To empower students to take control of their thinking processes when reading texts

Thought-Provoking Idea

After a series of lessons on think alouds, ask students how they might use this activity. Their answers might include the following:

1. Studying for a test
2. Getting more understanding from textbooks
3. Clarifying confusing parts in a library book
4. Sharing insights in literature response groups

Think alouds are also helpful for teachers to use when they wish to evaluate a student's ability to read with comprehension. By listening informally, teachers can identify the strengths and weaknesses in a student's awareness of reading strategies and how and when to use them. A more structured approach to using think alouds for assessing comprehension appears in an article by Suzanne Wade (1990).

Reading as Thinking

In the past two or three decades, reading instruction has changed considerably as teachers become increasingly aware of how children learn to read. "Recent research in comprehension and metacognition suggests that reading is a far more complex process that involves reasoning and problem solving rather than simply the accumulation of skills" (Wade, 1990, p. 442).

Constructing Meaning

At one time we believed that most competent readers got the same message when reading the same selection because, after all, what the author had to say was there in black and white! Now, however, we realize that many factors enter into getting meaning from text, and we find that active readers must construct their own meanings by integrating background experiences with new knowledge. The following factors may affect the way in which we interact with text and thus the meanings we construct:

- Personal feelings and emotions about the topic
- Prior knowledge of and experience with the subject
- Purpose and motivation for reading the selection
- Relevance and value for applying information to real-life situations
- Preconceived beliefs and perceptions

For example, children reading Gary Paulsen's *Hatchet,* a story of survival in the wilderness, might understand the story differently as follows:

- A child afraid of being alone and having to be resourceful might dwell on Brian's feeling of fear.

- A child with Scout training and knowledge of camping might clearly visualize scenes, experience a sense of adventure, and feel great empathy with Brian.

- A child living in the city with no outdoor experience might have trouble comprehending Brian's difficulties.

- A child reading *Hatchet* for an assigned book report might look for main ideas, details, or character development.

- A child about to go camping might read with a sense of purpose, focusing on ways to survive in the wilderness.
- A child convinced that the wilderness is a threatening and dangerous environment may have those beliefs confirmed.

Because of various backgrounds and purposes, each of these children will interpret the book differently.

Thought-Provoking Question

Reread the quotation from Wade in the first paragraph of this section. What background experiences affect your understanding of what she says?

The concept that reading is constructing meaning, not just repeating the author's words, has several implications for teachers, such as the following.

- Encourage children to think about what the selection means to them personally.
- Give children credit for responses that differ from yours or from those in the manual, if they make sense from the child's perspective.
- Provide opportunities for shy children to try out their meanings in small groups or with partners.
- Ask children to give reasons for interpreting the reading as they do.
- Show appreciation for diverse interpretations.

Thinking Before, During, and After Reading

Children who benefit most from reading think strategically as they read in order to make sense of the text. Beth Ann Herrman (1992, p. 428) defines *strategic reasoning* as "the complex thinking processes used before, during, and after reading and writing to construct meaningful interpretations of text and to create meaningful texts." Strategic reasoning includes making use of prior knowledge, forming predictions, monitoring "sensemaking," and constructing meaning. In this section, we will consider some ways to guide children's thinking before, during, and after reading. Here are two strategies you can use *before* children read a selection on cave dwellers.

Semantic map. Children brainstorm their ideas about cave dwellers, and the teacher places their words on a web around the central term *cave dwellers.* The children thus bring their prior knowledge to bear on the new selection. (Chapter 9 gives examples of semantic maps.)

Anticipation guide. The teacher gives the children some statements about cave dwellers and asks them to indicate whether they believe them to be *true* or *false*. Students then read the selection and once again mark the statements true or false. What they have read may cause them to change some of their beliefs. This activity encourages children to make predictions before reading and then verify or refute them after reading. Sample statements might be these:

Before	After	
_____	_____	The earliest people lived in caves.
_____	_____	Fire keeps animals away.
_____	_____	The first cave dwellers lived in Europe.

Semantic maps and anticipation guides prepare readers for the selection, help them predict and anticipate the content, and enable them to integrate prior knowledge with new material.

Cave Dwellers

Cave dwellers live in rock shelters or caves. The first humans probably avoided living in caves because they feared the wild animals that inhabited them. When people learned how to make fire, however, they were able to keep the animals away. The earliest cave dwellers lived in China 360,000 years ago, and some indigenous people still lived in caves until recently.

Most early cave dwellers were hunters and gatherers. We know this because of the piles of bones found in the caves. They made weapons and tools from bones, and sometimes they painted pictures on the walls. Later, people used caves mostly for burial, storage, and protection of their flocks in winter.

The following strategies are useful *during* reading.

Think alouds. Ask children to find partners and read the first paragraph about cave dwellers. Then have them stop and ask their partners the following questions:

• Does this make sense?

• Why do you think fire kept the wild animals away?

• Do you think anyone still lives in caves? Why do you think that?

Students can then continue reading and ask each other similar questions after the next paragraph. This activity causes them to create meaning, make inferences, and reflect on what they read.

Self-questioning. Students turn factual statements into *why* questions that they try to answer. In the passage about cave dwellers, they might ask themselves the following:

- Why did cave dwellers use bones to make weapons and tools?
- Why did they paint pictures on walls?
- Why did some indigenous people live in caves until recently?

Posing and answering questions such as these during reading causes students to be thoughtful readers.

After their reading, students find time for reaction, response, and reflection, which can occur in a variety of contexts. They should also return to their anticipation guides, but here are other options that address different ways of knowing.

Creative drama. By recalling and interpreting the main events in a selection, children are able to act it out. From the two paragraphs on cave dwellers, they might create a scene in a cave with someone carving tools or weapons from bones or someone returning from the hunt. More reading on this topic would furnish richer detail and allow students' imaginations to create ways in which cave dwellers might have interacted.

Art. Additional research on cave dwellers may yield reproductions of art found on walls of caves. Students may appreciate the ways that cave art represented what was significant to cave dwellers, and they can also create cave art of their own.

Writing as Thinking

Just as talking and reading are pathways to thinking, so is writing. As students write, they select ideas that are meaningful for them and record them for later perusal by an intended audience, which may on occasion consist only of themselves. When writing, students do the following:

- Review what they know and think
- Sort out ideas and select those that are most significant
- Shape their writing to suit the audience
- Choose words and phrases carefully to create the right meaning
- Affirm and reinforce what they know
- Clarify vague thoughts in order to communicate them to others
- Analyze and evaluate what they have written

Thinking Strategies During the Writing Process

Most of us are familiar with the writing process, which consists of the following procedures: topic search, rough draft, revision(s), editing, and publishing. During each procedure, students must think about what to do, as shown in Figure 5-4.

Figure 5-4. Thinking Strategies During the Writing Process

Topic Search
> Brainstorm possible topics.
> Evaluate feedback from peers.
> Narrow choices and make decisions.

Rough Draft
> Set thoughts and ideas on paper.

Revisions
> Ask yourself the following questions:
>> Does the lead sentence grab the reader's attention?
>> Is the organization logical?
>> Will it be understood and appreciated by the audience?
>> Did I omit anything significant?
>> Did I repeat material unnecessarily?
>> Is the writing style clear?
>> Could I find better words to express my ideas?
>> Do I want to make any changes based on others' suggestions?

Editing
> Seek and remedy possible points of confusion.
> Locate and correct errors in spelling, punctuation, and grammar.

Publishing
> Choose the most effective way to make the piece appealing to an audience.
> Decide what illustrations to use.
> Design an attractive cover.

Thought-Provoking Question

How do you teach children to think when they write? Here are some answers, and you may think of others.

1. Think aloud as you model writing on an overhead transparency.
2. Confer with students about their writing, asking them how they can clarify, expand, or create greater interest.
3. Ask for volunteers to share their writing and let students give constructive suggestions.
4. Read good children's literature and ask students to discover ways that authors make their books interesting.

Types of Writing That Stimulate Thinking

Unless students copy material directly from a source, they must think as they write. The following writing forms promote a variety of thinking strategies: journal writing, persuasive writing, fiction writing, and use of metaphor.

Journal Writing

Journal writing, says Regie Routman (1994), encourages thinking and makes it visible. Teachers don't usually grade or evaluate journals, so students feel free to express their ideas without fear of teacher judgment. Journals serve different purposes, including personal diaries not to be shared, math or social studies journals, literature response logs, and journals in which teachers respond on a regular basis. By dialoguing with students, teachers learn a great deal about them—their anxieties, values, and misunderstandings—and are thus better able to understand and guide them.

Journal time is a time for reflection: thinking over what a lesson or an experience means, pondering something of significance, or recording moments of joy or grief. Students too shy to talk about their thoughts and feelings can often express them in writing.

Persuasive Writing

Once thought to be too complex and advanced for elementary students, persuasive writing is now considered an acceptable genre if the teacher presents information at the students' levels (Burkhalter, 1995). Persuasive writing is difficult but challenging for three reasons:

1. The writer must take a position and defend it with valid reasons.
2. The student needs to organize thoughts in a different way from typical narrative writing.
3. The writer must convince readers of the merit of the position and anticipate possible objections.

Oral discussions, arguments, and debates prepare children to write persuasively, and an extensive body of knowledge about the subject helps the writer make a convincing case.

Current community or school issues are generally good topics for persuasive writing because children can easily relate to them and may have already formed opinions. I have seen many well-written editorials in student-produced school newspapers that present arguments for or against an issue. One example is an editorial about holding the Grand Prix in Melbourne, Australia. Angelina Fankhanel, the editor and a sixth-grade student, presents arguments against the race as follows:

Do you want the Grand Prix?

If you ask me, I would agree with the protesters. Number one, Albert Park Lake is a park. It is for children to play in, it is not for cars to go racing around! Just think of all the noise and air pollution that this race will cause! The parking is also a problem. Think of all the poor residents around the area. People will need somewhere to park so they will go to alleyways, and block other cars in. And of course now they have closed up the path that you would use to walk right around the lake. I would close it up just the day before the race. And one more thing—the ducks. Where would they go? They will be terrified of the cars! Plus they could run on the road and get run over, although they would fly away because of the noise that the cars will make. I think the race is a bad idea although it *is* a privilege for Melbourne.

Fiction Writing

Of all genres, fiction writing demands the most creative imagination. Here children are free to invent, fantasize, imagine, and create within the framework of a story. Most stories contain a setting (time and place), characters, a problem or conflict, and a resolution.

Good preparation for fiction writing is reading aloud and discussing a variety of types of fiction: folktales, myths, fables, science fiction, modern fantasy, and so on. Students need to discover authors' techniques, create story maps, and identify the text features that make stories work. Once they are aware of authors' effective strategies, children are ready to try their own hand at creating fiction.

Using Metaphor

Metaphors are figures of speech that enrich reading and writing through analogies or implied comparisons. When reading, children may interpret metaphors differently because of their diverse backgrounds, so a discussion of meanings would help students be aware of different perspectives. The title of this book is a metaphor that compares pathways to strategies, and the Introduction is a metaphor comparing a journey to reading a book. Poets often use metaphors to create images, as in Langston Hughes' "Dreams." Here Hughes tells us to treasure our dreams, for without dreams, life is no more than a bird that cannot fly or a barren, snow-covered field.

To create metaphors, children must think of ways that one thing is similar to another, despite their obvious differences. To help them see common attributes, ask them to brainstorm answers to questions like these:

- How is a horse like a car?
- How is a dream like a wish?
- How is a baby like a kitten?
- How is rain like a washing machine?

Then ask them to find ways to use metaphors in their writing.

In her book *Hailstones and Halibut Bones,* Mary O'Neill makes us see how colors represent images and feelings through metaphor. After reading several of the poems, Cindy Dowell asked her sixth graders to create some "color" metaphors. Here are some lines from their poems:

- Gray is the sky after it rains.
- Red is dresses just bought at the store.
- Red is an apple not eaten to the core.
- Blue is the tigers on the tiger team.
- Blue is the air that makes a bird float.
- Gray is the eye of a wee little mouse.

Writing and Thinking Across the Curriculum

When viewed as a thinking process, writing applies to all areas of the curriculum. In the opening vignette, Karen hardly knew what lesson she was teaching because reading and writing were so much a part of the math lesson. Regardless of subject and particularly with an integrated curriculum, writing guides students' thinking by helping them articulate, clarify, organize, reinforce, and review what they are learning. Figure 5-5 shows some specific ways to use writing and thinking strategies.

Figure 5-5. Using Writing and Thinking Activities Across the Curriculum

Subject	Activities
Math	Write number stories for others to solve.
	Write out the procedures used to solve a problem.
	Create and interpret graphs of real-life situations.
Science	Write science fiction based on futuristic concepts.
	Record observations and findings of experiments.
	Write step-by-step directions for conducting an experiment.
Literature	Keep a literature log of reactions to a story.
	Create new endings, invent new characters, or take a different point of view.
	Analyze an author's style and record examples to support your findings.
Health	Create ads that warn of health hazards for some products.
	Create menus for a balanced diet.
	Make a schedule for physical fitness routines.
Social Studies	Write an editorial about an event in history.
	Draw a political cartoon and write a caption.
	Identify a community or school issue and make a list of arguments for and against it.

Summary

Metacognition is the awareness of one's thought processes and the ability to monitor and control them. Students possessing metacognitive strategies read, study, and learn effectively because they think about their thinking. Modeling by thinking aloud during oral reading is one way that teachers can help students learn how to use their metacognitive powers. Think alouds help children become aware of ways to think about text.

Researchers have found that reading is a process of constructing meaning and that interpretations of text vary depending on individual experiences. Thinking occurs before, during, and after reading as students make predictions and anticipate content, use think alouds and ask themselves questions, and respond to the text.

Writing helps students clarify their thinking, and they learn a variety of thinking strategies as they engage in the writing process. Many types of writing are well adapted to promoting thinking strategies, such as journal writing, persuasive writing, fiction writing, and using metaphors. Writing occurs across the curriculum and enhances every subject.

References

Angeletti, S.R. (1991). Encouraging students to think about what they read. *The Reading Teacher, 45*(4): 288–295.

Baker, L. (1991). Metacognition, reading, and science education. In C. Santa and D. Alvermann (Eds.), *Science learning: Processes and applications.* Newark, DE. International Reading Association.

Baumann, J., Jones, L., and Seifert-Kessell, N. (1993). Using think alouds to enhance children's comprehension monitoring abilities. *The Reading Teacher, 47*(3): 184–193.

Browning, N., and McClintic, S. (1995). Acting, talking, and thinking like a writer: Sixth graders become authors. *Language Arts, 72*(2): 105–112.

Bull, G. (1989). *Reflective teaching.* Carlton South, Victoria: Australian Reading Association.

Burkhalter, N. (1995). A Vygotsky-based curriculum for teaching persuasive writing in the elementary grades. *Language Arts, 72*(3): 192–199.

Burns, M. (1995). Writing in math class? Absolutely! *Instructor, 104*(7): 40–47.

Burns, P., Roe, B., and Ross, E. (1996). *Teaching reading in today's elementary schools* (6th ed.). Boston: Houghton Mifflin.

Cambourne, B. (1988). *The whole story.* Auckland, New Zealand: Ashton Scholastic.

Collins, N. (1996). *Metacognition and reading to learn.* Bloomington, IN: ERIC Digest.

Commeyras, M. (1993). Promoting critical thinking through dialogical-thinking reading lessons. *The Reading Teacher, 46*(6): 486–493.

Cook, J. (1995). Integrating math and writing. *Teaching K–8, 25*(8): 22–23.

Coon, C. (1965). Cave dwellers. *World Book Encyclopedia.* Chicago: Field Enterprises.

Costa, A. (1986). Mediating the metacognitive. *Teaching skillful thinking.* Alexandria, VA: Association for Supervision and Curriculum Development.

Dixon-Krauss, L. (1996). *Vygotsky in the classroom.* White Plains, NY: Longman.

Emmitt, M., and Pollock, J. (1991). *Language and learning.* South Melbourne, Victoria Australia: Oxford.

Gabarino, J., and Stott, F. (1989). *What children can tell us.* San Francisco: Jossey-Bass.

Golley, F. (1965). Bat. *World Book Encyclopedia.* Chicago: Field Enterprises.

Goodman, K., Smith, E.B., Meredith, R., and Goodman, Y. (1987). *Language and thinking in school* (3rd ed.). New York: Richard C. Owen.

Grindler, M., and Stratton, B. (1995). *Using think alouds to develop strategic readers.* Paper presented at the 1st Combined Great Lakes and Southeast IRA Regional Conference, Nashville.

Herrmann, B.A. (1992). Teaching and assessing strategic reasoning: Dealing with the dilemmas. *The Reading Teacher, 45*(6): 428–433.

Lipson, M. (1996). Conversations with children and other classroom-based assessment strategies. In L. Putnam (Ed.), *How to become a better reading teacher.* Englewood Cliffs, NJ: Prentice-Hall.

Manning, M., and Manning, G. (1996). Writing in math and science. *Teaching K–8, 26*(4): 107–109.

Manzo, A., and Manzo, U. (1995). *Teaching children to be literate: A reflective approach.* Fort Worth, TX: Harcourt Brace.

Maria, K. (1996). Reading comprehension instruction for disabled readers. In L. Putnam (Ed.), *How to become a better reading teacher.* Englewood Cliffs, NJ: Prentice-Hall.

McCarthey, S. (1994). Students' understandings of metaphors in teachers' talk about writing. *Language Arts, 71*(8): 598–605.

McCormick, S. (1995). *Instructing students who have literacy problems.* Englewood Cliffs, NJ: Prentice-Hall.

O'Neill, M. (1989). *Hailstones and halibut bones.* New York: Doubleday.

Paulsen, G. (1987). *Hatchet.* New York: Bradbury.

Peterson, R., and Eeds, M. (1990). *Grand conversations.* Richmond Hill, Ont., Canada: Scholastic.

Routman, R. (1994). *Invitations,* (2nd ed.). Portsmouth, NH: Heinemann.

Turner, J. (1997). Starting right: Strategies for engaging young literacy learners. In J. Guthrie and A. Wigfield (Eds.), *Reading engagement.* Newark, DE: International Reading Association.

Vacca, J.A., Vacca, R., and Gove, M. (1991). *Reading and learning to read,* 2nd ed. New York: HarperCollins.

Wade, S. (1990). Using think alouds to assess comprehension. *The Reading Teacher, 43*(7): 442–451.

Wang, M., Haertel, G., and Walberg. (1994). What helps students learn? *Educational Leadership, 51*(4): 74–79.

Wilson, J., and Wing Jan, L. (1993). *Thinking for themselves.* Portsmouth, NH: Heinemann.

Wing Jan, L. (1991). *Write ways.* Melbourne, Victoria Australia: Oxford.

CHAPTER 6

Questioning Strategies

When I asked the teachers,

"What kinds of questions generate the most thoughtful responses?"

the teachers said:

- Open-ended questions, where there are really no correct answers.
- Questions that begin with: "Why do you think . . . ?" or "How do you feel about . . . ?"
- Questions that lead to other questions in order to continue and expand thinking about a subject.
- Questions that ask children to predict what will happen, solve problems, and reflect on what could have been different and how that difference would have changed the whole situation.
- Open-ended questions that ask children what they would have done or what they think might happen.
- Questions that cause children to "invent" new ways.
- Higher-order questions that the students can relate to in some way. They need to have enough information to think through the topic before reaching a conclusion.
- Questions that are about things that interest the children.

How would you answer this question?

Concepts to watch for

- The value of questioning
- Guidelines for effective questioning
- Types of questions that call for different kinds of thinking
- Benefits of student-generated questions
- Some structured questioning strategies

After reading *Jamie O'Rourke and the Big Potato*, Susie Andrews asked her sixth graders to put on their white thinking hats (based on deBono; see Chapter 1) and generate literal questions about the story. She divided them into groups and gave each group a word to start a question: *who, when, where, what,* or *why*. Working in groups, the children referred back to the story in order to construct their questions. Learning to form questions calls for a different type of thinking than searching for answers. When each group was ready, Susie asked the students to share their questions. In other sessions, students would wear different colors of hats and construct types of questions appropriate for the color they were wearing, thus focusing attention on one questioning technique at a time.

The Value of Questioning

Good questions lead children to inquiry and high levels of thinking. "All learning begins with questions," says Kenneth Chuska (1995, p. 7). "Questions cause interactions: thought, activity, conversation, or debate." The nature of the question determines the dynamics of the interactions, and well-designed questions encourage active student involvement in lessons.

Higher-level questions make us analyze, compare, interpret, hypothesize, reflect, create, evaluate, find new meanings, and stretch our imaginations. The skillful questioner causes children to do the following:

- Focus their attention on the issue(s) at hand
- Integrate new ideas with prior knowledge
- Examine their values and beliefs
- Apply knowledge to life situations
- Pursue areas of inquiry
- Explore ideas at various levels of thinking
- Form habits of thinking
- Verify and justify their positions
- Transfer knowledge to other areas
- Reflect on what they are learning

Questioning strategies have positively affected students' thinking and increased their learning (Hunkins, 1995). It only makes sense that students who regularly answer factual, low-level, short-answer questions do better on achievement tests that call for this type of response than students who don't practice answering such questions (Strother, 1989). Questions that make students think, however, enable them over time to make gains in achievement, expand their knowledge, and, in many cases, develop positive attitudes. Also, thinking-style questions often create enthusiasm for learning because students get more pleasure from reading and studying when they are thoughtfully engaged than when they are not (Hunkins, 1995).

Literal, factual questions are important for building an information base, but in themselves they are of little value for causing students to think. Unfortunately, most teacher questions call for short, factual, right-or-wrong answers (Bromley, 1992). Although open-ended, higher-order questions are more difficult for teachers to construct and respond to, they stimulate higher levels of thinking. Acceptable responses to these questions vary because they allow students to draw on previous experiences and view situations from different perspectives.

Thought-Provoking Question

How might children respond differently to the following question in terms of their values, needs, logic, and/or experiences: What would you do if you found $10 in a grocery store?

Asking Thought-Provoking Questions

Anyone can ask questions, but posing questions that promote learning and thinking takes time, thought, effort, and practice. Poor questions simply use valuable class time without benefiting anyone, so ask yourself the questions in Figure 6-1 when constructing questions worthy of discussion.

Thought-Provoking Question

What is a poor question?

Responding to Students' Answers

Because of its importance in getting students to think about their answers, the issue of *wait time* merits special attention. Wait time should

Figure 6-1. Evaluating Questioning Techniques

Is my question clear and specific? Do students know what I expect?

Does my question serve a worthy purpose, such as stimulating divergent thinking, searching for relationships, making judgments, or problem solving?

Do I encourage students to ask their own questions? If so, do I consider their questions respectfully?

Am I willing to accept more than one response to an open-ended question? Do I sometimes ask questions for which I don't know the answer?

Instead of insisting on a quick answer, do I allow students to grope, ponder, and discover the answer(s)?

Do I ask different types of questions to stimulate different types of thinking?

Do I conclude my lessons by asking reflective questions such as "What did we learn?" and "How does this knowledge help us?"

Do I encourage all children to be actively involved?

Do I sometimes encourage students to expand their answers by asking them to provide fuller explanations, clarify their ideas, or offer supporting evidence?

Have I established a classroom environment in which students feel comfortable enough to risk giving their best answers?

---

occur immediately after posing a question and also after the student responds, but before we react. These extra seconds provide time for students to consider their best answers and elaborate on their responses. Studies have shown that we normally wait only a second after asking a question before expecting a response, but a wait of 3 to 5 seconds can bring many benefits, such as the following (Hunkins, 1995):

- Increased length of responses
- Greater evidence of thinking
- More diversity of thinking
- Increased achievement
- More participation
- Greater confidence in knowledge of content
- Better likelihood of supplying supportive evidence
- Increased number of student-generated questions

Teachers also benefit from longer wait time by listening more carefully and thoughtfully to students' replies before reacting.

When responding to children's answers, our tendency is to evaluate them by making comments such as "Good idea," "That's right," or "Not exactly. Does anyone have the right answer?" Instead, we can keep the discussion open and encourage other responses by making noncommittal remarks, such as "Interesting" or "Thanks for sharing. Who else has an idea?"

We can use students' answers as bridges to further learning by asking the respondent to explain or clarify ("Can you tell us more?") or by asking the other students for their reactions ("What do you think of Mark's idea?"). Hunkins (1995) refers to *probing questions,* which lead the student to rethink or support the answer given. Often occurring in a series, these questions require the student to think at higher levels and justify answers. Probing questions, however, may intimidate children who lack the verbal ability to expand on their answers, as well as older students who are uncertain of their answers, so we should avoid sounding confrontational. In a community of learners, where rapport and trust have been established, students are less likely to feel threatened by probing questions.

Socratic questions "probe the underlying structure of our thinking" (Wilks, 1995, p. 19). They focus discussion away from the teacher and on the students, as in the following examples

- Can you help Brandon rephrase his question?
- Are you sure that's what you mean?
- Are Tyler and Andrea saying the same thing?
- Is there anything unusual here?
- Is anyone still confused?
- Who can summarize the discussion up to this point?

Thought-Provoking Idea

Follow up a question with probing questions that enable students to confirm, question, justify, or support the original response. Some examples of probing questions are the following:

1. How do you know?
2. What makes you sure?
3. Can you explain what you mean?
4. Can you give us an example?
5. Does anyone have another way to think about that?
6. Do you agree or disagree? Why?

Types of Questions

In Chapter 1 we looked at some models and types of thinking, which we can now consider as the basis for questioning. John Dewey advocated reflection and problem solving, and Hilda Taba proposed three stages of inductive thinking—concept formation, interpretation of data, and application of principles—all of which rely heavily on questioning. Edward deBono's thinking hats program suggests different types of questioning; Brian Cambourne's natural conditions for learning set the stage for a classroom where honest inquiry lessons flourish; and Benjamin Bloom's taxonomy of the cognitive domain classifies six major types of thinking. These models help us see how the types of questions we ask affect the kinds of thinking that students do. Figure 6-2 presents some thinking strategies followed by question starters and/or lead-in phrases that help us address each strategy. By varying the ways in which we introduce our inquiries, we can encourage students to learn to think in different ways.

Figure 6-2. Starters for Thinking Strategies

Strategy	Starters
Knowledge	Who, what, when, where, which, does, identify, define, list, recall
Comprehension	Interpret, compare, what are the relationships, contrast, explain in your own words, infer
Application	Demonstrate, how can you use it, where does it lead you, apply, test
Analysis	How, why, what are the causes, what are the consequences, analyze, classify, relate
Synthesis	Create, how else, what would happen if, develop, suppose, design, combine, predict, how about
Evaluation	Which is best, rate from good to bad, select, judge, decide which, how, why
Problem solving	What procedures, what plan, how, what is needed, what might work
Reflective thinking	What were you thinking, what does it mean, why is it important, what difference does it make
Inductive thinking	Discover, infer, what conclusions, what clues, what do you notice, observe

From any worthy theme, you can develop an array of questions that are appropriate for different developmental levels and effective for promoting various types of thinking. Figure 6-3 shows how the issue of reducing pollution in our environment can (1) be simplified for kindergartners and expanded for upper-grade students and (2) how various questions related to the theme can address different types of thinking (listed in parentheses following questions).

Figure 6-3. Reducing Pollution in Our Environment: Questions at Different Levels of Complexity to Promote Thinking Strategies

What can we do to keep our classroom looking nice? (application, discovery, exploration, creativity)

What is pollution? (knowledge, convergent thinking, comprehension)

What kinds of trash can we find in and around our school? (brainstorming, fluency, observing)

What are some other forms of pollution? (brainstorming, flexibility, divergent thinking)

How can we group various types of pollution? (classifying, organizing, analyzing)

What are some causes of pollution? (knowledge, cause and effect)

How can we find out what people are doing to reduce pollution? (inquiry, research, investigation)

Are the methods we are using to reduce pollution working well? (analysis, evaluation)

How do our pollution problems today compare with pollution problems a century ago? (comparison and contrast)

How can we create energy without polluting the environment? (synthesis, creativity, invention, originality)

What roles can we play in solving environmental problems? (problem solving, application, decision making, divergent thinking)

How do our pollution problems compare with those of other countries? (comparison and contrast, evaluation, analysis)

To what extent should the federal government be involved in reducing pollution? (critical thinking, evaluation)

What are some pollution problems we may face in the future? (predicting, elaborating, hypothesizing)

Do you believe that we are doing all we can to reduce pollution? Why do you think as you do? (point of view, evaluation, reasoning, reflecting)

If you were in charge of pollution control, what would you do? (decision making, strategies)

How can we use the knowledge we already have to find solutions to pollution? (transfer of learning, application, reasoning)

Educators have analyzed types of questions from many points of view. As we have seen, probing questions often result in deeper appreciation and more thoughtful responses. We looked at the role of self-questioning during think alouds in Chapter 5, and we will consider student-initiated questions in the next section of this chapter.

Questions may be closed (convergent) or open (divergent). Closed questions have only one correct answer (e.g., What is the capital of Delaware?), but open questions allow a variety of responses (e.g., Why was Delaware important during the early development of our country?).

Questions in the affective domain—those related to values and emotions—play an important part in helping us discover how we feel about things (based on Krathwohl's taxonomy, cited in Hunkins, 1995). Questions from both the cognitive and affective domains overlap because our emotions affect how we think, and our thinking affects how we feel. Beginning with the simple but crucial level of paying attention, affective questioning continues through additional levels to *characterization*, which means establishing and maintaining a set of consistent values. This highest level is seldom achieved during the school years, but we can make students aware of their attitudes and interests as we invite them to think about what matters to them. Figure 6-4 summarizes the five stages of the affective domain.

Figure 6-4. Levels of Affective Questioning

Levels	Characteristics	Questions
Receiving or attending	Conscious awareness, attention; willingness to participate; resistance to distractions	Which activity would you prefer to do?
Responding	Agreement and willingness to respond voluntarily; satisfaction from response	How do you like reading *Jumanji*?
Valuing	Acceptance of, preference for, and commitment to a value	What makes a good citizen? Can you be one?
Organization	Creating, identifying, and organizing concepts about values	Which character do you like best? Why?
Characterization	Understanding and accepting values to live by	What values should guide your life?

Student-Generated Questions

Being naturally curious, children want to know *why*, and they often ask questions that stump us. Instead of persisting with our own questions, we need to listen to and learn from the questions children ask. Dene Thomas (1988, pp. 554, 555), in her discussion of *why* questions, says the following:

> . . . the spirit of struggling with difficult, even unanswerable questions is what keeps learning alive. "Why" is so important because it sits at the very heart of learning: the spirit of curiosity, the purposes for which we set up a school system at all, the reasons we teach. Without why . . . the hows and whats don't matter very much.

Children who are constantly wondering, hypothesizing, and pondering become students who seek their own solutions, discover answers for their own satisfaction, and invent new ways to accomplish tasks. Curiosity leads them to question things as they are and wonder if other, perhaps better, options exist. "The hallmark of the good thinker, the good questioner, is the inquiring mind" (Hunkins, 1995, p. 19). We need minds like this to lead us into the future.

Lesson: Generating Questions That Stem From Curiosity

Near the beginning of the school year, Jane Bassett gave her fourth graders the opportunity to articulate their questions. She told them that she wasn't looking for answers today, just good questions. She offered to begin and asked, "I've always wondered: Why do we have mosquitoes, ticks, and fleas?" Quickly the children raised their hands as questions came to them. They generated nearly 50 questions in 15 to 20 minutes. Some may prompt serious inquiry, whereas others may continue to be sources of wonderment.

Among their questions were the following:

- Why do snapping turtles snap?
- Why do onions make you cry?
- Why do girls giggle so much?
- Why do things rot in your cupboard?
- How did AIDs get started?
- Why do carrots make you see better in the dark? Do they really?
- Why do we have to go to school?
- Why is the sky blue?
- Why do parents get divorced?
- How did space get made?
- Why is skin different colors?

Lesson continued on next page

Lesson continued from previous page

- Why can't we print our own money?
- Why don't motors get tired?
- Where do numbers end?
- How did the first person get made?
- Who made God?
- Why is snow white?
- When is the world going to end?
- Why is Alaska part of the United States when it's closer to Canada?
- When is the sun going to burn out?

Jane complimented the children on their thoughtful questions and suggested that they choose some to begin searching for solutions.

Encouraging Students to Generate Questions in the Classroom

Since children are naturally inquisitive, teachers should gradually transfer some of the responsibility for creating questions and posing problems to their students. At first students' questions may be unclear, poorly articulated, and factual (having only one correct answer). Given the chance, however, students can learn to form questions that generate discussion. Regie Routman (1994) tells of a class of third graders who came to reading discussion groups with their questions already written in literature logs. As each child asked a question, the class realized that some questions led to better discussions than others. One child admitted that her factual question was not very good because there was nothing to discuss.

With teacher modeling followed by practice in writing their own questions, student questions should become more open-ended and thought provoking. Regie Routman and Nancy Schubert (Routman, 1994) modeled ways to create open-ended questions based on the first six chapters of *The Lion, the Witch, and the Wardrobe* by C.S. Lewis. They stressed to their fourth graders the importance of constructing questions that had several possible answers. They then let the students work in groups of four to discuss and write their own questions while they walked around offering guidance as needed. Interest was high as students formed their questions and chose one "best" question to share with the class.

Thought-Provoking Question

What opportunities do you (or would you) give your students for asking and pursuing answers to their own questions?

Teachers have also used intriguing objects, photographs, guessing games, and reading and listening materials to stimulate curiosity and cause children to raise questions. For example, by bringing a mud puppy (salamander) to an elementary science class, a science teacher elicited an average of five questions from each student (Dillon, cited in Strother, 1989).

In a series of literature-based discussion lessons, Georgiana Sumner relinquished control of the questioning and allowed her second graders to create their own questions (Commeyras, 1995). Although Georgiana had her own ideas about the types of questions her children should be asking, she soon found that the children had other ideas and that their questions were bringing about openness and in-depth thinking. Analyzing videotapes and transcripts of the literature discussions, Georgiana found that student-generated questions were leading students to think critically by doing the following:

- Considering how the wording of the question could make a difference in its meaning
- Understanding story events
- Discovering reasons related to larger issues, such as the deaths of relatives
- Recognizing when differences of opinion are productive

Student questioning can occur in different situations throughout the day. In Chapter 5, we considered ways that students question themselves as they read and study in order to improve their comprehension. Students in an Explorer's Club meet three times a week during the last class period to investigate their own questions. They record their questions in their Wonderful Questions Journals, then collaborate as they pursue answers (Kligman, 1996). During morning conversation in a primary class, I watched several children take turns sharing something of interest with the class. The teacher permitted the other children to respond only by asking questions, not by making comments or sharing similar experiences. By doing so, the teacher was enabling the children to think of suitable questions that were focused on the topic being presented.

Our *why* questions are important for stimulating thinking, but so are those the students ask. When students initiate the inquiry, we do not have to motivate them. Their incentive to learn comes from within.

Responding to Student Questions

Initiating questions is not easy for students, who must find an opportunity to break into the discussion, articulate the question clearly so that others can comprehend it, overcome the fear of displaying ignorance or asking a "stupid" question, and take the risk of having the question be accepted or rejected. Our responses can either stifle or nourish student questioning. Ignoring a question sends the message that it is unimportant and not worth answering. Even worse, treating questions disdainfully humiliates students so that they won't risk asking them again. On the other hand, treating questions with respect and taking time to consider answers encourages students to value their questioning.

When responding to *why* questions, such as those listed earlier, teachers should avoid simply saying, "I don't know" or "Just because." Such replies offer no satisfaction (Thomas, 1988). Instead, in true Socratic style, teachers should try turning the question back to the questioner by saying, "What do you think?" This reply enables the child to continue puzzling over the situation and at the same time opens dialogue. Another acceptable response to a *why* question would be to admit that you don't know the answer but you will help the child find it. In some cases, such as if a child asks, "Why do we have to go to school?", you might either turn the question back or respond by giving reasons. Our responses should give some measure of satisfaction, but they should also nudge children to further exploration and discovery of the question that intrigues them.

Structured Plans for Questioning

Questions that naturally build on class discussions are perhaps most effective for stimulating thinking, but several structured programs exist for incorporating questioning with reading, learning of content, and creativity. Four of these that we will consider in this section are Question-Answer Relationships (QARs), Reciprocal Questioning (ReQuest), Inquiry Charts (I-Charts), and SCAMPER. The first two plans relate to thinking about what we are reading, the I-Chart procedure is an inquiry-based research program, and SCAMPER is a creative questioning strategy. The following selection about starfish is the basis for sample questions for the first three plans.

The Arms of a Starfish

A starfish is not really a fish. It is a sea animal in the family of echinoderms. It is usually shaped like a star and has five arms, but some starfish have such short arms that they look like a five-sided figure. Sun starfish have many arms. When an arm is broken, the starfish can grow a new arm. The underside of the arms on the starfish is covered with hundreds of tiny suction cups that enable it to move across the bottom of the sea.

Question-Answer Relationships

When using QARs to answer questions, the reader draws on both textual information and prior knowledge (Raphael, 1986). Information in the text is divided into two categories: *right there,* in which answers are directly stated, and *think and search,* for which the reader must look through several sentences or paragraphs to find the answer. Prior knowledge also has two categories: *author and you,* involving both the text and background experience, and *on my own,* which can be answered only from the reader's experience. Figure 6-5 shows the structure of QARs.

Figure 6-5. Organization of QARs

In the Book	In My Head
Right there	Author and you
Think and search	On my own

Based on the selection about starfish, you might ask the following questions for each of the QAR categories.

Right there: What is the scientific family name for starfish?

Think and search: What are some other sea animals that belong to this family?

Author and you: Can you visualize what a starfish looks like from the author's description?

On my own: Where have I seen starfish?

Taffy Raphael (1986) recommends beginning the questioning with *on my own* QARs so that students can recall what they already know about the text. Then ask *think and search* QARs that consist of text-based and inference questions, followed by *author and you* QARs. Finally, return to *on my own* QARs for extension activities.

Reciprocal Questioning (ReQuest)

ReQuest helps students think about their reading and asks them to form questions to ask the teacher (Manzo and Manzo, 1995). Since many children tend to ask lower-order, literal questions, you may need to model higher-order questions to encourage them to ask questions that require thinking. Figure 6-6 summarizes the ReQuest procedure.

As the children carry out the first step of ReQuest, they might ask the following questions about the title and the first sentence:

- What is this story about?
- What kind of arms would a starfish have?
- How many arms might it have?
- If it's not a fish, what is it?

In Step 2 the teacher continues asking questions, possibly modeling some higher-level questions, such as the following:

- If it isn't a fish, why is it called a *starfish*?
- How do you think the starfish got its name?

Figure 6-6. Reciprocal Questioning (ReQuest) Procedure

Step 1: Teacher and students read only the title and first sentence of a selection and look at any illustrations.
Step 2: The teacher turns the book face down, and the students ask the teacher questions about what they have read or seen. Students try to ask the kinds of questions the teacher might ask.
Step 3: After answering all the students' questions, the teacher asks additional questions, but only about the title, first sentence, and illustrations. The last question should always be: "What do you suppose the remainder of this section will be about?" (p. 288).
Step 4: Questioning proceeds through the next sentences in the same way, beginning with student questions and followed by teacher questions. You may conclude the reciprocal questioning when a reasonable purpose for reading has been established.
Step 5: After the ReQuest activity, students should continue reading silently for the purpose(s) that evolved.
Step 6: After the children have finished reading silently, the teacher asks them if they read for the right, or best, purpose.

- How might the starfish's arms be different from our arms?
- What do you suppose the remainder of the selection will be about?

The ReQuest procedure is effective for improving students' comprehension and questioning strategies. It has also improved teachers' questioning techniques. It can be used in all subjects and at all grade levels, and it helps students become independent readers and thinkers.

Inquiry Charts (I-Charts)

Suitable for any area of the curriculum, the I-Chart procedure begins with questions the teacher raises about a topic to be investigated (Hoffman, 1992). Students seek answers to the questions, and along the way they introduce new questions that occur to them as a result of their investigation. Students gradually assume more responsibility for the questioning, eventually taking over the teacher's role in discovering important questions to begin the inquiry process.

Returning to our example of the starfish, we see the teacher heading each of several columns with a question, such as the following:

- What are some other members of the echinoderm family, and what characteristics do these family members share?
- How do starfish survive?
- Why are starfish considered pests in oyster-breeding grounds?
- How do starfish "see" and "feel"?

Children then search for answers in various sources, record them under appropriate headings, and summarize their findings at the end of each column. During their research, they also add information under the headings of "Other Interesting Facts and Figures" and "New Questions."

Thought-Provoking Question

What are some topics for I-Charts that you might introduce to your students that correlate with their interests and with your curriculum guide?

SCAMPER

Instead of focusing on reading and research, SCAMPER is a framework for *creative questioning* that can apply to almost any situation at home or school (Eberle, 1987). SCAMPER also spurs students to think like inventors, composers, and designers by asking them to discover new possibilities and applications for existing products, stories, or ideas. SCAMPER is an acronym for the different mental processes people use as they apply creative thinking strategies. Figure 6-7 lists the key words and accompanying questions for the SCAMPER technique (adapted from SCAMPER Checklist, Eberle, 1987, p. 7).

Figure 6-7. SCAMPER Checklist

S .. Substitute	Who or what else? What other time or place?
C .. Combine	Combine what or whom? Combine purposes, ideas, or materials?
A .. Adapt	How to adapt, re-shape, tune-up, tone-down?
M.. Modify	How to change? Color, sound, motion, form, size, shape, taste, odor?
..... Magnify	Add what to make greater, higher, stronger, thicker, longer?
..... Minify	How to make less, smaller, lighter, slower, less frequent, shrink, reduce?
P .. Put to other uses	What new purposes, uses? Where or when else to use? How else to use?
E .. Eliminate	How to remove, omit, get rid of? What to cut out or simplify?
R .. Reverse	How to turn what around, upside down, inside out?
..... Rearrange	How to change order or sequence, find another pattern, regroup, redistribute?

Children may apply SCAMPER to a story or an object by asking themselves questions from the checklist. For instance, in *Cinderella* they might ask themselves how the story would be different if the following had happened:

- Cinderella had gone home at 1:00 A.M. instead of midnight (Substitute)
- Cinderella wanted to be a career woman (Modify)
- There had been no fairy godmother (Eliminate)
- Cinderella had been considered unattractive (Reverse)

In order to invent a better product, the student could take an existing product, such as a bicycle, and think of ways to improve it by asking questions from the SCAMPER checklist. For instance, would my bicycle be better if I did the following:

- Replaced the handlebars with a steering wheel (Substitute)
- Mounted a television above the front wheel (Combine)
- Added a small motor for going up hills (Modify)
- Took off the back wheel and rode it as a unicycle (Eliminate)

Such mental manipulations cause children to be flexible and open-minded as they approach new problems and challenges.

Summary

Higher-order questioning is essential for promoting thinking in the classroom. Of the various guidelines that help teachers prepare and present thinking-style questions, the use of several seconds of wait time is one of the most important.

Teachers should avoid asking confusing or pointless questions, but they should ask questions that lead students to think in different ways. Following frameworks of questioning advocated by leading educators, such as Bloom, Krathwohl, and Taba, makes us aware of how to construct questions that address different types of thinking. Probing questions cause students to think beyond superficial answers and to reflect on how they know or what reasons they can give to support their answers.

Students are capable of generating their own higher-level questions. Naturally curious, they already have numerous questions in their heads that they are eager to investigate. Teacher modeling, practice in creating questions, and opportunities to use them during discussions help children understand how to form questions.

Educators have developed several structured questioning techniques. The Question-Answer Response (QAR) strategy enables students to ask four types of questions about what they read, and Reciprocal Questioning (ReQuest) lets them interact with the teacher in constructing questions about reading material. The I-Chart is a framework for investigating a topic or theme by having children seek answers to questions, and SCAMPER encourages creative questioning.

References

Barnes, R. (1964). Starfish. *World Book Encyclopedia.* Chicago: Field Enterprises.

Barr, R., Sadow, M., and Blachowicz, C. (1990). *Reading diagnosis for teachers* (2nd ed.). New York: Longman.

Bromley, K.D. (1992). *Language arts: Exploring connections,* 2nd ed. Boston: Allyn & Bacon.

Cecil, N.L. (1995). *The art of inquiry: Questioning strategies for K–6 classrooms.* Winnipeg Man., Canada: Peguis.

Cecil, N.L. (1996). *Questions across the curriculum.* Presentation at the International Reading Association, New Orleans.

Chuska, K. (1995). *Improving classroom questions.* Bloomington, IN: Phi Delta Kappa.

Commeyras, M. (1994). Were Janell and Neesie in the same classroom? Children's questions as the first order of reality in storybook discussions. *Language Arts, 71*(7): 517–523.

Commeyras, M. (May, 1995). Tracing the evolution of research: From critical thinking to literacy partnerships. *NRRC News* 1–3.

Costa, A. (1991). *The school as a home for the mind.* Palatine, IL: Skylight.

Dillon, J. (1983). *Teaching and the art of questioning.* Bloomington, IN: Phi Delta Kappa.

Eberle, R. (1987). *Scamper on.* East Aurora, NY: D.O.K.

Grindler, M., and Stratton, B. (1995). *Using think alouds to develop strategic readers.* Presentation at the 1st Combined IRA Regional Conference Great Lakes and Southeast, Nashville.

Hoffman, J. (1992). Critical reading/thinking across the curriculum: Using I-charts to support learning. *Language Arts, 69*(2): 121–127.

Hunkins, F. (1995). *Teaching thinking through effective questioning,* 2nd ed. Norwood, MA: Christopher-Gordon.

Kligman, P. (1996). Questioning tips: An invitation to inquiry in reading. *The California Reader, 29*(3): 4–6.

Lange, J., and Lange, M. (1996). *Fostering critical and creative thinking in Title I classrooms.* Presentation at the International Reading Association, New Orleans.

Manzo, A. and Manzo, U. (1995). *Teaching children to be literate.* Fort Worth, TX: Harcourt Brace.

McKeown, M., Beck, I., and Worthy, M.J. (1993). Grappling with text ideas: Questioning the author. *The Reading Teacher, 46*(7): 560–566.

Routman, R. (1994). *Invitations* (2nd ed.). Portsmouth, NH: Heinemann.

Raphael, T. (1986). Teaching question-answer relationships revisited. *The Reading Teacher, 39*(5): 516–522.

Staab, C. (1996). Talk in whole-language classrooms. In V. Froese (Ed.), *Whole language: Practice and theory* (2nd ed.). Boston: Allyn & Bacon.

Strother, D. (1989). Developing thinking skills through questioning. *Phi Delta Kappan, 71*(4): 324–327.

Thomas, D.K. (1988). *Why* questions and *why* answers: Patterns and purposes. *Language Arts, 65*(6): 552–556.

Wasserman, S. (1992). *Asking the right question: The essence of teaching.* Bloomington, IN: Phi Delta Kappa.

Wilks, S. (1995). *Critical and creative thinking.* Portsmouth, NH: Heinemann.

Wilson, J., and Wing Jan, L. (1993). *Thinking for themselves.* Portsmouth, NH: Heinemann.

Wood, D. (1988). *How children think and learn.* Oxford, England: Basil Blackwell.

III

Integrating Thinking
Across the Curriculum

I asked the children,

"How can thinking in one subject help you think about another subject?"

and the children said:

I think and use the same skills for almost all subjects.

If you think about it, you have maps in math and social studies, thinking would help you in both subjects.

So Like English helps me in Science because I will now how to write a sentence

In math you learn equations and measurements. (like in science)

If you are using a certain method for studying for a test in one subject, if it is effective, you can use it to study in another subject.

If you learn how to solve problems in math you could apply the same skills in another subject, like science.

You can learn about something in one subject to help you work out a promblem in another subject.

If I were studying the Holocaust in S.S. class and had it also in Reading class, I could tie both information to learn more

If you are studying about the past in history and fossils in science one subject helps you think about another.

Because one subject such as math and Social Studies can Be related like with graphs and other kind of stuff.

The children had more difficulty understanding and answering this question than any of the others. Perhaps some were not transferring knowledge and processes from one curriculum area to another, and perhaps others were unaware of doing so. As you can see from their answers, however, they did recognize certain connections among subject areas.

We'll begin this section by considering ways that teachers can help students transfer thought processes and content from one content area to another. We've already considered the reading-writing connection in Chapter 5, and we will continue to see how teachers use reading and writing throughout the curriculum. Themes are the most obvious organizational pattern for uniting subjects around a common core, so we'll look at how to select and develop them. Children's literature also spans the curriculum with its rich, diverse selections and varied opportunities for responding, and some educators believe that curriculum integration is best attained through literature.

Addressing another way of knowing, graphic organizers allow children to visually display their knowledge and understanding through a variety of organizational strategies. In addition, technology enhances students' ability to manage their own learning and understand complex concepts.

Thus, students begin to integrate what they learn by seeing connections within themes, understanding ways that literature can enrich their knowledge and appreciation in all areas, discovering relationships through graphic organizers, and using technology to enhance and advance their understanding. In order to benefit fully from these experiences, students need time to reflect on what is meaningful for them and ways to apply new knowledge and concepts. As part of this reflection, they also evaluate their goals, their progress, their efforts, and their strengths.

CHAPTER 7

Integrated Learning With Themes

When I asked the teachers,

"How can thematic units help students see connections and relationships among ideas and concepts?"

the teachers said:

- Thematic units are like file folders in our brains. We sort different ideas, but we compile a network and put different ideas together. We can see connections among many different subjects. Fitting ideas together is like putting together puzzle pieces.
- Most concepts and ideas have a central theme. July 4 and Memorial Day could both fall under the theme of patriotism. By connecting certain ideas and concepts, we allow students to quickly grasp meanings.
- By using themes, a teacher can bring in related topics that may not normally be covered.
- Letting students come up with ways to expand the theme and guiding them through the process gives them actual experience with thinking in terms of relationships among ideas and concepts.
- A theme relates ideas and concepts by placing them all under the umbrella of the theme.
- By their very nature, theme studies make connections to the variety of areas that the particular theme touches.

How would you answer this question?

Concepts to watch for

- Rationale for integrating the curriculum
- Ways to help children transfer knowledge and procedures from one area to another
- How to connect mathematics to writing
- Ways to select and develop themes
- Methods of sharing information that consider multiple ways of knowing

---

Visiting a science class, I watched as second-grade students attempted to complete electrical circuits. Working in pairs, they experimented with different objects to discover what kinds of materials would cause the bulb to light and which materials had no effect. Kathy Cameron, the teacher, drew the children together to discuss their findings. She then gave them diagrams of circuits to label with the vocabulary words listed in the room. Again working together, the children wrote the appropriate words and glued their diagrams into individual theme books on electricity. In this class the children learned in a variety of ways: by discovery, discussion, interpreting diagrams, reading and writing new vocabulary words, and placing one more piece of information in their theme booklets.

Integrating the Curriculum

This chapter begins with integrating the curriculum, or finding ways of linking the language arts with each other as well as with the disciplines. An integrated curriculum should center around major understandings that relate to the students' interests and to your grade-level curriculum guide. A totally integrated curriculum that interrelates all subjects all day every day is difficult, if not impossible, to achieve, so strive instead for making connections across the curriculum whenever possible (Routman, 1994).

The integrated curriculum is a widely accepted means of enabling students to make connections and transfer knowledge (Hughes, cited in Lipson et al., 1993). Among its attributes are the potential for the following:

- Providing authentic learning experiences that are readily transferable to other situations
- Engaging students in a cyclical learning process that involves successive stages of formulating problems, forming concepts, applying, evaluating, reflecting, and modifying
- Encouraging students to gain insights, construct meaning, and apply new knowledge

- Promoting higher-order thinking and the ability to transfer concepts across subject areas

Another argument for an integrated curriculum is the lack of time for teaching all the subjects that the curriculum requires. For instance, in addition to the "basics," teachers may be expected to cover multiculturalism, computer literacy, drug awareness, and environmental studies. By integrating the curriculum, teachers can incorporate many of these issues in meaningful, interrelated ways.

Thought-Provoking Question

What efforts have you made or would you like to make toward integrating the curriculum?

In their answers to the question at the beginning of this section, a few children observed that thinking strategies and problem solving are useful in different subject areas. Indeed, thinking should be the core of an integrated curriculum, connecting subject areas and grade levels with such strategies as critical reading, problem solving, modes of inquiry, and study skills (Costa, 1991). Instead of science, math, or the arts being ends in themselves, children need to see how to apply the unique nature of each discipline to other situations. When this change in practice occurs,

> We will refocus from mastering content and concepts as an end, to the application of knowledge, the transference of cognitive strategies, and the tackling with confidence of new problems that command increasingly complex reasoning, more intricate logic and more imaginative and creative solutions (Costa, 1991, pp. 164-165).

Until this refocusing happens, the transference of thinking strategies is limited.

Reinforcing this concept, Michael Jaeger and his colleagues (1996) point out that learning traditional school subjects is quite different from using the disciplines as ways of learning. When studying school subjects, students simply acquire the knowledge associated with a particular discipline that has been uncovered and recorded by others. When students use the disciplines as ways of learning, however, they employ scientific methods or historical analysis to discover information for themselves. Using tools of various disciplines (i.e., graphing, recording, classifying), they conduct investigations and explore primary source materials to find answers.

Learning in themes or strands is natural for children in multiage classrooms, which combine two or three adjacent grade levels. Instead of trying to cover a specific curriculum for each grade level, teachers develop broad curricular themes and introduce thinking processes that involve all the children, who of course are performing at various developmental levels. For instance, students from kindergarten and grades one and two in a multiage classroom might be studying community helpers. Younger children would be looking at picture books and drawing pictures of them, and older ones would be reading and writing about them, but all would participate in discussions and activities. Teachers in multiage classrooms rotate topics for themes so that the same topic appears at two- or three-year intervals, as they encounter completely new groups of children. In a multiage classroom, the curriculum is based on the following (Mixed-Age Primary, 1994):

- Solving problems
- Making sense of written material and the social and physical environment
- Learning from hands-on, manipulative activities
- Reflecting on connections between their firsthand investigations and reports from others
- Availability of real-world materials, such as cooking supplies, musical instruments, art supplies, books, and measuring equipment
- Building the curriculum around children's interests and applications of real-world materials

Making Connections

During early childhood, children live in a holistic world. There are no artificial boundaries that separate observing ants in an ant hill, talking about them, and looking at a picture book about ants. Not until they enter school is such a theme divided into science, oral language, and reading. Making connections is a natural part of learning and discovery for the young child.

When answering the question at the beginning of this section, children connected content areas when they saw similarities between science and math (measurement), social studies and reading (the Holocaust), and science and history (fossils). They also saw relationships among processes when they observed that problem solving in math and science is similar, that graphs can be used to illustrate both math and social studies, and that effective study methods can be transferred from one subject to another. Unless students can see meaningful connections among disciplines and ways of learning, they are unlikely to make transfers to other subjects and life outside school. The example that follows illustrates some ways to make connections.

Theme: Making Connections With *Houses*

Immersed in a theme of *houses*, these fourth-grade students were exploring this concept from various perspectives. They brainstormed to create a list of about 50 types of houses, ranging from an igloo to a caravan to a holiday house. Using their imaginations, they drew their dream houses, constructed models of houses, and wrote acrostic poems about houses. By researching various sources, they made a list of facts about houses that they posted on the wall. They focused particularly on Japanese houses, which they linked to their lessons on the Japanese language.

Thought-Provoking Question

How many curriculum areas, ways of knowing, and thinking strategies are part of this theme? Can you think of additional experiences related to houses for making connections?

Students make connections through their experiences. When they say "This is like what we did before" or "This reminds me of . . . ," they are connecting what they are now learning to previous experiences. They use prior knowledge and experiences to make sense of new information. By providing students with meaningful, authentic experiences during the day, we help them transfer what they are learning in school to their lives out of school—a significant connection if school is to be a worthwhile learning experience. Parents can observe such transfers occurring when children use math to estimate expenses or budget allowances, apply problem-solving strategies to keeping squirrels away from the bird feeder, or use research skills to find out if a snake is poisonous. To help children make connections between school and their lives outside school, try asking them the questions that appear in Figure 7-1.

Thought-Provoking Question

What question(s) could you ask about a current or recent school topic that would help students transfer their knowledge to other situations?

Students see meaningful relationships in other ways as well. Children's literature is a powerful connector, as we will see in Chapter 8. Many great books enable children to attain insights and depth of understanding

Figure 7-1. Questioning Children About Making Connections

How can you use what we learned in school when you go home?

How does what we learned remind you of other things you already know?

How can you use what we learned today to become a better citizen?

What examples can you give of ways that you applied the problem solving strategies we use in school to other situations?

Can you think of other things that you could learn at school that would help you when you leave school?

How would it be different if we investigate _____ as a historian, a scientist, an artist, or a writer? What strategies might be the same?

in a variety of subject areas and to identify with characters and situations. As children begin to acquire strategies for studying, they'll find that similar techniques work for them across the curriculum. Here is where their own ways of knowing come into play, for some learn best by writing down important points, others by visualizing, others by creating a chant or simple melody, and some by outlining. Following are some examples of connections between various areas of the curriculum.

Connecting Mathematics and Writing

Although teachers can find authentic ways to integrate mathematics with many themes, they also realize that some math computational skills must be taught separately. Understanding processes, as opposed to memorizing math facts, however, can be enhanced by linking mathematics and language arts. The National Council of Teachers of Mathematics (1989) issued a document that views mathematics as a means of communication that involves discussing, reading, writing, and listening. In recent years teachers have discovered many ways to help children comprehend and solve math problems through oral and written language.

Meaningful math instruction centers on problem solving, or finding solutions to real-life situations involving numbers. In order to solve math problems, students have typically relied on trial and error or the process of elimination, but teachers are finding that discussion and writing often help children clarify their thinking about ways to solve problems. Students must use a variety of thinking strategies to analyze the problem, determine what is being asked, consider relationships among the elements, decide on a series of steps to follow, and evaluate the reasonableness of the answer. As children discuss and later write the procedures they used, they refine their understanding.

In many classrooms children are creating their own problems about real-life situations for others to solve (Winograd and Higgins, 1994/1995). As emerging scientists, engineers, architects, or city planners, children need to know how to recognize problems and find solutions to them. In Donna Strohauer's fifth-grade class, students make up purposeful problems about money, trading cards, or shopping; solve their own problems; share the problems and solutions; and then revise them based on reactions from their peers. Figure 7-2 lists some advantages of writing about math problems.

Figure 7-2. Advantages of Connecting Mathematics and Writing

Gaining deeper understanding of math concepts
Increasing reasoning powers in mathematics
Organizing ideas
Forming hypotheses that might lead to solutions
Clarifying thinking
Applying math facts to real-life situations
Making sense of mathematics
Identifying and articulating math problems
Using imagination and creative thinking to pose problems
Writing and thinking analytically to solve problems
Reflecting on answers to see if they make sense

In Melbourne, Australia, children all over the city were excited about the impending Grand Prix to be held in a local park. Many classroom activities centered on the race, and sixth-grade students in Mrs. Carter's classroom were absorbed in a theme study about the Grand Prix. When I visited, the students had already produced a class newspaper featuring the race, created raps and other forms of writing about it, and debated the issue of whether or not it should be held in the city. What particularly impressed me, however, was the math connection. On the board Mrs. Carter had written, "Create word problems about the Grand Prix." Below this was a list of suggested math-related topics that the students had brainstormed. These included the following:

ticket prices	cost of cars	brake time
length of pits	budget	drivers (age, height, etc.)
crowd statistics	gate takings	time (set-up, pull-down)
litres of petrol	drivers' salaries	actual race lap times
noise levels	cost of extra security	merchandise sold (souvenirs)
fast food consumed	qualifying lap times	

From this list, students saw many real-life applications for learning mathematics.

Christine Gordon and Dorothy Macinnis (1993) found another form of writing about mathematics, dialogue journals, to be useful in their classrooms for both students and teachers. As the students wrote, they explained what does and doesn't work when they try to solve math problems. They were also thinking about what might help them learn better and gaining insights into their own learning processes. As the teachers read their students' entries, they became aware of the students' difficulties and could see how they needed to improve their instructional techniques. They also became aware of their students' development as mathematical thinkers.

Thought-Provoking Idea

Read Jon Scieszka's *Math Curse* to your students. Ask them to begin looking at everything that happens to them as a math problem needing a solution and to keep a journal of what they find.

Connecting Science and Reading

Science taught with textbooks seldom motivates children to learn, so many teachers approach science with hands-on activities (Guthrie and Alvermann, 1996). Students learn to think like scientists by observing, predicting or hypothesizing, conducting experiments, collecting data, and writing reports. Instead of reading from a single textbook, students gather and sort through information by reading a variety of texts, including straightforward informational materials and picture books that evoke emotional responses. They also review a variety of materials in reference books, on video, and on CD-ROM. They connect new information to old information, check long-held theories against new data, and confirm or reject ideas based on their own observations and discoveries.

When reading is regarded as a problem-solving process, reading and science follow similar procedures (Padilla, et al., 1991). Knowledge of reading thus transfers to an understanding of scientific processes. In reading, the student reads the text, makes inferences, and draws conclusions; in science, the student carries out an experiment, interprets the results, and draws conclusions. In addition, both science and reading ask the student to make and verify predictions and to be aware metacognitively of how well they understand what they are reading or the activity they are performing.

Connecting Thinking to Movement, the Creative Arts, and the Language Arts

Approaching any subject through multiple ways of knowing enhances its worth and engages students whose primary ways of learning are through movement, music, drama, or visual art. Pat Jordan, an elementary physical education teacher, finds ways to challenge her students' thinking and problem solving strategies through movement. Here are two activities she uses.

Designing a game. The principal created a contest, and the winning homeroom would be able to spend Friday night in the gym. Your class won, but all the basketball goals had been removed from the gym. Your job is to make a game that everyone can play with the remaining available equipment (which is given). Describe the game and the rules, draw the playing area, and name the game.

Crossing a river. Your job is to get your team across an imaginary river (actually, the gym floor) using the available equipment, including ropes and scooters. You must work cooperatively with other members of your team and consider the special needs of any students who are physically challenged for your team to win.

Musical, dramatic, and artistic expression are vital ways of communicating and developing understanding. Keeping rhythm with drumbeats during a simulation of an African safari, playing madrigal music while studying the Middle Ages, or learning folk songs during a pioneer study add new dimensions to the curriculum. Artistic expression is particularly helpful in developing appreciation for literature (Carroll et al., 1994). Students bring literature to life as they become storytellers, actors in Readers Theater and creative drama, or artists and illustrators in the creation of their own publications. The following example shows how one teacher involved her students in art.

Aware of the parallels in visual processing between reading and writing and the visual arts, Ann Alejandro (1994) tells how she brought her at-risk second and third graders to reading and writing through art. Ann believes that analyzing the components of paintings—shape, texture, mood, conflict, and color—calls for the same thought processes as interpreting the elements of written text, such as words, spelling patterns, genres, metaphor, and style. Ann discarded work sheets and skill materials in favor of famous paintings, which she presented to her class as slides, transparencies, and reproductions in books. Prompted by Ann's passion for art, the children immersed themselves in the paintings, exclaiming over such features as background, foreground, media, and mood. As young art critics, they brainstormed feelings portrayed by the paintings, compared artistic styles, and observed contrasts between cool and warm colors. The children then turned their attention to writing; they drafted their descriptions, revised them, published them, and read each others' works. A field trip to an art museum added to their fervor for art and served as a continuing resource for reading and writing throughout the remainder of the year.

Thematic Units

Students need to be able to see meaningful connections between content and process. Thematic units can help students become aware of these connections and realize that different subjects share similar patterns and concepts (Lipson et al., 1993). By learning about frogs, for instance, children connect the environment, characteristics of animals, and stories about frogs with their own experiences. Such learning piques their curiosity so that they want to know more about related areas, such as other amphibious animals and the ecology of a pond.

A *thematic unit* is a framework for organizing learning around a central concept or goal, such as the environment or the Civil War, rather than a subject, such as history or science. It spans many areas of the curriculum and usually continues for several weeks. Thematic units differ from the units that teachers once taught, for traditional units simply consisted of teaching a topic within a discipline for an extended period of time. I remember teaching a social studies unit on transportation to third graders. During the last hour of each day for about three weeks, students engaged in a variety of activities related to transportation, but I still taught basal reader stories for reading, spelling words from the spelling book, science lessons about insects, and so forth. There was no continuity across the curriculum. In a thematic unit on transportation, however, my third graders would be reading and writing about transportation, creating lists of spelling words related to the topic, computing distances and speeds in math, and learning the basics of aerodynamics and power transmission in science. Figure 7-3 shows some advantages of teaching with thematic units.

Thought-Provoking Question

What can go wrong with thematic units? Here are some answers. Perhaps you can think of others.

1. Choosing an unworthy topic for a theme
2. Making artificial, contrived connections
3. Using activities that are irrelevant to the theme
4. Presenting content and strategies in isolation

Figure 7-3. Advantages of Thematic Teaching

Creates links between what children are learning and their own lives

Supports the integration of the curriculum

Enables children to look at the big questions

Gives authentic purposes and provides real audiences for learning

Uses reading and writing as functional tools for learning instead of as ends in themselves

Enables the class to collect and use vast amounts of materials on the theme because learning focuses on one major topic

Encourages cooperative learning as students work collaboratively

Supports parental involvement as parents contribute to the theme

Gives all children, especially in inclusion classes, ways to learn and contribute

Provides opportunities for students to learn according to their strengths and individual ways of knowing

Allows children to make decisions, use various thinking strategies, pursue their own inquiries, pose and solve problems, construct knowledge, examine issues critically, and become independent learners

A variation of thematic units is *theme cycles*. Thematic units may not be linked to one another, but in theme cycles, new themes grow out of questions and problems related to former themes. Thus, theme cycles are recursive and spiraling, with new inquiries building on prior investigations (Altwerger and Flores, 1994; Harste et al., 1988). For example, a theme study on career choices might lead to space exploration or recent medical developments. The role of the teacher in both units and cycles is to serve as guide, facilitator, demonstrator, supporter, and mediator in helping students grow in knowledge and understanding (Andrews-Sullivan and Negrete, 1994).

Selecting Themes

Since many themes cover a period of several weeks, selection of appropriate topics is critical. Valuable time can be wasted if the theme is inappropriate and results in little learning. The answers to the previous "thought-provoking question" give some practices that cause themes to be ineffective, but here we will turn our attention to selecting worthy themes. Some considerations are the following:

- Students' interests (based on a survey or observation)
- Curriculum guide
- Topics of local interest (e.g., a new city park)
- Ideas from other teachers, particularly in a team-teaching arrangement
- Availability of supporting materials and resources
- Themes from literature-based reading series

The topic should not be so broad that it lacks focus, but it should be broad enough to allow for investigations of special related issues. Above all, be sure that you are enthusiastic about the topic yourself in order to transmit your zeal to the students. You can negotiate topics for themes, allowing students to have input but keeping in mind district mandates and your own views on their value.

Regie Routman (1994) warns us that many so-called themes are no more than collections of activities centered around a topic (e.g., mice, bears, dragons). In such cases, themes fail to provide opportunities for developing important concepts and transferring knowledge and skills. They are often irrelevant to students' lives and unlikely to meet educational goals and objectives. Instead of teachers putting so much energy into developing cute, artificial correlations, Routman advises us to select topics that are natural, meaningful, and worthwhile.

Figure 7-4 shows some major topics that could be the basis of worthy thematic units. Along with the topics are suggestions for related goals and major concepts.

Figure 7-4. Topics for Worthy Themes

Electricity (usefulness, potential danger, ways to produce, sources, relation to magnetism)

Insects (traits, characteristics, life cycles, effects on the environment)

Weather (effects of changing atmospheric conditions, weather cycles, significance of cloud formations, how to predict)

Energy (importance of conservation, alternative forms, how it is produced and used, meeting demands, resources)

Cultural diversity (contributions, customs, and origins of various cultures)

Inventions (how they change society, significant inventions and inventors, processes for inventing)

Space exploration (effects, development, leaders, potential, components of the solar system)

Developing Thematic Units

Thematic units vary considerably in development and application. They usually last for several weeks or as long as student interest remains high. Teachers can usually adapt basic concepts from themes to a wide range of grade levels and the abilities of special learners, include a variety of thinking and learning strategies, and help students find activities that support different learning styles or intelligences. Team teaching is often part of the planning and development of themes, particularly when themes extend across grade levels or become schoolwide. Some themes, however, may develop as the result of a single class's inquiry into a topic of special interest. Although no standard procedure for developing themes exists, the plan that follows incorporates many of the practices usually found in thematic units. The thinking strategies listed after student activities are those most likely to be used, but some strategies may not be activated for every topic and others may also be used in some cases.

Major Goals or Understandings

Remember that a thematic unit must contain concepts that are sufficiently important to justify the time, effort, and resources involved. They should have social and/or academic significance and evolve from teacher selection, student interest, and curriculum guidelines. You should refer to them as the unit progresses to make sure that you keep on track.

Introducing the Theme

As you introduce the theme, your two major purposes should be to generate prior knowledge and create interest. Children are generally eager to share what they already know, and if the students had a major role in selecting the topic, motivation is built in. A good selection from children's literature, a motivational resource person, or an exciting video are effective introductory activities, but the best is student-initiated inquiry. Two strategies that are useful for generating prior knowledge and creating interest are semantic mapping and K-W-L, which are shown in the sample theme in Figure 7-5. Because her class is bilingual, Elena Castro (1994) wrote introductory charts for her theme in both English and Spanish.

Thinking strategies: Recalling, brainstorming, classifying, divergent thinking, elaboration, fluency, flexibility, inquiry, predicting, seeing relationships.

Each of the questions in the second column could be a subtopic worthy of investigation. As children find answers, they may list them on charts. Some teachers add another column on *How We Can Find Out*, thus inviting children to list possible resources for conducting their investigations.

Figure 7-5. Thematic Unit on *Oceans*

Major Goals or Understandings

The world's oceans have many distinctive features.

The oceans' resources are important to us in many ways.

Oceans influence climate.

There is much plant and animal life in the oceans.

The exploration of oceans offers many possibilities.

Introducing the Theme

Ask the students to help you create a semantic map by telling you words that they associate with *oceans*. Then ask them to help you place the words in categories and label each category. The map at the beginning of the unit might look like this.

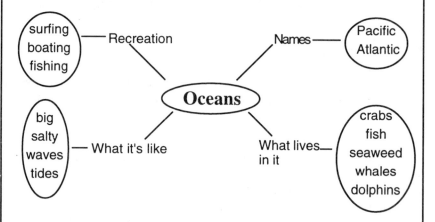

You may expand semantic maps during the unit as the children uncover new information, and you may also use them as a way of summarizing data at the conclusion of the unit. More information on creating semantic maps is found in Chapter 9.

The K-W-L procedure refers to *What We K̲now, What We W̲ant to Know,* and *What We L̲earned.* The children begin by telling you what they already know, which you put in the first column, and then they ask questions about what they want to know, which you list in the second column. The third column is added later as students find information, but you may actually want to have a separate L chart for each subtopic that groups of children investigate. The example shows only the first two columns.

figure 7-5 continued on next page

figure 7-5 continued from previous page

Oceans

What We Know	What We Want to Know
Cover most of the earth	What are oceans like (how deep, big)?
Have salt water	What use are they to us?
Provide recreation	How do people explore the ocean?
Move (waves, tides)	What kinds of fish live there and how do they live?
Deep-sea divers	

Procedures

Based on the major goals and the children's questions, students divide into five groups:

- Features of the oceans
- Usefulness of the oceans to people
- Plant and animal life in the oceans
- Exploration of oceans
- Effects of oceans on climate

Groups conduct investigations and participate in activities, which may include the following:

- Collecting resource materials, including trade books, reference materials, videos, and computer programs
- Inviting or interviewing a scuba diver, an oceanographer, or an authority on sea life
- Exploring the Internet
- Visiting an aquarium or the shore of an ocean
- Organizing information in a logical order; working out any contradictions; considering what is essential and what is irrelevant

Groups consider plans for sharing information, and their projects may take one of the following forms:

- Construction of a globe showing the different oceans with labels identifying major bodies of water
- Simulation of an ocean exploration team recovering a sunken ship
- Written report with graphs summarizing findings

figure 7-5 continued on next page

figure 7-5 continued from previous page

- Musical production with sea chanties (published music and student-created songs)
- Model of a relief map of the bottom of one of the oceans
- Computations, charts, and tables of tides
- Art display of various forms of sea life (drawings and three-dimensional models)

Student Reflections and Self-Evaluations

At the conclusion of the thematic unit, children ask themselves such questions as the following:

- What did I learn from studying about oceans?
- Has what I learned change the way I used to think? If so, how?
- How can I use the knowledge I now have about oceans?
- What more do I need or want to find out?
- Who would like to know what I've learned? How will I share?
- Did I do my best work?
- Did I make worthwhile contributions to my group? If so, what were they?
- What was easy or difficult for me to understand? Why was that?

Students may consider these questions by writing answers to them or by discussing them with you and/or other students.

Curriculum Areas Covered

Reading and writing: Investigating source materials, writing reports, reading related trade books, making charts.

Geography: Location of worlds' oceans, influence on climate, map and globe study.

Social Studies: Influence of oceans on economy, lifestyles.

Mathematics: Ocean currents, distances, areas, making graphs.

Health: Inclusion of sea foods in diet.

Science: Ecology of the ocean.

The arts: Exploring oceans through art, drama, and music.

References (Trade Books)

Cerullo, M. (1993). *Sharks: Challengers of the deep*. New York: Cobblehill.

Cole, J. (1992). *The magic school bus: On the ocean floor*. New York: Scholastic.

Jeunesse, G., and Cohat, E. (1990). *The seashore*. New York: Scholastic.

Koch, M. (1993). *World water watch*. New York: Greenwillow.

figure 7-5 continued on next page

figure 7-5 continued from previous page

Pallotta, J. (1986). *The ocean alphabet book.* Watertown, MA: Charlesbridge.
Patent, D. (1984). *Whales: Giants of the deep.* New York: Holiday House.
Simon, S. (1988). *How to be an ocean scientist in your own home.* Philadelphia: Lippincott.

Procedures

An effective way to begin the investigation into a theme is to let students select special-interest groups that relate to the main topic. These may evolve from the semantic map, K-W-L procedure, the I-Chart (explained in Chapter 6), signing up for a subtopic related to the major understandings, or some other means. Each group then gathers data, organizes material, and decides how to share information with the audience (usually the rest of the class). Although the students can identify some of the resources, you should have an abundant supply of reference materials, as well as ideas for field trips, people to interview, artifacts, and activities related to the creative arts. Sharing may be through visual art, movement, music, drama, written reports, charts or graphs, or any meaningful way of transmitting information.

Thinking strategies: Organizing, decision making, problem solving, comparing and contrasting, concentrating, creative thinking, imagining, interpreting, investigating, logical thinking, observing, point of view, reasoning, seeing relationships, planning strategies, summarizing, synthesizing.

Reflection and Self-Evaluation

Students reflect on what they have learned by thinking over what they know now that they didn't know before and by finding ways to integrate new knowledge with former attitudes and perceptions. They may also reflect on how this new information can affect their lives, both in and out of school. They can also evaluate their participation in the unit, their contributions, and the extent of their work.

Thinking strategies: Analysis, application, critical thinking, evaluating, hypothesizing, imagining, interpreting, predicting, developing point of view, reasoning, transferring learning.

Teacher Follow-up

As you also reflect on the unit, consider how well you and the students met your major goals or understandings. You might ask yourself these questions:

- Did most students grasp the major understandings?
- Did I have sufficient resources to enable students to carry out their investigations?

- Could I help students locate other resources?
- Did I work well with other teachers in planning and developing the theme (if a team situation)?
- Did student interest remain high?
- Did I offer ample opportunities for students to apply thinking strategies?
- Were there opportunities for students to use a variety of learning styles and intelligences?
- What changes could I make to improve this theme study if we do it again?

You will also need to evaluate each student's work, especially if you must give a grade. You should observe progress continually, and you should consider both the process (the ways in which the student moves toward the goal, such as organizational skills) and the product (the concrete result, such as a report or dramatic reenactment). Be sure to consider the student's self-evaluation as well as your own assessment of progress.

Many children are reluctant to take active roles in selecting thematic units and participating in them if their previous school experiences have been totally teacher-directed. They may be bewildered when asked what they would *like* to study, regard cooperative work as "cheating," and feel that they aren't learning because they are not reading from textbooks (Ramirez, 1994). Be patient with these children, guiding them gradually into decision making and independent learning until they feel confident and willing to take risks.

Thought-Provoking Question

What are some specific ways that you might encourage the reluctant participant?

Summary

Curriculum integration makes sense because it provides authentic learning experiences that children can transfer to other situations, promotes higher-order thinking, enables children to apply new knowledge, and focuses on thought processes instead of separate subjects. As children transfer knowledge and insights from one area of the curriculum to another, they make meaningful connections both within the classroom and to their lives outside school.

Connections across the curriculum occur in many ways, but the connection between mathematics and writing is particularly strong. As children write problems for others to solve and as they write out procedures that they follow when solving problems, they clarify their understanding of story problems. Strong connections also exist between science and reading and between the creative arts and language arts.

Thematic units provide a framework for integrating the curriculum. When selecting topics for themes, be sure to choose a topic worthy of study, one that corresponds with curriculum guidelines, and one that interests both you and the children. Your students should have some voice in the selection.

At the beginning of the theme, establish major understandings or goals that will guide your study. You can introduce the theme in a variety of ways, but be sure to generate students' prior knowledge and create interest. Semantic maps and the K-W-L procedure are two effective ways to do this. During thematic units children often work in groups that investigate the major understandings. They search through resource materials, find information, organize data, and prepare their findings to present to an audience. During the process, they use multiple intelligences and a wide variety of thinking strategies. At the conclusion of the thematic unit, students reflect on their learning and evaluate themselves as participants.

References

Alejandro, A. (1994). Like happy dreams—Integrating visual arts, writing, and reading. *Language Arts, 71*(1): 12–21.

Altwerger, B., and Flores, B. (1994). Theme cycles: Creating communities of learners. *Primary Voices, 2*(1): 2–6.

Andrews-Sullivan, M., and Negrete, E. (1994). Our struggles with theme cycle. *Primary Voices, 2*(1): 15–18.

Baskwill, J. (1988). Making connections. *Teaching K–8, 19*(8): 42–43.

Black, S. (1994). Beyond age and grade. In *Staying focused on the children.* Peterborough, NH: Society for Developmental Education.

Bull, G. (1989). *Reflective teaching.* Carlton South, Victoria: Australian Reading Association.

Carroll, J., Ahuna-Ka'Ai'Ai, J., Chang, K., and Wong-Kam, J. (1993) Integrated language arts instruction. *Language Arts, 70*(4): 310–315.

Carroll, J., Wong-Kam, J., Chang, K., and Jacobson, H. (1994). Linking language arts with creative arts. *Language Arts, 71*(1): 60–66.

Castro, E. (1994). Implementing theme cycle: One teacher's way. *Primary Voices, 2*(1): 7–14.

Cordeiro, P. (1992). *Whole learning, whole language and content in the upper elementary grades.* Katonah, NY: Richard C. Owen.

Costa, A. (1991). *The school as a home for the mind.* Palatine, IL: Skylight.

Cudog, B. Theme cycle as a vehicle for transformation: One principal's story of change. *Primary Voices, 2*(1): 20–25.

Cushman, K. (1994). The whys and hows of the multi-age primary classroom. In *Staying focused on the children*. Peterborough, NH: Society for Developmental Education.

Ford, M. (1990). The writing process: A strategy for problem solvers. *Arithmetic Teacher, 38*(3): 35–38.

Fortescue, C. (1994). Using oral and written language to increase understanding of math concepts. *Language Arts, 71*(8): 576–580.

Goodman, K. (1986). *What's whole in whole language?* Portsmouth, NH: Heinemann.

Gordon, C., and Macinnis, D. (1993). Using journals as a window on students' thinking in mathematics. *Language Arts, 70*(1): 37–43.

Greene, B. (1993). Integrating processes in the language arts. *Language Arts, 70*(4): 323–325.

Guthrie, J., and Alvermann, D. (1996). Linking language arts to science. *NRRC News*. University of Georgia and University of Maryland, College Park: National Reading Research Center.

Harste, J., Short, K., and Burke, C. (1988). *Creating classrooms for authors*. Portsmouth, NH: Heinemann.

Hoffman, J. (1992). Critical reading/thinking across the curriculum: Using I-Charts to support learning. *Language Arts, 69*(2): 121–127.

Jaeger, M., Lauritzen, C., and Davenport, M.R. (1996). The role of the disciplines in integrating curriculum. *The Reading Teacher, 50*(1): 64–66.

Lipson, M., Valencia, S., Wixson, K., and Peters, C. (1993). Integration and thematic teaching: Integration to improve teaching and learning. *Language Arts, 70*(4): 252–262.

Lukasevich, A. (1996). Organizing whole-language classrooms. In V. Froese (Ed.), *Whole language* (2nd ed.). Boston: Allyn & Bacon.

The mixed-age primary: What and why. (1994). In *Staying focused on the children*. Peterborough, NH: Society for Developmental Education.

National Council of Teachers of Mathematics, Commission on Standards for School Mathematics. (1989). *Curriculum of evaluation standards for school mathematics*. Reston, VA: National Council of Teachers of Mathematics.

Padilla, M., Muth, K.D., and Padilla, R. (1991). Science and reading: Many process skills in common? In C. Santa and D. Alvermann (Eds.), *Science learning: Processes and applications*. Newark, DE: International Reading Association.

Pike, K., Compain, R., and Mumper, J. (1994). *New connections*. New York: HarperCollins.

Ramirez, L. (1994). Reflections. *Primary Voices, 2*(1): 33–34.

Roberts, P. (1993). *A green dinosaur day: A guide to developing thematic units in literature-based instruction, K–8.* Boston: Allyn & Bacon.

Routman, R. (1994). *Invitations* (2nd ed.). Portsmouth, NH: Heinemann.

Santa, C., and Alvermann, D. (Eds.). (1991). *Science learning: Processes and applications.* Newark, DE: International Reading Association.

Scieszka, J. (1995). *Math curse.* New York: Viking.

Shoemaker, B. J. (1991). Education 2000 integrated curriculum. *Phi Delta Kappan, 73*(10): 793–797.

Thompson, G. (1991). *Teaching through themes.* New York: Scholastic.

Weaver, C. (1990). *Understanding whole language.* Portsmouth, NH: Heinemann.

Winograd, K., and Higgins, K. (1994/1995). Writing, reading, and talking mathematics: One interdisciplinary possibility. *The Reading Teacher, 48*(4): 310–318.

Woods, R. (1994). A close-up look at how children learn science. *Educational Leadership, 51*(5): 33–35.

CHAPTER 8

Children's Literature as a Pathway to Thinking

When I asked the teachers,

"How can children's literature promote thinking?"

the teachers said:

- Because children are comfortable with children's books, teachers can ask nonthreatening, thought-probing questions.
- Children may be able to think through some stories and apply them to real-life situations.
- Children's literature allows children to encounter things that they have never experienced before or to see familiar situations in a new light.
- Picture books create moods through their use of color, line, and texture, thus eliciting emotions that might not be felt in a verbal, factual description.
- Children can relate to a concept once it has been presented in a story.
- Children's literature lets students view situations from a different perspective and encourages them to be more open-minded.
- A teacher can read all but the ending of a book and then let students think about how they want the book to end.
- Instead of showing children the illustrations, I like them to think and visualize their own pictures.

How would you answer this question?

Concepts to watch for

- How children's literature enhances thought processes
- The concept of envisionment
- Reader response theory
- Responses to literature that cause students to think
- Specific books that foster thinking strategies

In a first-grade class, Val Ferguson was conducting a writing workshop. The children were eagerly writing creative stories or more chapters for their books. Watching the children work and reading their stories on bulletin boards, I was amazed at the diverse topics they chose and the inventiveness of the stories.

During a break in her conferences with these young writers, I asked Val how she enabled them to write such complex and interesting stories. She told me that the children know they will have periods of time to write at least four mornings every week, but even more important, she reads to them frequently from a wide variety of fascinating storybooks. She captures their imaginations with exaggerated expression and by changing her voice to match the voices of her characters. Soon, she said, they can't wait to invent stories of their own!

Promoting Thinking With Children's Literature

In Chapter 1 we considered a variety of frameworks for thinking strategies, all of which can be readily applied to children's literature. For example, when teachers use deBono's types of thinking or advanced levels of Bloom's taxonomy to guide their literature lessons, children learn to think from different perspectives and on more complex levels than if they were simply to recall the story. Most stories begin with problems, proceed through ways to overcome them, and ultimately arrive at solutions, so awareness of problem-solving strategies helps students anticipate story structure.

Individuals construct meaning as they read; that is, they interpret the words of the author in terms of their experiences, prior knowledge, and values or attitudes. Through reflection and personal associations, each reader arrives at a slightly different meaning for the text. Consistent with this constructive aspect of reading are *transactive theories* (Rosenblatt, 1994), which view the reading process as a transaction or exchange of ideas between the reader and the text. Figure 8-1 gives some ways that readers interpret text through the interactions of their own thoughts and the words of the author (Allred, 1996).

Figure 8-1. Thinking Strategies During Interactive Reading

Readers interact with the text by the following means:
- Tapping into prior knowledge of content
- Considering relevant personal experiences
- Making predictions about what might happen
- Visualizing settings and situations
- Empathizing with characters
- Connecting this text with other materials they have read
- Associating characters with other people, other characters, or themselves
- Allowing themselves to wonder and ponder as they read
- Viewing situations in terms of their own cultures and backgrounds
- Continuing to reflect on what they have read as they get fresh insights and share ideas with others

Instead of seeking one predetermined correct answer to a question about a piece of literature, many teachers today value children's unique interpretations of what they read. Almost any interpretation is valid as long as the reader can justify it. Children arrive at a variety of interpretations due to their cultures, experiences, values, family influences, and so on. In order to understand why some children think as they do, Michelle Commeyras and Jodie Guy (1995) suggest that teachers consider links between events in children's lives outside school and the ways in which they interpret literature. Understanding different cultural and linguistic aspects of children's backgrounds should help teachers appreciate ways that children arrive at different interpretations.

Envisionment

Believing that literature plays a role in developing sharp, critical minds, Judith Langer (1990, 1995) sets forth the concept of *envisionment*, which she describes as

> dynamic sets of related ideas, images, questions, disagreements, anticipations, arguments, and hunches that fill the mind during every reading, writing, speaking, or other experience when one gains, expresses, and shares thoughts and understandings (1995, p. 9).

Essentially, envisionment is the reader's understanding of a text at a particular time. A student's envisionment of a literary selection changes and grows as new ideas unfold; for instance, the reader realizes that some ideas are no longer important and that it is necessary to reinterpret others.

By understanding how envisionment works, teachers can offer students instructional support that will help them to think more clearly when they read literature.

Envisionment consists of four options, or *stances*, with each stance offering a different way to gain ideas. Figure 8-2 describes the kind of thinking the reader does during each stance. These stances are not linear and can recur at any point during the reading.

Figure 8-2. Stances of Envisionment

First Stance: Being Out and Stepping In

Readers "step in" by relating personal experiences and prior knowledge to the text and by using any available clues for making meaning. Surface features provide initial ideas about the characters, plot, setting, and situation.

Second Stance: Being In and Moving Through

Readers become immersed in developing understandings by using personal knowledge and the text to stimulate thinking about the selection. By making connections among thoughts and ideas, readers develop awareness of the sense of a story or the feel of a poem.

Third Stance: Being In and Stepping Out

Readers use new understandings to expand or modify existing knowledge and experiences. They consider how new insights from their reading can affect their own lives in terms of values, beliefs, attitudes, or emotions.

Fourth Stance: Stepping Out and Objectifying the Experience

Now readers reflect on the reading experience by considering the selection objectively and thinking critically about the literary elements and allusions.

During the process of envisionment, students seek to make sense by relating emerging ideas to the whole piece, trying to go beyond the information given by asking questions and forming hypotheses, and reflecting on their lives and the human condition in general (Langer, 1990, 1995). Here are some types of open-ended questions that encourage students to move beyond their initial interpretations.

- How would you respond to this piece?
- In what ways is this meaningful to you?
- What are some implications?
- How can you connect what you read to your personal knowledge or experiences?

- How would you compare this piece with others you have read?
- How would you evaluate the author's work?

Thinking Strategies Related to Literature

Several of us at Tennessee Technological University designed a project for using literature to support and expand thinking strategies for 140 students in grades three through six over a nine-week period (Ross and Stephens, 1989). We focused on three strategies: analysis of story structure (predicting, sequencing, and generating alternatives), analysis of literature by comparison and contrast (seeing relationships, classifying, and inferring), and imagery (creating mental pictures and interpeting poetry). As a result of pre- and post-testing, the only significant gains were for sixth graders in awareness of story structure and for fourth, fifth, and sixth graders in strategies related to comparison and contrast. Overall, however, the project created a great deal of interest in children's literature and made students more aware of thinking strategies they could use while reading.

One offshoot of this study resulted from our desire to move students from literal recall to abstract, higher-order thinking. We began by reading several Aesop's fables to the students and then leading them to discover the morals for each through class discussions. We encouraged them to think in broad generalities and underlying themes instead of brief, concrete summaries. Figure 8-3 shows their perceptions of the moral in "The Town Mouse and the Country Mouse." In keeping with developmental stages, which move children from concrete to abstract thinking, the fifth and sixth graders came closer to expressing their ideas as morals than did the third and fourth graders, who were still quite literal.

Figure 8-3. Children's Perceptions of Morals

The mouse liked beans, peas, and bread better than ale, cake, and jelly.

I would rather be able to eat freely than run for my meal.

City mouse wants junky things. Country mouse wants stuff that's good for him. Everyone has their own opinion about their lifestyle.

The country mouse didn't like to eat with a dog barking and lots of loud noises. We would like to be in peace without loud noises.

I'd rather eat in peace than in fear.

The country mouse did not like the city because he had to be on the run. The city mouse didn't like the country because he liked the ale, cake, and jelly.

The country mouse would rather be safe at home than on the run and scared all the time.

Thought-Provoking Question

How would you rank the morals in Figure 8-3 from literal to abstract?
Which, if any, are actually morals?

Literature has the potential for causing thinking to occur, from anticipating what will happen to responding to events. The following examples show some thinking strategies that are likely to occur when children read literature.

Activating Prior Knowledge

Drawing on prior knowledge and experiences when beginning to read helps the student make connections and construct personal meaning. You can help students do this in the following ways (Hennings, 1992):

- Recalling ideas about the topic
- Discussing meanings with others
- Brainstorming related words and ideas
- Webbing ideas to show interrelationships among them
- Charting and outlining to organize thinking
- Drawing pictures and writing sentences about what is known

Predicting

By predicting what they are about to read, students anticipate what is to come so that comprehension is easier. When predictions don't work out, students need to adjust their thinking in light of new evidence or changes in the story line. Here are some guidelines for students to follow when making predictions:

- Look at the illustrations to get an idea of the subject.
- Read the title and think what it may mean.
- Preview the selection to see what it's about.
- Call on relevant prior experiences and knowledge.
- Consider your knowledge of story structure to anticipate what might happen next.
- Look for clues that might cause you to change your predictions.

Visual Imagery

Students can understand, appreciate, and enjoy reading more if they can visualize what's happening than if they just read the words. Mental images make stories come alive. The following guidelines for students may help them create visual images as they read:

- Select a scene from a favorite story and draw a picture of it. Write or tell someone about the scene you drew.
- Discuss with a partner what you see in your mind as you read a story together.
- Focus on each of the senses related to the story. Can you imagine how something feels, smells, looks, tastes, or sounds?
- Read a descriptive paragraph. Close your eyes and visualize the author's description.
- Write a description for someone else to visualize. Try to include as many sensory images as you can.

Making Connections

For literature to be meaningful, students should be able to connect story events and characters to incidents in their own lives. Making connections helps them understand ways to work through problems, apply new information, find relevance for their own lives, appreciate cultural diversity, and develop coping skills. Following are some questions students might ask themselves when making connections:

- What would I have done if I'd been the main character?
- How might I change as a result of reading this book?
- How can this book help me deal with my own problems?
- Has this book enabled me to appreciate people who are different than I am? If so, how?
- What information can I use from this book to help me do the things I want to do?

Responses to Literature

Children can respond to literature in dozens of ways. Many of these are cute little activities that fail to relate meaningfully to the selection. Such activities may be fun and interesting, but they do not support thinking about literature. Too often, related activities, such as making a mural of a scene from a story, absorb much of the time that could be spent reading, reflecting, and discussing. Although the arts have a place in interpreting literature, be sure that the activity advances the appreciation of the literary selection enough to warrant the time and effort. Don't let the tail wag the dog!

Some form of response generally enhances literary appreciation, but don't require a response for every book that is read. Children may sometimes prefer to read and reflect for themselves, simply for personal enjoyment.

Before engaging children in response activities, make sure that they have read or heard the entire selection. Without a complete awareness of the unfolding story, they will be limited in their interpretations and perspectives.

Reader Response Theory

Louise Rosenblatt (1994), a leading reader response theorist, proposes two ways of responding to literature: *aesthetic* and *efferent*. Aesthetic responses are personal, subjective, and emotional, whereas efferent responses are knowledge-based and factual. As we read, we generally find ourselves moving back and forth along a continuum between these two types of responses, or stances. The purpose of the reading should determine the dominant response. Efferent responses are more appropriate for analyzing texts and acquiring information, but aesthetic responses are better suited to developing literary appreciation and awakening feelings. Features of aesthetic responses include the following (Cox and Many, 1992; Ross, 1994):

- Making meaningful associations and connections
- Focusing on images, feelings, and sensations
- Recalling related ideas, knowledge, attitudes, and impressions
- "Living through" the literary experience
- Choosing a preferred form of response (drama, visual art, music, dance, writing)
- Discussing thoughts, insights, and ideas with others
- Actively visualizing situations

Patricia Polacco's *Pink and Say* shows us how a book can evoke both efferent and aesthetic responses. In the story, based on Polacco's ancestor's experiences during the Civil War, Pink, a young African American soldier, rescues Say, a badly injured young White soldier. Pink takes Say home, where Pink's mother nurses Say back to health, but then the two boys are captured; Pink is hanged and Say barely survives at Andersonville prison. Along with learning some factual information about the Civil War, we experience the fears and tragedies that touched the two boys who fought in it. The power of this story comes not from recounting events during the War (efferent response) but from the emotions it generates (aesthetic response).

Some questions that can trigger personal interpretations are given in Figure 8-4.

Figure 8-4. Questions That Generate Aesthetic Responses

What thoughts or ideas occur to you as you read this selection?

How would you illustrate this story?

What seems especially real to you?

What part caused you to react strongly (to be upset, happy, disappointed, or something else)? Why?

How did the author make you feel as you did?

What words were especially interesting or unusual?

How could you be part of this story?

With which character do you identify most? Why?

Have you ever lived through a similar experience? What was it?

Does this selection remind you of something else—a television show, a film, an experience, or another book?

After reading this selection and discussing it with others, what new insights or ideas do you get?

How would you like to respond to this selection?

Thought-Provoking Idea

Instead of using textbooks for teaching content area material, use a variety of informational trade books, which are more likely to evoke aesthetic as well as efferent responses. Children will find it easier to absorb, understand, and retain information if they become emotionally involved than if they just learn facts.

Types of Responses

When selecting response activities, consider your goals for teaching literature. If you're trying to develop understanding and appreciation, then suggest response activities that help your students reach this goal. Responses to thinking questions and active participation in discussions do more to promote an appreciation of literature than activities that amount to little more than busy work. Avoid work sheets and activity books that call for predetermined correct answers.

Oral Responses

Long before children enter school, they respond to literature by interacting with others during shared book reading. They predict, anticipate, point, giggle, worry, repeat familiar phrases, exclaim over the illustrations, answer questions, and ask some of their own. For children who have heard stories from their early days, response to literature is natural. Entering school, they look forward to more story times. For children who have never experienced stories, responses come more slowly and may take some coaxing.

Whether with a partner or the entire class, children who participate in discussions have opportunities to share their views and hear what others think. Not only is personal interpretation important for understanding literature, so are the insights that come from social interaction. Students broaden their perspectives as they hear other points of view, and they sharpen their insights as they become aware of nuances they may have missed. As the teacher, you can facilitate discussion by helping readers create their unique envisionments, think critically about what they read, and respond aesthetically and/or efferently to the selection. The questions given in Figure 8-4 can serve as prompts for personal interpretations. In addition, you can promote an understanding of literary elements by asking questions that cause readers to identify one or more themes, consider the growth and realism of characters, examine the effects of the setting on the developing story, identify the problem, and reflect on events leading to its solution. Several types of discussion can stimulate good thinking about literature, as shown in the following formats.

Think-Pair-Share. In the Think-Pair-Share arrangement, children find partners with whom they share their thoughts. Before they begin reading, the teacher identifies stopping points in their books. As they reach each stopping point, the students pause to think about what they've read, take notes about their ideas, talk in pairs about their thoughts, and share interesting ideas with the entire group. Students then continue reading until they reach the next stopping point and begin the cycle again. This procedure is particularly helpful for students with disabilities, who often need support as they read stories (Rasinski and Padak, 1996).

Literary Peer-Group Discussions. Believing that children benefit from peer-group discussions of literature, Dorothy Leal (1993) divided students into groups of six and read aloud one book a week to each group. She paused three times during each reading to let the children discuss their thoughts and ideas. The students themselves served as catalysts for the discussions by sharing prior knowledge and constructing new meanings based on the collaborations of group members. They also helped each other find meanings and explain problems that other students hadn't discovered on their own. Being free to explore their ideas, correct or not, encouraged children to create and investigate new interpretations.

Literature Response Groups. Sometimes referred to as literature circles, literature response groups enable students to select what books they will read, meet in groups with others who have chosen the same book, read to an agreed-upon stopping place, write their thoughts in literature logs, and discuss their responses to each portion of the book. Through such discussions, children express their views, hear what others think, and often readjust their own thinking in light of others' perspectives.

For instance, Katherine Paterson's *Bridge to Terabithia* spawned a variety of responses. Readers related their own family lifestyles to those of Jess and Leslie, seeing advantages and disadvantages for each lifestyle. They reacted differently to Leslie's death; many were shocked by its unexpectedness, others accepted it as part of the plot development, and some related to it because they knew of another child's death. Still others focused on the imaginary kingdom of Terabithia, likening it to one they had at some time created or imagined.

Collaborative Reasoning. Students participating in collaborative reasoning meet in groups to discuss central questions about the books they have read (Waggoner et al., 1995). These central questions ask children to take a stand on one side or the other of a major issue in the story. For instance, a central question for Phyllis Reynolds Naylor's *Shiloh* might be: Should Marty keep the beagle or return it to its owner? The questions must permit several interpretations that can be justified from the text so that children can offer a variety of valid perspectives, based on the text and their prior knowledge. This format encourages students to think in a reasoned manner and to consider different viewpoints.

Thought-Provoking Question

What would be a good central question for a fairy tale, such as *Little Red Riding Hood* or *Cinderella*?

Junior Great Books. The cornerstone of the Junior Great Books curriculum is shared inquiry (Criscuola, 1994). It consists of four interrelated features: discussion focusing on personal interpretations, selected literature that is rich in meaning, discussion that is focused and directed by the teacher, and acknowledgement of students' efforts to explain their thinking and react to each others' ideas. Good interpretive questions for discussion are those that relate directly to the text but can yield more than one valid response. For further information about this program, call the Great Books Foundation at (800) 222-5870.

Written Responses

Through discussion children learn to think about literature in different ways, and they realize that there can be a wide range of valid interpretations. The same kinds of thinking can extend into written responses, especially if they follow the same types of prompts suggested earlier in this chapter.

After Beverly Mackie read *The Little Red Hen* to her second graders, she asked them to think about the hen's attitude and what might have made a difference. Jonathan Justice believed that the hen was selfish and could have taught the animals a lesson (Fig. 8-5). Diane Bowman read a variety of legends to her fourth graders, discussed the characteristics of legends, and then asked the children to write their own legends. Katie Mahan applied the features of a legend to a contemporary scenario, as in Figure 8-6.

Exposure to literature gives children ideas for creating innovations on published works or for writing their own stories. With a little guidance, children readily pick up story structure, characterization, action, and language patterns. After reading "Sarah Cynthia Sylvia Stout Would Not Take the Garbage Out" (in Shel Silverstein's *Where the Sidewalk Ends*), children can write a similar poem with phrases that relate to their own experiences with garbage. Stacy Ross reads a wide variety of patterned books and asks her kindergartners to write innovations on them. For instance, the children wrote their own similes based on *Quick as a Cricket* and their own versions of *Good Morning Sunshine*, based on Margaret Wise Brown's *Goodnight Moon*. Taking their cues from Mary Ann Hoberman's *A House Is a House for Me*, one child wrote,"A book is a house for words," and another wrote, "A cornucopia is a house for fruit."

As we saw in the opening vignette, Val Ferguson motivated her first-grade students to write by reading captivating stories to them on a regular basis. Sometimes the stories inspired the children to write individually, and at other times the class worked together to construct variations of a story. A group-constructed big book resulted from *Meg and Mog* (by Nicoll and Pienkowski), a story about a witch (Meg) and her cat (Mog) who think up spells. Mimicking the language patterns found in the book, the children dictated their own spells to Val, as in the following example.

A Weather Spell

No more puddles
Rain and muddles
Black clouds go away
Fire, sun, rays
Blue, sky, light
Make a sunny day.

Figure 8.5. Response to *The Little Red Hen*

The Little Red hen
I think the Little red hen
was selfish
with her friends
because she cud of taut them
a lesson by talking to them.

Figure 8.6. A Contemporary Legend

♡ *Me* ♡

My name is Katie, and I am the fastest shopper around. I can buy clothes in five minutes, and I can buy accessories in two minutes and C.D.s in 1.5 seconds! the people at the mall expect me there every day! I Know them all by their names too! If you try to stop me I'll buy you!

♡Katie Mahan

Children can record thoughtful reactions to what they read in response journals, or literature logs. In their journals, students need not worry about mechanics or spelling, but only about expressing their ideas or speculations. One type of response journal is the double-entry journal, which consists of two columns on each page (Tompkins, 1997). In the first column the student writes a selected quotation from the book, and in the second column the student writes a reaction to it, which may be a question, comment, or personal reflection. When Karen Fesler asked her sixth graders to use double-entry journals, Elizabeth Branch McGhee responded to selections from *Bunnicula* (Howe), and Corey Hinton based her entries on *The Witch of Blackbird Pond* (Speare). Figure 8-7 shows some excerpts from their journals.

Responding Through the Arts

The arts—music, visual art, and drama—play major roles in students' responses to literature. Not only do they enable students to respond through multiple intelligences, they also open up new ways to explore literature. Whether creating contemporary raps based on a story or interpreting poetry by its cadences, musical/rhythmic learners become more deeply involved in literature than if they had simply read the words. For all students, but especially for visual/spatial learners, the richly colored, textured illustrations in picture books stimulate aesthetic responses. In wordless picture books, such as Molly Bang's *The Grey Lady and the Strawberry Snatcher,* children create their own story line by following the pictures.

Although illustrations inspire response, stories without pictures cause the reader to create mental images from the words alone in order to visualize what is happening. *Visualization,* inner vision constructed by the reader, is a powerful way to comprehend and interpret stories. Working with two primary classes, Ruth Hubbard (1996), along with the children's teachers, found that memory images had a positive effect on how these children made meaning and found connections as they read. The children reported that they used their imaginations in new ways when they drew pictures of mental images in visual response logs.

When I asked fourth graders in Jane Bassett's class how they made pictures in their minds as they read, they were quick to respond. Annette recalled the beautifully illustrated fairy tale books she had as a young child. She now thinks back to these illustrations, but she also uses her imagination to go beyond them and see new pictures that relate to what she is reading. Referring to Judy Blume's *Tales of a Fourth Grade Nothing*, Jamay said that the scene where Fudge threw food reminded her of the time her little brother smeared mashed potatoes on the wall. Christian told us he creates mental images by using his own experiences along with the details the author gives, and Rick said he closes his eyes and imagines from the author's description.

Figure 8.7. Excerpts From Double-Entry Journals

Bunnicula

In the Text	My Response
"Cute Little bunny?" "That's what you think. He's a danger to this household and everyone in it.	Chester sounds frightened, but also Like a hero about warning everybody at his house about the bunny.
"That Bunny got out of his cage last night"	Chester is sounding suspicious about that bunny.

The Witch of Blackbird Pond

There's a pair just Like mine, Judith, and a pair for you, Mercy.	This sentance tells me that Kit is very loving and a giving person.
From the first moment, in a way she could never explain, the Medows claimed her and made her their own.	This sentance tells me that when Kit has a problem, she will always come to the Medows.

Thought-Provoking Question

How do the pictures in your head compare with those the illustrator creates? How do you feel about viewing a film after reading the book, when you had to create your own images?

Creative drama involves students in thinking, imagining, and responding every step of the way. Basing their drama on a familiar story, children improvise scenes, create dialogue, and interpret characters according to their understanding of the story. Here the bodily/kinesthetic and interpersonal learners shine as they act out the story through movement and interactions with other performers. Not intended for formal presentation, creative drama lets children develop and refine communication skills and experiment with story interpretations.

Selecting Books That Promote Thinking

Most good children's books cause students to reflect on the content, identify with situations and/or characters, and make connections to their own lives. If one of your goals is to promote thinking, however, choose books that offer additional mental stimulation.

Some books invite critical and creative responses because the authors deliberately create puzzling situations for young readers. These authors delight in mystifying audiences with books that cause children to ponder magical events, discover answers to riddles by studying illustrations, consider uncommon points of view, apply their imaginations, examine their values, or solve problems. For example, you can count on Chris Van Allsburg to add a touch of mystery to his stories, and David Macaulay sets up multiple story episodes with strange, interconnecting features in *Black and White* and *Shortcut*. In *The True Story of the Three Little Pigs!,* Jon Scieszka challenges readers to consider the wolf's point of view, and Graeme Base perplexes his audience with an unsolved mystery in *The Eleventh Hour*.

In Figure 8-8 you'll find other stories that provoke readers to careful analysis and thoughtful response. After each entry is a question intended to initiate discussion, but you can probe more deeply by following up with additional questions, such as "Why?", "How do you know?", or "What makes you think so?"

Figure 8-8. Books That Stimulate Thinking

Mystery Books

The Stranger. Chris Van Allsburg. Who *is* the stranger?

The Wretched Stone. Chris Van Allsburg. What does the wretched stone represent?

The Eleventh Hour. Graeme Base. Who spoiled the party?

June 29, 1999. David Wiesner. Where did the vegetables really come from?

The Polar Express. Chris Van Allsburg. How did the bell get under the boy's tree? Could *you* hear it ring?

Bad Day at Riverbend. Chris Van Allsburg. What's really happening in this western town?

Point of View

The True Story of the Three Little Pigs! Jon Scieszka. Do you agree with the wolf or the pigs?

Two Bad Ants. Chris Van Allsburg. Should the ants take the sugar? In what ways do things appear different from an ant's perspective?

Round Trip. Ann Jonas. How is it possible for scenes to change by turning the book upside down?

Tuck Everlasting. Natalie Babbitt. Is it a good thing to live forever?

Grandfather's Journey. Allen Say. How is it possible to love one place as much as another?

Hey, Al. Arthur Yorinks. How did Eddie's and Al's adventure change their view of home?

Note: Alvin Granowsky has written a series of classic tales (published by Steck-Vaughn) from the antagonist's point of view.

Imagination

Hailstones and Halibut Bones. Mary O'Neill. How do colors make you feel?

Tuesday. David Wiesner. Where did the frogs come from? What do you predict will happen next Tuesday?

Oh, the Places You'll Go! Dr. Seuss. Where would you like to go? What would you like to be?

How Much Is a Million? David Schwartz. How would you visualize how much a million is?

Free Fall. David Wiesner. Where does the boy go on his magical dream adventure? Where would you go in your dreams?

Where the Wild Things Are. Maurice Sendak. Where would *you* go in your imagination?

Figure 8.8 continued on next page

Figure 8.8 continued from previous page

Values

Rainbow Fish. Marcus Pfister. How did Rainbow Fish make friends? What can we do to make friends?

Frederick. Leo Lionni. What things are most important in life?

Yo! Yes? Chris Raschka. Who can be a friend?

Song and Dance Man. Steven Gammell. What are elderly people really like?

Mirette on the High Wire. Emily McCully. What does it mean to have courage? Can we help someone else find courage?

Problem Finding and Problem Solving

Tops and Bottoms. Janet Stevens. How does Hare get the money to buy back his land?

Counting on Frank. Rod Clement. How does the boy find problems? Can you think of some others?

Caleb. Gary Crews. What happens to Caleb?

Math Curse. Jon Scieszka. How can everything be a math problem? How could everything be a science problem?

Miss Nelson Is Missing. Harry Allard and James Marshall. What really happened to Miss Nelson?

Hatchet. Gary Paulsen. What were some problems Brian faced and how did he solve them?

Obervation and Discovery

I Spy. Jean Marzollo. Can you find the answers to the riddles in the pictures?

Where's Waldo? Martin Handford. Can you find Waldo?

Errata: What's Wrong With This Picture? Hemesh Alles. What doesn't belong in each picture? (This is definitely for older children!)

Animalia. Graeme Base. What items can you find that begin with the featured letter on each page? Can you find the boy in the striped shirt and jeans on each page?

Who's Hiding Here? Yoshi. Can you find the camouflaged animals?

Look! Look! Look! Tana Hoban. What do you think each picture is? Turn the page to find out if you are right.

Thought-Provoking Question

What other books have you found that stimulate thinking and lead to diverse interpretations?

Summary

This chapter explores the possibilities that children's literature offers for promoting thinking strategies. It begins with a discussion of the ways in which children construct unique, personal meanings by blending their own experiences with what the author is saying. Envisionment makes us realize that our understanding and interpretation of literature grows as the story unfolds and we reflect on its meaning. Some types of thinking strategies that readers typically use are activating prior knowledge, predicting, visual imagery, and making connections.

Reader response theory, as advocated by Louise Rosenblatt, tells us that readers can respond aesthetically, with emotions, or efferently, by searching for information. In most cases, readers respond somewhere along a continuum between these stances, often varying their responses as they continue reading. In order to encourage students to think aesthetically as they read, you can ask a variety of questions related to feelings, making connections, and personal reflections. Valuing personal interpretations is important if children are to become thoughtful readers.

Readers can respond to literature orally, in writing, and through the arts. Some formats for oral responses include Think-Pair-Share, literature circles, and Junior Great Books; written responses may take the form of story innovations or response journals. Response through the arts addresses multiple intelligences by involving students in the rhythm of poetry, the illustrations in picture books, and the movement and interactions that are part of creative drama.

References

Allred, C. (1996). *Teaching literature-based reading from three perspectives.* Presentation at Tennessee Council of Teachers of English, Gatlinburg, TN.

Cairney, T. (1990). Intertextuality: Infectious echoes from the past. *The Reading Teacher, 43*(7): 478–484.

Commeyras, M., and Guy, J. (1995). Parole officers and the king's guards: Challenges in understanding children's thinking about stories. *Language Arts, 72*(7): 512–516.

Considine, D., Haley, G., and Lacy, L.E. (1994). *Imagine that.* Englewood, CO: Teacher Ideas Press.

Cox, C., and Many, J. (1992). Toward an understanding of the aesthetic response to literature. *Language Arts, 69*(1): 28–33.

Criscuola, M. (1994). Read, discuss, reread: Insights from the Junior Great Books program. *Educational Leadership, 51*(5): 58–61.

Davenport, M.R., Jaeger, M., and Lauritzen, C. (1995). Negotiating curriculum. *The Reading Teacher, 49*(1): 60–62.

Galda, L., and West, J. (1995). Exploring literature through drama. In N. Roser and M. Martinez (Eds.), *Book talk and beyond.* Newark, DE: International Reading Association.

Hennings, D.G. (1992). *Beyond the read aloud.* Bloomington, IN. Phi Delta Kappa.

Hubbard, R.S, Winterbourne, N., and Ostrow, J. (1996). Visual responses to literature: Imagination through images. *The New Advocate, 9*(4): 309–323.

Karolides, N. (Ed.). (1997). *Reader response in elementary classrooms: Quest and discovery.* Mahwah, NJ: Lawrence Erlbaum.

Langer, J. (1990). Understanding literature. *Language Arts, 67*(8): 812–816.

Langer, J. (1994). A response-based approach to reading literature. *Language Arts, 71*(3): 203–211.

Langer, J. (1995). *Envisioning literature.* Newark, DE: International Reading Association.

Lauritzen, C., Jaeger, M., and Davenport, M.R. (1996). Contexts for integrating curriculum. *The Reading Teacher, 49*(5): 404–406.

Leal, D. (1993). The power of literary peer-group discussions: How children collaboratively negotiate meaning. *The Reading Teacher, 47*(2): 114–120.

Madura, S. (1995). The line and texture of aesthetic response: Primary children study authors and illustrators. *The Reading Teacher, 49*(2):110–118.

McGee, L. (1996). Response-centered talk: Windows on children's thinking. In L. Gambrell and J. Almasi (Eds.), *Lively discussions.* Newark, DE: International Reading Association.

Oyler, C., and Barry, A. (1996). Intertextual connections in read alouds of information books. *Language Arts, 73*(5): 324–329.

Peterson, R., and Eeds, M. (1990). *Grand conversations.* New York: Scholastic.

Pradl, G. (1996). Reading and democracy: The enduring influence of Louise Rosenblatt. *The New Advocate, 7*(1): 9–22.

Ralston, M., and Sutton, W. (1996). Literature in a whole language program. In V. Froese (Ed.), *Whole language: Practice and theory* (2nd ed.). Boston: Allyn & Bacon.

Raphael, T., Goatley, V., McMahon, S., and Woodman, D. (1995). Promoting meaningful conversations in student book clubs. In Roser, N., and M. Martinez, (Eds.), *Book talk and beyond.* Newark, DE: International Reading Association.

Rasinksi, T., and Padak, N. (1996). *Holistic reading strategies.* Englewood Cliffs, NJ: Prentice-Hall.

Rosenblatt, L. (1991). Literature—S.O.S.! *Language Arts, 68*(6): 444–448.

Rosenblatt, L. (1994). The transactional theory of reading and writing. In M.R. Ruddell and H. Singer (Eds.), *Theoretical models and processes of reading* (4th ed.). Newark, DE: International Reading Association.

Rosenbloom, C.S. (1991). From *Ox-Cart Man* to *Little House in the Big Woods:* Response to literature shapes curriculum. *Language Arts, 68*(1): 52–59.

Ross, E. (1994). *Using children's literature across the curriculum.* Bloomington, IN: Phi Delta Kappa.

Ross, E., and Stephens, K. (1989). Connecting thinking, language, and literature. *Ohio Reading Teacher, 23*(3): 9–15.

Rothlein, L., and Meinbach, A.M. (1991). *The literature connection.* Glenview, IL: Scott Foresman.

Ruddell, R. (1992). A whole language and literature perspective: Creating a meaning-making instructional environment. *Language Arts, 69*(8): 612–620.

Stoodt, B., Amspaugh, L., and Hunt, J. (1996). *Children's literature: Discovery for a lifetime.* Scottsdale, AZ: Gorsuch Scarisbrick.

Tompkins, G. (1997). *Literacy for the 21st century: A balanced approach.* Upper Saddle River, NJ: Prentice-Hall.

Tompkins, G., and McGee, L. (1993). *Teaching reading with literature.* New York: Merrill.

Waggoner, M., Chinn, C., Yi, H., and Anderson, R. (1995). Collaborative reasoning about stories. *Language Arts, 72*(8):582–589.

Children's Books

Allard, H., and Marshall, J. (1977). *Miss Nelson is missing.* Boston: Houghton Mifflin.

Alles, H. (1992). *Errata: What's wrong with this picture?* San Marcos, CA: Green Tiger.

Babbitt, N. (1975). *Tuck everlasting.* New York: Farrar, Straus, & Giroux.

Bang, M. (1980). *The grey lady and the strawberry snatcher.* New York: Four Winds.

Base, G. (1986). *Animalia*. New York: Abrams.

Base, G. (1989). *The eleventh hour*. New York: Abrams.

Blume, J. (1972). *Tales of a fourth grade nothing*. New York: Dutton.

Brown, M. (1947). *Goodnight moon*. New York: Harper.

Cauley, L. (1984). *The town mouse and the country mouse*. New York: Putnam's.

Clement, R. (1990). *Counting on Frank*. Auckland, New Zealand: William Collins.

Crews, G. (1996). *Caleb*. Grawn, MI: Publishers Distribution Services.

Galdone, P. (1973). *The little red hen*. Boston: Houghton Mifflin.

Gammell, S. (1988). *Song and dance man*. New York: Scholastic.

Handford, M. (1987). *Where's Waldo?* Boston: Little, Brown.

Hoban, T. (1988). *Look! Look! Look!* New York: Scholastic.

Hoberman, M.A. (1982). *A house is a house for me*. New York: Penguin.

Howe, D. and J. (1983). *Bunnicula*. New York: Atheneum.

Jonas, A. (1990). *Round trip*. New York: Greenwillow.

Lionni, L. (1966). *Frederick*. New York: Pantheon.

Macaulay, D. (1990). *Black and white*. Boston: Houghton Mifflin.

Macaulay, D. (1995). *Shortcut*. Boston: Houghton Mifflin.

Marzollo, J. (1992). *I spy*. New York: Scholastic.

McCully, E. (1992). *Mirette on the high wire*. New York: Scholastic.

McGovern, A. (1963). *Aesop's fables*. New York: Scholastic.

Naylor, P.R. (1991). *Shiloh*. New York: Atheneum.

Nicoll, H., and Pienkowski, J. (1994). *Meg and Mog*. London: Heinemann.

O'Neill, M. (1989). *Hailstones and halibut bones*. New York: Doubleday.

Paterson, K. (1977). *Bridge to Terabithia*. New York: Crowell.

Paulsen, G. (1987). *Hatchet*. New York: Bradbury.

Pfister, M. (1992). *The rainbow fish*. New York: North-South.

Polacco, P. (1994). *Pink and Say*. New York: Philomel.

Raschka, C. (1993). *Yo! Yes?* New York: Orchard.

Say, A. (1993). *Grandfather's journey*. Boston: Houghton Mifflin.

Schwartz, D. (1985). *How much is a million?* New York: Scholastic.

Scieszka, J. (1989). *The true story of the three little pigs!* New York: Viking.

Scieszka, J. (1995). *Math curse*. New York: Viking.

Sendak, M. (1963). *Where the wild things are*. New York: Harper & Row.

Seuss, Dr. (1990). *Oh, the places you'll go!* New York: Random House.

Silverstein, S. (1974). *Where the sidewalk ends*. New York: Harper & Row.

Speare, E.G. (1958). *The witch of Blackbird Pond*. Boston: Houghton Mifflin.

Stevens, J. (1995). *Tops and bottoms*. San Diego: Harcourt Brace.

Van Allsburg, C. (1985). *The polar express*. Boston: Houghton Mifflin.

Van Allsburg, C. (1986). *The stranger*. Boston: Houghton Mifflin.
Van Allsburg, C. (1988). *Two bad ants*. Boston: Houghton Mifflin.
Van Allsburg, C. (1991). *The wretched stone*. Boston: Houghton Mifflin.
Van Allsburg, C. (1995). *Bad day at Riverbend*. Boston: Houghton Mifflin.
Wiesner, D. (1988). *Free fall*. New York: Scholastic.
Wiesner, D. (1991). *Tuesday*. Boston: Houghton Mifflin.
Wiesner, D. (1992). *June 29, 1999*. Boston: Houghton Mifflin.
Wood, A. (1990). *Quick as a cricket*. Auburn, ME: Child's Play.
Yorinks, A. (1986). *Hey, Al*. New York: Farrar, Straus, & Giroux.
Yoshi. (1987). *Who's hiding here?* Saxonville, MA: Picture Book Studio.

CHAPTER 9

Graphic Organizers

When I asked the teachers,

"Why are graphic organizers (e.g., semantic maps and Venn diagrams) useful for helping students understand concepts and see relationships?"

the teachers said:

- Some children have to see a concept as well as hear it.
- Graphics are very helpful for visual learners. Students can see similarities and differences.
- Graphic organizers are more concrete to students, who often assist in constructing the items and can then view them.
- Some concepts and relationships are not easily understood. Graphic organizers separate and classify, enabling the learner to store information in a logical manner.
- They make the connection between concepts in a concrete, visual way, which may then help students organize them in their minds.
- To see lines drawn between things helps students see how these things are related. They can also see that these relationships can go in many different directions.

How would you answer this question?

After reading Bernard Waber's _An Anteater Named Arthur_ to her second graders, Beverly Mackie asked them to tell her some of Arthur's problems. As the children dictated their answers, Beverly created a web in the following manner:

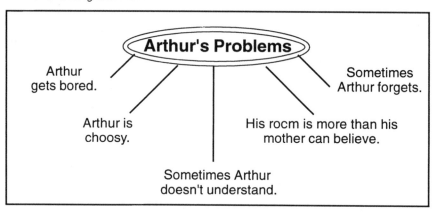

Beverly led the children in a discussion of how Arthur's mother needed to be patient instead of getting angry, and then she added another problem for Arthur: Sometimes Arthur doesn't pay attention. She asked the children to think about what happens when they don't pay attention, and she and the children created another web that looked like this:

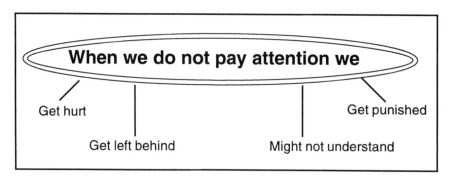

With these simple graphic organizers, Beverly helped the children focus on the story's key points and relate one of Arthur's problem's to their own lives.

An Overview of Graphic Organizers

A *graphic organizer* is a visual representation that shows relationships among concepts, ideas, topics, or story elements. It is a mental map that makes thinking visible (Burke, 1993), or a cognitive map that shows the important aspects of a concept arranged in a visual pattern (Cassidy, 1989). It enables children to grasp main ideas and organizational structures easily and quickly, as we can see from Beverly's simple maps. You are probably already familiar with such graphic organizers as semantic maps and Venn diagrams.

A major advantage of using graphic organizers is their appeal to special learners. Poor readers, who are easily discouraged by long written passages, eagerly pick up information from sparsely labeled visual aids, and visual/spatial learners see at a glance what is important for them to know. Graphic organizers benefit slow learners, who need structure, organization, and a clear format (Lehman, 1992), as well as gifted students, who may have difficulty analyzing long written texts (Cassidy, 1989).

Thought-Provoking Question

Which of your students might benefit most from graphic organizers?

A great deal of higher-level thinking goes into the interpretation and construction of graphic organizers. Students must think logically, critically, creatively, and analytically. By causing students to think about things in new ways, graphic organizers enable them to see connections that might have otherwise eluded them. Students must figure out the language and structure of graphic organizers in order to make sense of them. To construct one that other people will understand, students must think how best to represent the information graphically. Students go well beyond literal recall of text by developing rich networks of semantic or conceptual relationships.

As a child, Sara Fanelli created *My Map Book* (1995). In it she reveals who she is and what is important to her through a series of brightly colored, hand-labeled drawings, with occasional comments that express her thoughts and feelings. She created a map of her stomach by showing the location of the foods she had eaten, her family with lines that show connections among relatives, her daily schedule ending in star-studded dreams, her neighborhood with the locations of friends' homes, and her heart holding what is most precious to her. In constructing her maps, Sara found a creative way to portray her ideas, a way that visual/spatial learners would no doubt find extremely appealing.

Thought-Provoking Idea

Ask your students to map who they are or what matters to them. The only words they can use are labels and an occasional comment to tell how they think or feel about what they've drawn.

Teaching With Graphic Organizers

Graphic organizers provide an alternative to textual materials and offer an enjoyable, provocative way to learn. They can represent both print and nonprint information, such as videotapes or audiotapes, and you may find them useful as a framework for introducing new material, interpreting information, and summarizing key points. Much learning results from the discussions surrounding their construction and interpretation.

You can use graphic organizers in all areas of the curriculum and at any grade level. In kindergarten and the lower grades, keep the format simple and use pictures instead of words if the words are too difficult for the children to read. Graphic organizers are particularly useful for helping children learn vocabulary, enabling them to develop concepts in various subject areas, and helping them understand literature.

Thought-Provoking Idea

Look through the books you currently use for instruction to find examples of graphic organizers. Use these as a basis for discussion and observe how students respond.

When you introduce a particular type of graphic organizer, be sure that the children are familiar with the topic so that they have the background to understand what it represents. When they try to construct their own graphics, model what you expect them to do and give clear, precise directions. Let them become comfortable with one format before introducing another. Allowing children to work with partners or in groups lets them discuss their ideas and make decisions. Figure 9-1 shows some questions that students might ask themselves as they read or create graphic organizers, and the steps in Figure 9-2 suggest how to teach students to use graphic organizers.

Figure 9-1. Self-Questioning for Graphic Organizers

When interpreting a graphic organizer, students might ask themselves the following questions:

- What does this structure represent?
- Do I have the background knowledge to interpret it?
- What do these words mean in this context?
- How is the information arranged?
- What kinds of relationships are involved?
- What conclusions can I draw?
- How does this help me understand?

When constructing graphic organizers to help others understand information, students might ask themselves the following:

- What is the best format to use to show this information?
- How can I show relationships so that others can understand what I'm trying to say?
- What are the best words to use to make my meaning clear?
- Can I think of another way to represent this information?
- Have I left out anything important? If so, how can I add it?
- Have I given the graphic organizer a title that will help the viewer know what it represents?

Figure 9-2. Steps in Teaching Students to Use Graphic Organizers

Explain what graphic organizers are, how they can help us learn, and how we can use them.

Choose a topic that is familiar to the children and simple to represent graphically, such as making a semantic map of their school.

Model the procedure for constructing a graphic organizer with the whole class and encourage student input.

While constructing it, talk about your reasoning for developing it in a particular way. Point out that there are often many ways to represent information.

Distribute uncompleted or partially completed copies of the type of graphic organizer you modeled.

Ask the children to get into pairs or groups and choose a topic to work through, or to complete the topic you've already begun.

Let them work through the graphic organizer as you monitor them.

Encourage the children to share their graphic organizers with other groups and to consider alternatives.

Types of Graphic Organizers

Anyone can invent graphic organizers to represent concepts or show relationships; in many cases there are no absolute forms to follow. In fact, much of their appeal lies in their flexibility and adaptability. Teachers have found certain types to be particularly helpful, however, such as those that follow. To give you an example of a graphic organizer and provide an overview of this section, I've created one in Figure 9-3 that shows the types to be presented.

Sequence

Teachers have told me that sequence is one of the hardest concepts for children to understand, yet it is one of the most logical and essential for comprehending stories and information. We'll look at three types of graph-

Figure 9-3. Semantic Map of Graphic Organizers

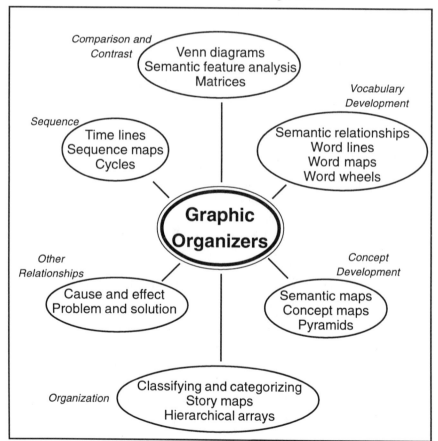

ics that can help children see sequential or time-order relationships: time lines, sequence maps, and cycles.

Time Lines

Beginning with a child's experiences is always a good way to develop an understanding of concepts, so model a time line by asking the children to dictate the order of events in a typical school day. Your time line might resemble the one in Figure 9-4. You could simply write the events first and add the times later. After students grasp the idea, ask them to create their own time lines for what they did last Saturday or Sunday. Remind them that all events must be given in the correct order. Insertions are allowed if they think of additional occurrences later. You can use the same basic structure to help them find the sequence of events in a story or identify the steps in operating a computer. Once the children are comfortable with this procedure, let them apply it to content area learning. One example would be for a small group to decide which events are most significant in the history of the United States, place them in order below the time line, and write the dates of the events above the line.

Figure 9-4. Time Line for Events in a School Day

8:30	10:00	10:50	11:10	11:30	12:00 to 3:00
Language Arts*	Math	Recess	SSR**	Lunch	Thematic Unit (Science, Social Studies, the Arts)

*Integrated reading, writing, listening, and speaking related to the thematic unit

**Sustained Silent Reading (a period of free reading for all)

Sequence Maps

Sequence maps can represent story events, episodes in history, or steps in a science experiment. They consist of a series of statements and may have a pictorial graphic that relates to the subject. Sometimes an arrow leads from one event to the next to help readers follow the sequence. For young children, limit the number in the series to four or five, but older children can work with a greater number. The example in Figure 9-5 is based on Donald Hall's *Ox-Cart Man* and uses the outline of the ox-cart to carry the series of statements.

Cycles

Also suitable for focusing on a sequence of events, cycles represent a circular pattern in which there is no beginning or end. One event leads to another, and so on, until returning to the initial event. For example, in *If*

Figure 9-5. Sequence Map of *Ox-Cart Man*

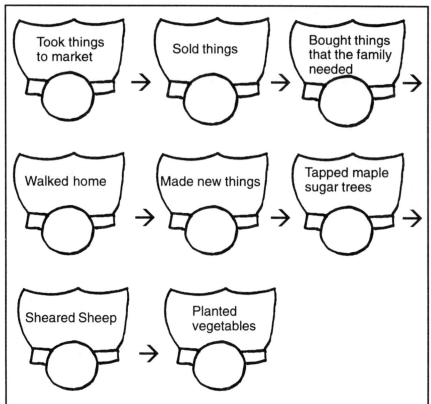

You Give a Mouse a Cookie (Numeroff), the mouse begins by wanting a cookie, which makes him want a glass of milk. The story proceeds through a series of related events, until he returns to wanting a cookie again to go with a glass of milk. Each event is part of the cycle.

Children may be able to understand cycles by thinking of their daily cycles that begin with getting up in the morning, going through a series of events, going to bed at night, and once again getting up in the morning. Thus, through stories and familiar experiences, you can help children begin to understand more complex cycles, such as the cycles of the moon, weather cycles, and life cycles. Figure 9-6 is an example of a butterfly's life cycle.

Comparison and Contrast

Children make comparisons as a matter of course, both in and out of school. They compare brands of tennis shoes, parental privilege and dis-

Figure 9-6. Life Cycle of a Butterfly

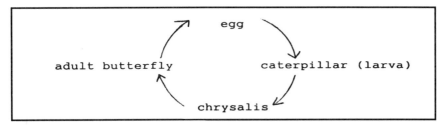

cipline policies, fast food restaurants, books they've read, and so on. Graphic organizers extend children's natural tendency to compare and contrast by providing frameworks for thinking about similarities and differences. Here are examples of the following frameworks: Venn diagrams, semantic feature analysis, and matrices.

Venn Diagrams

Widely used for showing similarities and differences, Venn diagrams consist of two overlapping circles with similarities shown in the overlapping portion. Individual criteria unique to each topic are listed in the outer parts of the corresponding circles, as in Figures 9-7 and 9-8. Figure 9-7 compares features of two children's books, *Miss Rumphius* (Cooney) and *My Great-Aunt Arizona* (Houston). After studying different groups of Native Americans, students from Eva Hearn's sixth-grade class created the Venn diagram shown in Figure 9-8, which compares Native Americans of the Plains with those of the Eastern Woodlands.

Semantic Feature Analysis

Particularly useful for developing vocabulary and concepts in the content areas, semantic feature analysis shows how two or more members of a group are alike or different. Items from the group are listed down the side of a grid, and features that they may or may not possess are listed across the top. The following markings are used:

+ for the presence of a feature
- for the absence of a feature
+,- to indicate that it is sometimes present and sometimes not
? for uncertainty about its presence or absence

Researchers have found semantic feature analysis to be useful for vocabulary development, content area instruction, and prereading activities. Research also supports its effectiveness with learners of various age groups, diverse ethnic groups, and varied reading abilities (Pittelman et al., 1991). Figure 9-9 is an example of semantic feature analysis that compares the features of urban, suburban, and rural communities.

Figure 9-7. Venn Diagram of Two Books

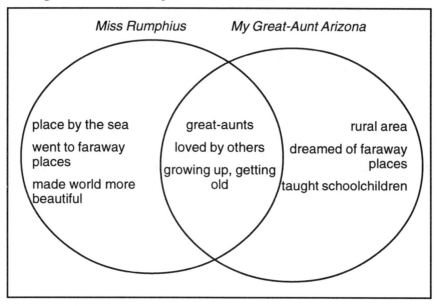

Figure 9-8. Venn Diagram of Groups of Native Americans

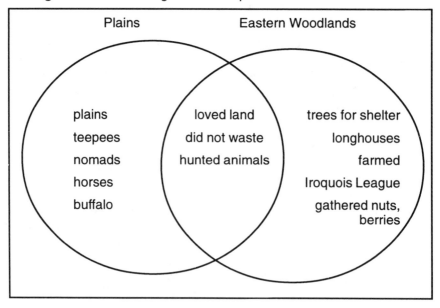

Figure 9-9. Semantic Feature Analysis: Communities

	Has a name	Big buildings	Houses	Farms	Malls	Schools
Urban	+	+	?	-	?	+
Suburban	+	+,-	+	-	+	+
Rural	+	-	+	+	?	+

Matrices

Similar to the grid for semantic feature analysis, a matrix is a graphic display of symbols, items, or numbers that are related in some way. You can use matrices to record and compare data and then evaluate information based on the results. Denise Brison set up a matrix for her third graders in which they compared the nutrients in various brands of cereal to decide which brand was most nutritious. Her matrix looked like the one in Figure 9-10 before the children filled in the percentage of daily values for each nutrient beside the brand.

Figure 9-10. Matrix for Comparing Nutrients in Cereals

Brand	Vitamin A	Vitamin C	Calcium	Iron	Thiamin	Riboflavin
A						
B						
C						
D						
E						

Susan Wilks (1995) suggests a type of matrix that causes children to make judgments about what they believe or understand. She asks them to consider if actions are rude, somewhat rude, or not rude at all; if things are very different, somewhat different, or not different; and if answers to statements are definite, unknown, or not possible. Along this line, you might construct a matrix about what children like, dislike, or don't care about, as shown in Figure 9-11. Children put a checkmark in the column that matches their feelings, and you may want to use the results for class discussion or to guide instruction.

Vocabulary Development

Students need to know not only the dictionary definitions of the words they encounter, but also the fine nuances that make meanings precise. Graphic organizers offer a variety of ways to help children discover exactly what words mean and how to use them. They enable students to

Figure 9-11. Matrix on Likes and Dislikes

	Like	Dislike	Don't Care
Sharing my ideas			
Figuring things out for myself			
Spending time with my family			
Babies			
Old people			
Working in groups			
Helping someone			

perceive relationships among words, activate prior knowledge, use a framework for study and review, and find problem-solving strategies for learning words.

Semantic Relationships

The graphic organizer for semantic relationships helps students understand synonyms, antonyms, and other relationships that might or might not exist between words. Students place a checkmark in the appropriate column to indicate the relationship they believe exists within a pair of words. Working with partners or in small groups, children analyze each pair of words to determine the type of relationship that exists. When meanings are unclear or the answer is disputed, the children can turn to the dictionary to support their views. Discussions about each word pair serve to clarify, reinforce, or redirect understandings of words.

Vocabulary development should originate in a meaningful context; therefore, several of the graphic organizers that follow are based on a story rich in vocabulary and powerful in meaning: *The King's Fountain* by Lloyd Alexander. This story tells of a poor, courageous man's attempt to save the water supply for his village. He pleads with a scholar, a merchant, and a metalsmith to ask the king to relinquish his idea of constructing a splendid fountain that would cut off the water supply to the villagers. When the others refuse to go, the poor man successfully confronts the king himself. Figure 9-12 is an example of a graphic organizer that uses words from this text (Ross, 1994).

Fourth graders in Carol Fuller's class experimented with another type of semantic relationship by creating compound word dominoes. Working in groups, the children placed a single compound word in the center of a piece of paper and built new compound words from it, as shown in Figure 9-13.

Figure 9-12. Semantic Relationships

	Same	Opposite	Related	Unrelated
clever-glib				
lofty-humble				
splendor-glory				
ponder-tremble				
flesh-blood				

Word Lines

Word lines, or linear arrays, display words along a continuum from one extreme to the other, such as *hot* to *cold* or *beautiful* to *ugly*. Along the continuum are intermediary words arranged in progression. You can provide a list for students to place in order, or they can generate their own lists. This activity helps students recognize fine distinctions in word meanings, and discussion again helps them determine proper placement. Figure 9-14 is an example of a word line and is also based on *The King's Fountain* by Alexander (Ross, 1994).

Figure 9-13. Compound Word Dominoes

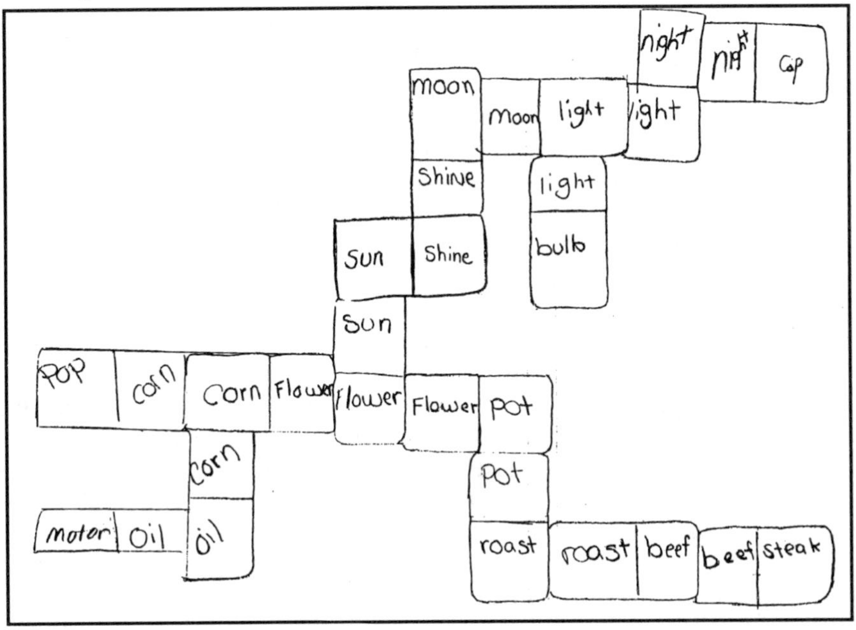

Figure 9-14. Word Line

murmur	stammer	speak	shout	roar

Word Maps

Concept-of-definition word maps help students understand words in terms of definition or classification, similarities or properties, and examples (Schwartz and Raphael, 1985). The key word is located in the center of the word map, and questions about the word are placed above each section that requires responses, as shown in Figure 9-15 (Ross, 1994). You can use word maps with any type of reading program and adapt them for students in any grade at any level of reading competence, including very poor and beginning readers (Duffelmeyer and Banwart, 1992/1993).

Figure 9-15. Word Map

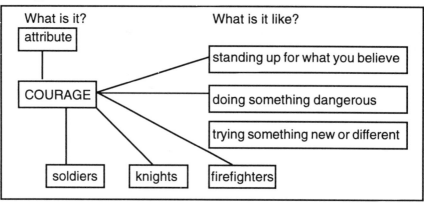

Word Wheels

Students are often confused when they find that a single word can have multiple meanings. In order to help them understand this, involve them in constructing word wheels. Once again, place the key word in the center, or in this case the hub, of the wheel. Then draw spokes radiating from the center to carry the various meanings of the word, as shown in Figure 9-16 (Ross, 1994). Ask the children to brainstorm as many meanings as they can for the key word, and write brief definitions on the spokes. When the children understand how to construct word wheels, they can make their own, with the dictionary as a reference.

Figure 9-16. Word Wheel

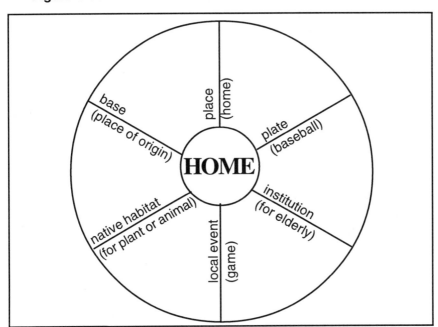

Concept Development

Graphic organizers such as semantic maps, concept maps, and pyramids can help children enrich their understanding of concepts. Through class discussion children can draw on their prior experiences and integrate new ideas in order to extend their somewhat limited knowledge. As their ideas are recorded on graphic organizers, they become aware of new possibilities and may indeed have an "aha" experience.

Semantic Maps

Semantic maps serve a variety of purposes: accessing prior knowledge, clustering information, finding labels for clusters, and calling for specific vocabulary. They are useful throughout thematic units, first for introducing them, then for expanding or correcting the initial maps as new information is acquired, and finally for summarizing and reviewing at the end of each unit.

The procedure begins when you present a word that is central to the theme to be studied. Ask the children to brainstorm words or phrases that relate to the theme, and either place them in clusters as you go or list them at the side to be clustered later. The children should help you decide which words go together. When they disagree, they experience a wonderful learning opportunity as they attempt to justify their reasons for word placements within certain categories. Labeling the clusters of words (details) causes the children to think of appropriate comprehensive terms (main ideas). Such clustering and labeling is actually a form of outlining, because the central word becomes the title, the labels become the headings, and the individual words become the topics under the corresponding headings. After reading *Little House in the Big Woods* (Wilder), third graders in Barbara Moss's class worked in groups to organize the items found in the store at Pepin. One group produced the semantic map found in Figure 9-17, and Julie Gibbons' map (Figure 9-18) shows four ways to find directions.

Concept Maps

Similar in form to semantic maps but more complex, concept maps show relationships among concepts. They increase children's ability to organize and represent thoughts, and they encourage divergent and reflective thinking. Strategies apply across a wide range of disciplines and readily transfer from one subject to another (Wilson and Wing Jan, 1993).

Begin with a topic and invite the class to brainstorm related ideas together. Ask students to think about which ideas are most important and

Figure 9-17. Semantic Map for Pepin Store

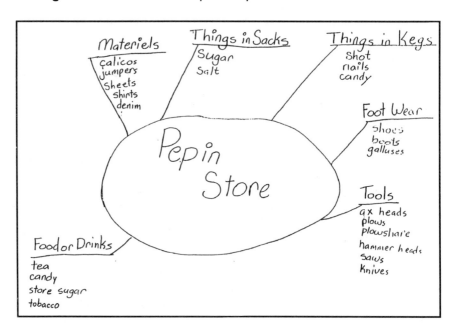

how concepts are interrelated. Let them suggest ways to show connections, perhaps by drawing arrows or writing information on connecting lines. After you have modeled concept mapping, encourage students to develop their own maps. Many possibilities exist, so students are free to explore a variety of ways to present information. See Figure 9-19 for an example of concept mapping.

Pyramids

Pyramids are simply a way to show how concepts can move from general terms to specific examples or vice versa. Choose a broad concept and ask students to brainstorm words that relate to that concept in more specific ways. Record these words and ask the children to choose those that gradually become more specific. If you use the procedure in reverse, begin with a specific term and become more inclusive. For example, you might begin with the name of your school and continue with the name of the town or city, county, state, country, continent, hemisphere, and so on. An example of a pyramid appears in Figure 9-20. Groups of fourth graders in Carol Fuller's class created variations of the pyramid by beginning with a general term identifying several specific related terms and adding descriptors for each specific term (Fig. 9-21).

Figure 9-18. Semantic Map for Finding Directions

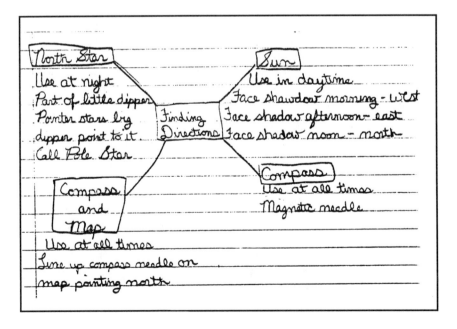

Figure 9-19. Concept Map

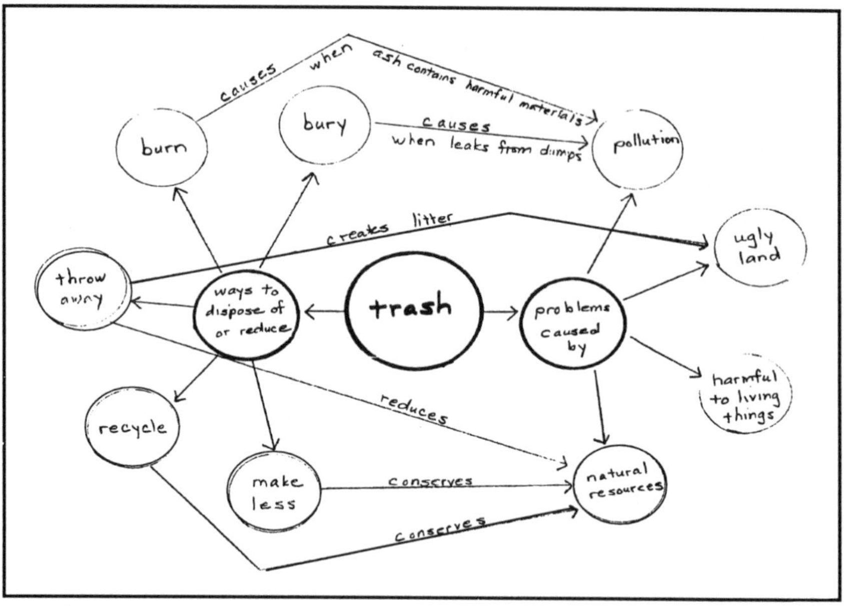

Organization

Many types of graphic organizers help us understand ways that things are organized, including several of the examples already given as well as flow charts, organizational charts, and structured overviews. For many of us, looking at an organization chart of our government is much clearer than reading several paragraphs explaining how the government is organized. Here we will consider classifying and categorizing, story maps, and hierarchical arrays.

Classifying and Categorizing

Children begin classifying and categorizing early in life as they arrange objects by size, color, or function. In preschool they may put all the blocks of the same size and shape together on a shelf, or they may cut out pictures of things that belong in a kitchen. These are beginning steps in logical, orderly thinking. As they get older, they use the same mental processes to classify words and concepts by their commonalities.

When constructing a table for placing words in categories, you may begin by giving major concepts and a list of words for the children to place under the appropriate headings. You may vary this procedure by providing a list of words and asking students to identify appropriate categories for themselves. As they arrive at their own labels for categories,

Figure 9-20. Pyramid

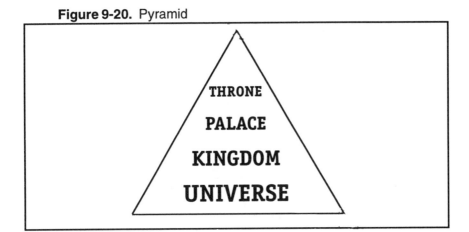

Figure 9-21. Pyramid With Descriptors

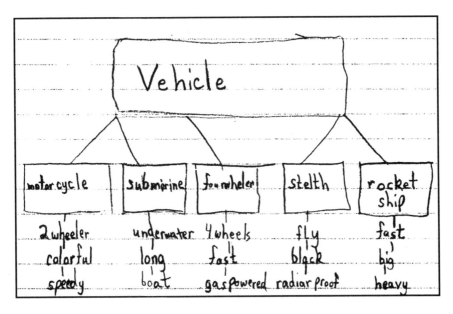

they need to think inductively in order to discover relationships among words. Figure 9-22 is an example of a graphic organizer with the names of categories given and a list of words to be placed under the appropriate headings. The words are from *The King's Fountain*.

Figure 9-22. Vocabulary Categories

Action	Feelings	Speech

Word list:

angry	golden tongue	pounded	dismayed	trudged
smash	strike down	hopeless	confused	downcast
climbed	heavy-hearted	eloquence	seized	hesitant
message	cloudy words	glib words		

Story Maps

Story maps can assume many forms. They may be a sequential series of events, a semantic map of characters with their names and character traits, or a concept map showing important relationships among events. In a transitional K–1 class I visited, Gloria Vick had read the children a story and asked them to create a story map by drawing pictures of the beginning, middle, and end. Another teacher used the formula of setting, characters, problem, and solution, and still another format appears in Figure 9-23 (Cassidy, 1989). Story maps help children focus on literary elements, but they do little to enhance their appreciation and aesthetic responses unless provision is made for doing so. For example, to the map below you might add "How I feel about this story," "Reflections," or "My personal response."

Figure 9-23. Story Map

Title:

Setting:

Characters:

Problem:

Events:

Solution:

Hierarchical Arrays

Hierarchical arrays represent connections among different levels or classifications. They vary in structure depending on the type of relationships being presented and the concepts to be analyzed (Cooper, 1993). They are useful for comparing and contrasting words and concepts, especially after students have read content-area material. Figure 9-24 shows an array created by Felicia Shoulta, a third grader in Denise Brison's class. The class had been learning about ecosystems, and Felicia chose mountains as her area of research.

Figure 9-24. Hierarchical Array

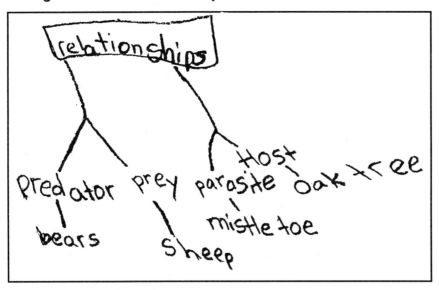

Other Relationships

Ways to represent ideas, show relationships, and portray linkages are virtually limitless, but we have covered many of those that teachers find useful. Two more areas bear mention because of their significance for thought processes: cause and effect and problem and solution. Graphic representations of these strategies are simple and direct.

Cause and Effect

Cause-and-effect relationships exist in nearly every area of the curriculum. In math we add two numbers together (cause) and get the total (effect); in science we plant a seed and water it (cause), and a plant begins to grow (effect); in social studies we study issues related to dissension over slavery (cause) and learn about the Civil War (effect). Understanding cause-and-effect relationships is often difficult for children, so it may be helpful for them to see a graphic representation of what makes something happen (cause) and its outcome (effect).

Sometimes causes and effects for a single event are multiple, but begin by focusing on situations in which one cause brings about one effect. Numeroff's *If You Give a Mouse a Cookie* is useful both for cyclical organizers, as suggested earlier in this chapter, and cause-and-effect relationships. A cause-and-effect map of the first part of this book might look like the one in Figure 9-25.

Figure 9-25. Cause-and-Effect Map

If You Give a Mouse a Cookie

Cause	Effect		Cause	Effect
Give cookie →	Wants milk		Give milk →	Needs straw
Drinks milk →	Needs napkin		Sees mirror →	Needs trim

Problem and Solution

Children frequently encounter problems in both their academic work and their lives out of school. They need to find ways to solve these problems, and a graphic organizer may help them focus on what the problem is, consider viable alternatives, and select the best possible solution(s).

Chapter 1 presented a lesson on problem solving in which the students were so nervous about their six-week test that they couldn't answer the questions. They sought help and reached solutions that relieved them of much of their anxiety. This problem-and-solution situation might be graphically represented as shown in Figure 9-26.

Summary

Graphic organizers enable us to see relationships and grasp concepts quickly because of their form and simplicity. They are mental maps that cause us to focus on what is important. They appeal to all learners, but they offer special advantages to poor or reluctant readers and visual/spatial learners.

Graphic organizers offer an alternative to textbook reading, and the discussions surrounding their interpretation and construction cause students to reason, analyze, make decisions, and think critically and cre-

Figure 9-26. Problem-and-Solution Map

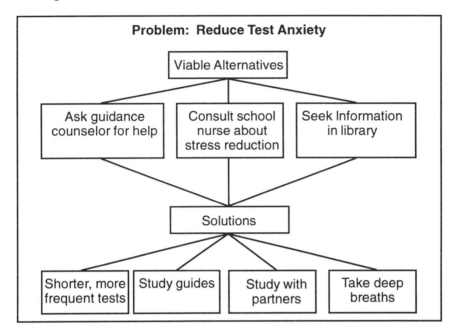

atively. They are useful at any grade level, and they are especially effective when students build on each other's ideas as they work in pairs or
small groups. When teaching students to read or make graphic organizers, teachers should first model the procedure, being careful to explain
the reasoning behind it, and then let children work collaboratively.

Appropriate for any subject, graphic organizers come in many forms
and serve a variety of purposes. In this chapter they are organized by the
following topics: sequence, comparison and contrast, vocabulary development, concept development, organization, and other relationships (cause
and effect, problem and solution).

References

Abromitis, B. (Ed.). (1994). *New directions in vocabulary*. Rolling Mead-
ows, IL: Blue Ribbon Press.

Alexander, L. (1971). *The king's fountain*. New York: Dutton.

Alvermann, D. (1991). The discussion web: A graphic aid for learning
across the curriculum. *The Reading Teacher, 45*(2): 92–99.

Blachowicz, C., and Lee, J. (1991). Vocabulary development in the whole
literacy classroom. *The Reading Teacher, 45*(3): 188–195.

Bromley, K. (1991). *Webbing with literature*. Boston: Allyn & Bacon.

Bromley, K., Irwin–De Vitis, L., and Modlo, M. (1995). *Graphic
organizers*. New York: Scholastic.

Bromley, K., Irwin–De Vitis, L., Modlo, M., and Pease, D. (1995). *Graphic organizers: An authentic assessment tool.* Presentation at the College Reading Association, Clearwater, FL.

Burke, K. (1993). *How to assess thoughtful outcomes.* Palatine, IL: IRI/Skylight.

Cassidy, J. (1989). Using graphic organizers to develop critical thinking. *Gifted Child Today, 12*(6): 34–36.

Cooney, B. (1982). *Miss Rumphius.* New York: Penguin.

Cooper, J.D. (1993). *Literacy: Helping children construct meaning* (2nd ed.). Boston: Houghton Mifflin.

Duffelmeyer, F. and Banwart, B.H. (1992/1993). Word maps for adjectives and verbs. *The Reading Teacher, 46*(4): 351–353.

Dunston, P. (1992). A critique of graphic organizer research. *Reading Research and Instruction, 31*(2): 57–65.

Fanelli, S. (1995). *My map book.* New York: HarperCollins.

Hall, D. (1979). *Ox cart man.* New York: Viking.

Hawk, P. (1986). Using graphic organizers to increase achievement in middle school life science. *Science Education, 70*(1): 81–87.

Heimlich, J. and Pittelman, S. (1986). *Semantic mapping: Classroom applications.* Newark, DE: International Reading Association.

Houston, G. (1992). *My great-aunt Arizona.* New York: HarperCollins.

Invitations to literacy. (1996). Boston: Houghton Mifflin.

Lehman, H. (1992). Graphic organizers benefit slow learners. *The Clearing House, 66*(1): 53–55.

MacLachlan, P. (1985). *Sarah, plain and tall.* New York: Harper & Row.

Manzo, A., and Manzo, U. (1995). *Teaching children to be literate: A reflective approach.* Orlando: Harcourt Brace.

Marzano, R., and Marzano, J. (1988). *A cluster approach to elementary vocabulary instruction.* Newark, DE: International Reading Association.

McCormick, S. (1995). *Instructing students who have literacy problems.* Englewood Cliffs, NJ: Merrill/Prentice-Hall.

Numeroff, L.J. (1985). *If you give a mouse a cookie.* New York: Scholastic.

Pittelman, S., Heimlich, J., Berglund, R., and French, M. (1991). *Semantic feature analysis.* Newark, DE: International Reading Association.

Rafferty, C., and Fleschner, L. (1993). Concept mapping: A viable alternative to objective and essay exams. *Reading Research and Instruction, 32*(3): 25–34.

Ross, E. (1994). Vocabulary graphics. *Tennessee Reading Teacher, 23*(1): 2–4.

Schwartz, R., and Raphael, T. (1985). Concept of definition: A key to improving students' vocabulary. *The Reading Teacher, 39*(3): 198–205.

Tompkins, G. (1997). *Literacy for the 21st century: A balanced approach.* Upper Saddle River, NJ: Merrill/Prentice-Hall.

Waber, B. (1967). *An anteater named Arthur.* Boston: Houghton Mifflin.

Wilder, L.I. (1953). *Little house in the big woods.* New York: Harper & Row.

Wilks, S. (1995). *Critical & creative thinking.* Portsmouth, NH: Heinemann.

Wilson, J., and Wing Jan, L. (193) *Thinking for themselves.* Portsmouth, NH: Heinemann.

CHAPTER 10

Using Technology to Stimulate Thinking

Betty D. Roe

When I asked the teachers,

"How can technology stimulate thinking?"

the teachers said:

- The students can visually see what they have been studying.
- There are many computer simulation programs that require problem solving.
- Technology helps to organize thoughts and supplies up-to-date resource materials.
- Technology can stimulate thinking by using colorful graphics.
- Students are challenged to think and act before a computer responds.
- Using the Internet can help children to explore ideas.
- When using the Internet, students can make their own decisions, visit different web sites, and discuss what they find.
- There are programs that make kids create and think in new ways.

How would you answer this question?

Concepts to watch for

- Ways computers can be used to teach thinking
- How different computer software contributes to different types of thinking strategies
- Thinking challenges posed by use of the Internet
- Technology use as a component of classroom research and presentations
- The relationship of programming to thinking strategies
- How the use of CD-ROMs and laser discs can enhance instruction in thinking strategies
- Values of television and videocassette recorders as tools for thinking

---

Two classes of middle-school students from a rural county in Tennessee were paired with students in a university reading-methods class. They read the book *Bridge to Terabithia* on the same schedule and e-mailed their reactions to it to their partners. The university students knew that predicting before reading helps to set purposes for the reading and involves the use of higher-order thinking. Many of the university students modeled the prediction process in their e-mail transmissions on early chapters of the book. Soon the middle-school students were initiating the prediction process, or at least making predictions of their own after their partners made predictions. The university students tried to always give reasons for their predictions, and the middle-school students followed the lead on this also. In this way, some of the university students introduced their partners to the technique of *foreshadowing*, a common device used by writers to help their readers anticipate coming events.

Other types of thinking were encouraged during these electronic literary discussions. The knowledge level of Bloom's taxonomy was evident as the students discussed who the characters were, what happened, and where the action took place. They exhibited the comprehension level when they described the characters and setting, compared the characters with each other and with people they knew, and compared the setting with their own homes and schools. Students were thinking on the level of analysis when they speculated on why Jess's family members acted as they did, why Jess's art work was not appreciated by some of the characters, why Jess defended Leslie when she wanted to run, why Jess didn't call Leslie before he went to Washington, and so on. They were thinking on the level of synthesis when they predicted events, and they were thinking on the level of evaluation when they judged the reactions that Jess's family had to his art, when they considered the validity of

Leslie's family's lifestyle, when they judged the trick that Jess and Leslie played on Janice, and when they decided whether Jess was right to take his sister to Terabithia after Leslie's death.

Computers and the Development of Thinking Skills

Today the technology that is getting the most attention is computer technology. You can use computers to develop thinking at different levels. Drill-and-practice programs promote literal thinking, but simulation programs and interactive text programs, which both have outcomes affected by the user's decisions, promote critical thinking, and programs that allow students to create new products, art work, or stories clearly promote creative thinking. Word processing and desktop publishing programs allow the creation of written works of varying levels of complexity and creativity.

Karen Wanamaker (1996), in a unit on Laura Ingalls Wilder books, uses the *Oregon Trail* simulation program produced by Minnesota Educational Computing Consortium (MECC) to help her students understand the experience of traveling during the era of covered wagons. The *Oregon Trail* program puts the user in the position of an expedition leader who must make decisions along the way about items to purchase, the distance to travel, stops, and hunting for food. *Africa Trail* (MECC) is a simulation that introduces students to African cultures, re-creating a bicycle trek of 12,000 miles across Africa. The users participate in activities such as buying spare parts for their bikes, deciding on the pace of the travel, deciding what to do during stopovers, and choosing partners with whom to travel. As in the Oregon Trail simulations, participants have to make decisions based upon what happens along the way (Holzberg, 1995). Using simulations allows students to form and test hypotheses about why things work as they do.

You can use database programs to promote classification and comparison-and-contrast ability, and these programs can provide information to be used in problem solving. For example, students could construct a database to categorize books used in a unit of study or perhaps all of the books in the classroom collection. On the other hand, they could use a commercially prepared database program to locate information about a topic of study. In order to do this, students must learn how to use *sort* and *find* functions to make comparisons from the information in the database. These qualities of databases lead educators to believe that the creation of databases and work with existing databases enhances higher-order thinking in the students (Hartson, 1993; Hunter, 1985; Lai, 1991).

A common application of database search strategies is on-line searches of library holdings. Using such a database requires knowledge of the search procedures; for example, choosing an Author, Title, or Subject search and entering the known information in the correct form. For a Subject search, key words need to be identified as likely locators, and the student has to be flexible enough to try various options if the first attempt fails to produce the needed material (Grabe and Grabe, 1996). When students find items in the search, they need to think critically to decide if the entries are relevant to the current need.

Use of individual electronic mail (e-mail) exchanges and mailing lists (via list servers) can promote thinking at any level, depending upon the purpose of the communication. If individual e-mail addresses are assigned, your class or individual students can subscribe to mailing lists related to various topics. Mail sent to these mailing lists is distributed to all subscribers. A person can send a message asking for help or information, offer help or information that was requested by someone else, or just make comments. Some subscribers simply read the interchanges about the topic without interacting personally.

Ferdi Serim's New Jersey elementary-school students sent electronic messages to children from the contaminated area around the Chernobyl Nuclear Station, who were in the United Kingdom to experience a contamination-free environment in order to build up their lost immunities. Ferdi's class discussed the situation, wrote individual messages, and saved text files containing their messages. Ferdi bundled the messages into a single text file and sent them. The class received a reply from two Byelorussian teachers who were accompanying the children. This experience sparked reading about the disaster and discussion of related topics, such as ecology and energy needs. Later, the students got to meet Anatoly Voronov, creator of Glasnet (the network that provides individual Russians with Internet access). After the visit, Voronov sent the class uncensored firsthand accounts of an armed rebellion in Moscow. What a stimulus for serious study that was! One of the sixth graders, who met Voronov and e-mailed Russian students, later won an essay contest about significant learning experiences with networks that was open to U.S. students from pre-kindergarten to twelfth grade. She said, "I still can't get over the fact that I was talking to kids that were looking at tanks rolling by. Everybody has a place they want to visit, and I can get there quicker just by using the telecommunication method" (Serim and Koch, 1996, p. 27).

Newsgroups or discussion groups can also promote thinking at any level. They are essentially electronic bulletin boards about particular topics. Messages are posted to a particular location, and users can go to this location and read the ongoing dialogue and post their own comments and questions, if they desire.

Thought-Provoking Question

Would you want your students to have free access to *all* the newsgroups on the Internet, considering the fact that in many of them there is no censoring of the comments made, and comments may be made by *anyone* in the world?

There are also on-line projects of various types that offer challenging interactions with others. "Commercial networks, such as National Geographic KidsNet, structure telecommunications projects around scientific themes, such as acid rain or weather" (Grabe and Grabe, 1996, p. 25). These projects are international and involve students in hands-on experiments, data collection, and comparison of their findings with other students worldwide. The students are assisted by a professional scientist in tracing geographic patterns in the data gathered (Sharp, 1996). It is easy to see how critical analysis would be involved in such interactions and in the classroom debates about the issues that follow the experience.

Research projects require the use of multiple resources for data collection and synthesis of this information into a coherent whole. Every step of a research project involves thinking. Data collection can take place in traditional ways, but technological resources are now playing a large part in student research. As mentioned before, for example, library holdings may be searched electronically.

Electronic dictionaries, encyclopedias, and atlases may be used for projects, and they may contain not only text and still pictures but also sound, video clips, and animation. Hyperlinks may allow the student to click with the mouse on a term in one article and be taken to a definition, a pronunciation, a picture (motion or still), or a related article. Icons may be used to cue the user to the type of material that is linked to the term. Using reference materials that are organized in this manner requires the student to engage in nonlinear thinking in order to locate the most relevant and useful information for his or her purposes. The student can copy material to a clipboard and print it out for later use.

Internet searches are the most challenging of the many ways to locate information with the computer. The Internet is hundreds of thousands of computers throughout the world, all connected so that other computer users can access them (Serim and Koch, 1996). You can obtain information in many forms (text, sound, video, and graphics) from the Internet.

The World Wide Web (WWW) is a portion of the Internet that has a graphical user interface and hyperlinks that allow users to click a mouse on special words or symbols and be automatically transported to web locations that are related to the currently addressed document. This process obviously facilitates research activities (Ryder and Graves, 1996/1997).

Browsers are used to make locating addresses on the Internet easier. There are text-only browsers (e.g., *Lynx*) and graphic browsers (e.g., *Netscape* and *Microsoft Explorer*). If a text-only browser is used, no graphics will be viewable, but the text of the various sites can be read, and it is often much faster to access only text, because graphics may take a long time to load, resulting in extensive wait time. The graphic browsers can be told to retrieve text only, if you want to speed up the search. A person using a graphic browser has to decide how important the graphics are to the specific purpose of the search. If you know the address to which you want to go, you can key it into the appropriate slot on the browser's screen, and the browser will go to that location. However, if you don't know specific addresses, you may choose to use a search engine (e.g., *Alta Vista* or *Webcrawler*) to locate appropriate material. These search engines will do key word searches. Some of them offer sophisticated searches that allow such things as the specification of AND to look for the presence of both of the connected terms and OR to look for either of the specified terms (Boolean searches). Doing such searches causes students to use logic in choosing terms. The searches may result in far more hits than the student wishes to check. In this case, thinking is necessary to decide how to limit the search. Some of the hits will not be relevant. The search engine will not be likely to discriminate between a monarch that is a king and a Monarch butterfly, for example. Some hits turn out to be completely inexplicable. Students will need to be flexible enough to examine each one and eliminate irrelevant ones without becoming unduly concerned.

Thought-Provoking Question

What can you do if students find that they get so many hits when they search that they don't want to work through them all? What if they don't get many hits with their chosen key words or if they get irritated and frustrated with irrelevant hits?

In Princeton, New Jersey, Janet Woods's first-grade classes have researched topics such as volcanoes, space shuttles, and weather on the Internet. They also use e-mail, and the international e-mail they received interested them in learning more about reading maps and globes. The middle-school students in Princeton also do research on the Internet, and ESL students from Central and South America look up soccer scores from their native countries (Serim and Koch, 1996).

Because nobody is in charge of checking web pages on the Internet for accuracy before they are published (or after, for that matter), there is often inaccurate information on Internet sites. Make your students aware of this fact, and encourage them to check information in more than one source before they use it. They can note if the material is documented in any way and can check the documentation. If they know who the originator of the site is, they may be able to decide if that person is a credible source. You can also give them some addresses of web locations that are reliable sources of information, such as the Library of Congress site (http://www.loc.gov) or NASA's Internet in the Classroom (http://quest.arc.nasa.gov/interactive.html). The process of evaluating collected information is a critical thinking activity.

Sites of interest can be bookmarked by the browser that students are using and returned to without having to type in the address again. However, the web is constantly changing, and a site that is available today may be gone tomorrow. Students would do well to gather the information from a relevant site while they have it in view. Of course, they may print or save to disk information that they find, making perusal possible at a future time.

One way that you may involve your students with Internet and electronic reference searches is to develop Anticipation Guides for thematic studies and to require the students to use these resources to check the information they fill in on the guides. Figure 10-1 is an example.

Internet contests may spark critical thinking. Ferdi Serim discovered that National Public Radio, as a part of its coverage of the Internet, was sponsoring an Internet Hunt, composed of six questions that had to be answered using only Internet sources. Serim and several sixth graders worked on strategies to use to locate the answers. He then sent in a file containing their answers and strategies. This unlikely team won the Hunt with complete and correct answers, beating teams from several universities (Serim and Koch, 1996).

Another way to lead students to do critical thinking is to give them a critical thinking task or question (Ryder and Graves, 1996/1997). Follow with a class discussion that calls attention to information that is relevant to the task. Then provide a graphic organizer (perhaps a semantic map) to focus their attention on information that can be found on the Internet. (Anderson-Inman and Horney [1996/1997] suggest the use of an outlining and diagraming program called *Inspiration*® for creating concept maps.) Let the students work in groups to consider different aspects of the critical thinking task. Finally, have each group share the collected information with the class and give other class members copies of the graphic organizer involved in the information collection. All the students should use information from the different groups to complete the critical thinking task.

Figure 10-1. Anticipation Guide

Here are some statements about American Indians. Do you agree or disagree with them? Tell why you agree or disagree and then find support for your answers with information from the Internet or a CD-ROM encyclopedia. Document the sources of your information.

Agree   Disagree   There were many more American Indians at the time of the American Revolution than there were when Columbus first came to America.

Agree   Disagree   At the time of European settlement of America, Cherokee Indians were farmers and hunters with permanent homes.

Agree   Disagree   Sequoyah invented a written language for the Cherokee. No other person is known to have accomplished such a task alone.

Agree   Disagree   Because the Cherokee had sided with the Whites during the war against the Creeks in 1813 and a Cherokee leader had saved Andrew Jackson's life during one battle, Jackson was very supportive of the Cherokee while he was President of the United States.

Older students can use the Internet to make alphabet books of information about some high-interest topic, such as animals. They can work in groups to find information on the Internet about each animal that they have chosen to represent a letter, and they can then add this information to their books. The results of the work of all groups can be combined to form a complete book. Pairs of older students can meet with pairs of younger students to share their class alphabet book. Finally, the four students can work together to find other animals on the Internet to form another book. The older students can help the younger ones to learn to do searches with a search engine (Cotton, 1996).

Even primary-grade children can learn to use the Internet, and Eileen Cotton (1996) believes that children who have been exposed to computer games will be ahead in the hierarchical logic needed to find their way through menus and along information trails. Young children can learn to do simple searches with the help of a search engine; older children can learn to use Boolean and other complex search techniques.

Publishing and Presentations

Desktop publishing programs can offer students an opportunity to produce creative posters, banners, and greeting cards and can allow a class to work cooperatively to produce a newsletter or magazine. Desktop publishing programs allow the incorporation of both text and graphics, the use of a variety of fonts, and the flowing of text around graphics. Planning page layout is as much a thinking task as writing the copy to be included. It involves the consideration of aesthetic effect, readability, and content composition. Copy can vary from literal reports of events to critical analysis of school situations in editorials to creative profiles of people or treatment of upcoming events. You can allow students to assume the roles of reporters, editors, design specialists, and so on, and each one can see how his or her contribution is necessary for the whole. The discussion necessary for coordinating such activity will involve much critical analysis and synthesis of ideas; students will compare and contrast options, consider causes and effects of visual appeal as they arrange material on the pages, and evaluate the overall effect of each decision.

Thought-Provoking Question

How does page design in desktop publishing activities involve higher-order thinking?

Through presentations, students can inform their classmates about a topic or persuade them to accept a position on an issue. Programs that allow students to develop multimedia presentations—complete with text, graphics, animation, and sound, as well as audiotape and videotape clips—cause the students to make decisions about information to present, sequence of presentation, fonts for text, screen design, transitions, and other features. The purpose of the presentation will affect these decisions. Use of these programs definitely promotes problem-solving abilities in students. The middle-school students in the opening vignette produced an mPower presentation based on the reading of *Bridge to Terabithia*. They worked cooperatively in groups and shared their reactions to the book with their university partners.

Developing multimedia presentations goes well with thematic units. In a Florida middle school, a unit on the ecology of a swamp area near the school and a nearby lake was enhanced when the students worked in teams to take soil samples, observe plant and animal life, and photograph the experience. They scanned the photographs and included them with HyperCard presentations that they developed. In addition to their firsthand experiences, they searched the Internet for information on some topics and used *The Great Ocean Rescue* (Tom Snyder Productions), a simulation about marine life and ecology, to enhance the unit study. They proceeded with open-ended inquiry to help them understand the problem they were studying (Mancini, 1995)—clearly a higher-order thinking process.

Greeno and Hall (1997) describe an experience that a group of middle-school students had with a computer modeling environment called "HabiTech," part of a curriculum unit called "LifeLines" that was developed at the Institute for Research on Learning. The students made recommendations to Alaska about alternative policies for controlling wolf populations on public lands. To support their recommendations, they built simulation models of a biological system that had wolf and caribou populations. The students read information from a database and constructed models based upon this information. One student used the computer program to build a link between the number of caribou in Alaska that die each year and the number of wolf packs that are hunting them, and found that "as more wolves are killed fewer caribou will be eaten." His group discussed a policy recommendation to the state that hunters be allowed to kill wolves in order to allow the caribou population to stabilize. Students can present a project like this to their classmates in a variety of ways, using various visuals, such as tables, graphs, and networks. Much higher-order thinking goes into the development of the computer model and the analysis of its implications, and even more goes into choosing the best mode for presenting the results to classmates. The classmates, in turn, must think critically as they analyze the presentation and its logic and effectiveness.

Some students may want to publish on the World Wide Web. Students can create their own web pages (Cotton, 1996; "Wired Education," 1996). By using codes in HTML (HyperText Markup Language), you and your students can turn text into a web page. There are editing tools that simplify the process of using HTML, some editors that allow the creation of web pages without directly inserting HTML codes, and some word processors that can produce documents in HTML form. You may set up a web page and use it for publication of your students' work on various class projects, as well as for publication of information about the class and/or school that students compile and design. The design can even involve hypermedia, with links that include multimedia offerings. Students can also publish magazines and newspapers on the Internet, with contributions from students worldwide (Serim and Koch, 1996). Planning web page designs and contents involves students in higher-level thinking, and the Internet provides students with a worldwide audience for their writing.

Thought-Provoking Question

What worthwhile things might your students publish on the World Wide Web? Could they manage the creation of a web page? What help might they need from you?

For the ultimate in creative thinking activities, you may want to involve your students in a MUD or MOO, "Interactive virtual worlds players construct as they go along. . . . These environments encourage students to collaborate to build their own worlds, and to explore historical and virtual worlds" (Serim and Koch, 1996, p. 92). Some MUDs and MOOs are just games, but some educators are designing them specifically for K–12 students. They embody discovery learning and interactivity and promote problem solving and communication strategies.

Programming

Heide and Henderson (1994, p. 47) believe that "[p]rogramming provides a medium for developing thinking skills, exploring, experimenting, and problem solving. When students program, they are able to create and control applications, as opposed to being at the mercy of commercial software." Logo is a programming language that students, even preschoolers, can use. With Logo, children can do such things as create graphics, control robotic devices, and make music. Causing devices to follow directions to perform desired maneuvers is a high-level problem-solving activity.

CD-ROMs and Laser Discs: Input for Thinking Activities

CD-ROMs and laser discs bring images into the classroom that provide the content for thought processes. Optical Data's *Kinderventures* program has five modules that help to give young children an expanding view of the world. The program includes videodiscs, CD-ROM activities, music, hands-on activities, read-aloud stories, literature, and manipulatives. The technology components are intertwined with the more traditional ones to offer a multisensory approach to learning. The *Math Around Us* module lets children explore numbers, solids and shapes, and early measurement concepts. It is designed to help the children learn how to solve problems flexibly. Each of the activities in this module presents a question to investigate and also includes a question at the end to extend children's mathematical thinking. Optical Data also has a *Windows on Math* and a *Windows on Science* program for elementary- and middle-school grades that include videodiscs. The math program attempts to make math concepts seem more real through a mix of media and activities. It presents problem-solving opportunities in the context of real-life situations. A Science Station CD-ROM is also available to encourage further investigations (Zimmerman, 1996).

A number of CD-ROMs can enhance study of other cultures, group work on thematic units, and writing of research papers. They include *500 Nations: Stories of the North American Experience* (Microsoft Corporation), *Journey to the Source: An Expedition Along the Yangtze* (Grid Media), and *One Tribe: An Interactive Encyclopedia of People and Cultures* (Virgin Sound and Vision) (Holzberg, 1995).

Several good sources for learning about archeology are *Archaeologica* (Hyper-Quest), *Introduction to Archeology* (E.M.M.E. Interactive), *Maya Quest* (MECC), and *Voyage in Egypt* (E.M.M.E. Interactive). In *Introduction to Archaeology* the users have to reconstruct the past by identifying attributes of the person who became a buried skeleton. In the process, they must consult documents and interview experts, among other activities that are clearly conducive to the enhancement of thinking strategies. In *Maya Quest* users visit Mayan ruins, decipher hieroglyphs, reconstruct monumental sites, and try to discover reasons that the Mayan civilization collapsed—clearly higher-order thinking activities (Holzberg, 1995). *Science Sleuths* (Videodiscovery) is a CD-ROM program that encourages middle-school students to solve humorous mysteries that introduce science concepts. They are asked to do research, perform tests, and present evidence. There are six levels of difficulty that require the students to use different resources and that have different solutions (Stearns, 1995).

Thought-Provoking Question

How can CD-ROMs and laser discs enhance the teaching of thinking strategies?

Math Heads (Theatrix Interactive) lets students create characters' faces, clothing, and the like, and students can have the characters compete on "Math Head TV" for points and prizes, in order to learn pre-algebra and problem-solving. Some areas covered by the program are reasoning, relationships with fractions, solving word problems, and developing estimating skills, all areas that require some higher-order thinking (Allen, 1997).

Figure 10-2. Model Interdepartmental Project

This model project has evolved over several years at St. Mary's Episcopal School, an all-girls, private school in Memphis, Tennessee.

St. Mary's sixth graders use modern computer technology and the combined expertise of several teachers to return to the "days of olde when knights were bold." As Ann Petersen (personal communication, September 10, 1996), the literature teacher, explained it:

> Every year my class reads the Newbery Award–winning book *The Door in the Wall* by Marguerite de Angeli. We discuss the book and listen to music from the time period ("Scarborough Fair," "The Ash Grove," and "Greensleeves"), read Shakespearean sonnets, and view illuminated manuscripts and illuminate our own initials. We also listen to music from the musical *Camelot* and discuss Arthurian legends. We learn about monks, troubadours, heraldry, royalty, the Black Plague, jousting, castles, and border wars with Scotland and Wales.
>
> At the same time, the girls study Europe in the Middle Ages in their social studies classes. There they discuss many of the same topics, as well as new ones, such as knights, the Crusades, and the influence of the Catholic Church. Students research the topic on CD-ROM encyclopedias to gather information about this time period.
>
> Last year the element of art was added to the project. The art teacher and the social studies teacher worked together to develop background on the architecture of castles. Slides were shown and lectures were given. Student research was done with the librarians' help and then the girls worked in small cooperative groups to construct clay models of Gothic castles and cathedrals. The finished products were beautiful and quite authentic-looking.
>
> Our computer teacher brought the most recent component to the Castle Project. She purchased the CD-ROM program *Destination: Castle*, an award-winning, introductory multimedia program from Edmark's Imagination Express. It provides medieval backdrops, music, cut-and-paste characters that can be animated, text tools for writing and sound tools for recording; there is even a dictionary of archaic terms. The computer teacher assigned children to work in pairs to create a story that was set in the Middle Ages and to bring it to life as a computer presentation. The social studies teacher and I gave the students a list of vocabulary words that had to be included in their final product. The stories were to be creative but true to the time period. The students used music, voice recordings, sound effects, animation techniques, scenic backgrounds and literary elements to form the stories.
>
> The finale for the Castle Project was the presentation of selected computer stories on a big-screen monitor to the principal, parents, grandparents, and the fifth grade. The stories were also printed out in color for display.
>
> Our Castle Project seems to be more successful and popular each time it is done, as we have drawn more teachers into the collaboration and made it truly cross-disciplinary.
>
> *Destination: Castle* is available for the Macintosh (which we used) and for DOS.

Televisions and Videocassette Recorders (VCRs): Tools for Thinking

Television has a prominent place in the lives of elementary school children. It is also a very accessible tool for classroom use. Television programs have the ability to make abstract ideas clearer to students by giving them an avenue other than words to the meaning of processes and events.

One of the drawbacks to the use of educational television for instructional purposes used to be scheduling—the program came on at a particular time and had to be watched then, if the teacher planned to get any educational value from it. Now, paired with a VCR, a television can deliver the instructional programming whenever it fits into the school day, not just when it is broadcast. (Note: You must follow the rules for taping of programs for educational use so that you do not violate copyright laws, but most programs can be taped for this purpose if they are used within a reasonable time and erased.) Of course, there are prerecorded videotapes available on any topic that you might want to present to your class. These use television as a delivery medium.

Valerie Lyle, a fifth-grade teacher in Illinois, had her students watch the segment of the television documentary *500 Nations* that was about the Mayas. The students then discussed the program segment in small groups; did library research on the Mayas, the Aztecs, and the Incas; and finally wrote a persuasive paper about which culture they would prefer (Strommen, 1995). This television presentation sparked critical thinking in order to discuss and choose a stance for the paper, problem solving as the students searched the library for further resources, and creative thinking as they wrote the paper. If computers had been available to Lyle's students, their use of technology could have included electronic encyclopedias, Internet searches, and word processing software for the production of the paper.

Television is a good tool for encouraging thinking strategies because there are many aspects of programming and advertising that can be critically analyzed. You need to teach your students to look at advertising critically, recognizing propaganda techniques and unrealistic claims that are meant to persuade buyers. You also need to teach them to analyze programming for its realism and values. You could follow up clips from a program supposedly set in a rain forest, for example, with a discussion of whether the rain forest was real and how they could tell, as one teacher has done (Strommen, 1995). Students then view the program with a scientist's eye and decide whether the setting is authentic or not, a valuable critical thinking activity. Books read in class can also be compared to the television movies or videos of the same selection, as the middle schoolers and university students in the opening vignette did with *Bridge to Terabithia*. The students discussed through e-mail the differences between the book and the video and if there were valid reasons for the differences. Most of the students were disgusted with the amount of detail that was left out of the video and the details that were changed "for no reason at all." They were particularly disturbed that in the video Leslie's father gave Jess the dog, for they believed that the book made a good point about Leslie's relationship with her father, when it showed that he was unable to part with Prince Terrien. They did recognize the reasons for some of the changes, however, and acknowledged that collapsing two different teachers into one character was probably dictated by the length of the video. Still, some maintained that the video downplayed the importance of the music teacher to Jess by merging her with the homeroom teacher, who was less empathetic.

Karen Wanamaker (1996) uses videos of *The Little House on the Prairie* television program to compare with segments of the *Little House* books. For example, she shows a video segment that includes a Christmas scene and then has the children read Chapters 18 and 19 of the book in order set the stage for them to compare and contrast Laura's Christmas with one of theirs.

Televisions and VCRs can also be teamed to allow students to create videos for viewing by the class. Students can first create original stories or poems, factual articles about school events or study topics, or profiles of each other based on interviews that they plan and conduct. Then they can work together to make these part of a video production (Strommen, 1995). Students may need to write transitions between readings or recitations by different students. This activity would entail an analysis of the various presentation pieces and the determination of connecting ideas or themes. The students who work the camera will need to choose camera angles, decide when to zoom in for close shots, and use appropriate transitions, such as fade-in and fade-out techniques. These activities also involve critical and creative thinking.

For distance-learning television programs, sometimes students and teachers can interact through telephone or fax communications, some criticisms of the passive educational television of the past. The ability to question the teacher of the television class or make comments encourages more thinking on the part of students. In addition, the classroom teacher is generally expected to be involved in the lesson as well (Strommen, 1995).

Thought-Provoking Question

What is a good way to encourage students to think critically about television programs?

Summary

There are many ways that you can use computers to teach thinking strategies and to provide practice in the use of these strategies. Different computer software encourages different levels of thinking. Some types of programs that you may use are drill-and-practice, simulation, interactive text, word processing and desktop publishing programs, and database programs. You may also use many electronic reference books for research. Use of the computer for electronic mail, Internet newsgroups or discussion groups, and Internet searches of web sites can all encourage higher-order thinking. Development of multimedia presentations involves a large number of thinking activities, as does programming the computer to perform tasks.

CD-ROMs and laser discs provide much content for thinking, as well as possibly providing interactive experiences of a variety of types. Television also can provide content, and it can be paired with a videocassette recorder to present content either from prerecorded tapes or from tapes that students have created themselves. Television programs for distance learning now sometimes allow interaction between students and teachers at remote sites through fax machines and telephones.

References

Allen, D. (1997). Teaching with technology: Math and science motivators. *Teaching K–8, 27*(4):16–17.

Anderson-Inman, L., and Horney, M. (1996/1997). Computer-based concept mapping: Enhancing literacy with tools for visual thinking. *Journal of Adolescent & Adult Literacy, 40*(4): 302–306.

Cotton, E.G. (1996). *The online classroom: Teaching with the Internet.* Bloomington, IN: ERIC Clearinghouse on Reading, English, and Communication.

Grabe, M., and Grabe, C. (1996). *Integrating technology for meaningful learning.* Boston: Houghton Mifflin.

Greeno, J.G., and Hall, R.P. (1997). Practicing representation: Learning with and about representational forms. *Phi Delta Kappan, 78*(5): 361–367.

Hartson, T. (1993). Kid-appeal science projects. *Computers in Education, 20*(6):33–36.

Heide, A., and Henderson, D. (1994). *The technological classroom: A blueprint for success*. Toronto: Trifolium Books.

Holzberg, C. S. (1995). Buyer's guide: Cross-cultural adventures. *Electronic Learning, 15*(3):38–41.

Hunter, B. (1985). Problem solving with data bases. *The Computing Teacher, 12*(8):20–27.

Lai, K. (1991). Integrating database activities into a primary school curriculum: Instructional procedures and outcomes. *Computers in the Schools, 8*(4):55–63.

Mancini, G.H. (1995). Special report on middle schools: Charting the course? *Electronic Learning, 15*(93): 22–23, 26.

Ryder, R.J., and Graves, M.F. (1996/1997). Using the Internet to enhance students' reading, writing, and information gathering skills. *Journal of Adolescent & Adult Literacy, 40*(4):244–245.

Ryder, R.J., and Hughes, T. (1997). *Internet for educators*. Columbus, OH: Prentice-Hall.

Serim, F., and Koch, M. (1996). Netlearning: Why teachers use the Internet. Sebastopol, CA: Songline Studios and O'Reilly and Associates.

Sharp, V. (1996). *Computer education for teachers* (2nd ed.). Madison, WI: Brown & Benchmark.

Stearns, P.H. (1995). Software-at-a-glance—Fresh new finds: *Science Sleuths. Electronic Learning, 15*(3):43.

Strommen, E. (1995). Television catches its second wave. *Electronic Learning, 15*(3):30–37, 57.

Wanamaker, K. (1996). *Learning from Laura*. Presented at the Tennessee Reading Association Conference, Gatlinburg, TN.

Wired education— The Internet: A valuable, integral part of the teaching process. (1996). *Curriculum Administrator, 30*(8):8.

Zimmerman, L. (1996). *Windows on science: The "write" language arts program for your students*. Presented at the Tennessee Reading Association Conference, Gatlinburg, TN.

IV

Creating Independent Learners

I asked the children,

"When do you need to be able to think outside school?"

and the children said:

> I think outside of school for whenever I go to the store. I use math!

> Weither you smoke or go to cdlege or what you eat and stuff like that.

> so when some one ask you to take drugs you can think about it.

> To know what to do

> So you can make diesouns between right & Wrong.

So you may solve personal problems, and problems that occur at home. Also so you can make decisions, like what to do with friends or family.

To make choices like not doing drugs.

To work out problems at home and at church and when you are with your friends

It's important to learn to think so you can make your own disisions in life!

When you are being pressured to do something you think is bad.

As we can see from the children's answers to this question, many are aware of how they use thinking strategies to make decisions about drugs, family problems, and so on. Few realize, however, that they will soon face increasingly complex problems, which make even greater demands on their ability to think through situations and make wise choices.

The sooner that children learn to think for themselves, the better they will be able to deal with day-to-day decision making and problem solving. If we place them in situations that cause them to think, allow them to take risks, and give them opportunities to evaluate the results, we are preparing them to be thoughtful, responsible adults.

This section consists of a single chapter, yet it is the culmination of all that has gone before. In the other chapters we considered different theories about thinking and recognized that students have preferences for certain ways of knowing, as in the theory of multiple intelligences. We recognized the importance of providing a comfortable emotional environment for thinking to flourish, and we saw the value of social interaction. We realized that children examine their thoughts through reading and writing and that questioning leads them to consider a variety of viewpoints. We saw how children learn to think as they make connections across the curriculum and expand their ways of knowing through thematic units, children's literature, graphic organizers, and technology.

In this chapter, we will look at how well children can apply their thinking strategies to real-world situations and use them to deal with issues that affect their lives. The chapter begins with encouraging students to reflect on their learning and evaluate the effectiveness of their work, and it concludes with helping them find ways to transfer thinking strategies from school to the outside world.

CHAPTER 11

Developing a Sense of Responsibility

When I asked the teachers,

"How can teachers help students to become responsible, independent learners?"

the teachers said:

- Give them more choices and more responsibility.
- Trust them to make responsible, valid decisions and to follow through and see the consequences of those decisions, good or bad.
- Give more opportunities in the classroom for students to make their own decisions about their learning.
- Reassure them that there are no silly questions. Teach them to be question askers—to research, read, and seek answers!
- Give the students positive reinforcement when they make decisions and take responsibility.
- Be a role model by showing how you make decisions and implement them.
- Guide them and allow them to find the answers or figure out how to solve their own problems.
- Let students set goals for themselves and evaluate their progress toward these goals.

How would you answer this question?

Concepts to watch for

- The importance of reflecting for learning
- The value of setting goals
- Types of self-evaluation
- Ways that teachers can help students make a transition from teacher-direction to self-regulation
- Ways that teachers can facilitate independent learning
- Applications of thinking strategies to real-life issues

Lesley Wing Jan's sixth-grade students were finding answers to questions about an excursion they were planning to Wilson's Prom. When some questions were followed by "Why?" or "Why not?", Lesley helped the children realize that they could use *because* to connect their statements to their reasons instead of writing two short sentences. During the lesson, Lesley helped them find other ways to make their writing clear.

At the conclusion of the lesson, Lesley asked the students to close their eyes and think about what they had learned. They then shared what they had learned with the class. Through this process of reflection, Lesley helped the children recall what was meaningful to them and internalize her teachings.

Reflection

Reflection is the thoughtful consideration of the meaning and implications of experiences; it is a way to develop intrapersonal intelligence. Reflection enhances students' abilities to assume responsibility for their learning, and it leads to metacognitive thinking which in turn leads to improved decision making (Wilson and Wing Jan, 1993). In the classroom, reflection may refer to the way in which a learner is able to see the value of a skill or process and apply it to future situations. For instance, the students in the previous vignette may realize that *because* is a useful connector and may thus use it on other occasions.

Because each teaching day is so full, it is tempting to rush from one lesson into another. Taking a few moments for students to reflect on a lesson, however, is time well spent because it helps students sort out what is meaningful and think of ways to apply new knowledge to other situations. Reflection locks in learning instead of letting it drift off into a soon-to-be-forgotten realm.

Setting conditions in which reflective thinking may occur involves providing opportunities for reflection through modeling and guidance during whole-class discussions, offering recognition and support for good thinking, and setting aside time for students to reflect. You model by explaining how a recent experience affected or changed you, and you guide by leading children to discover meanings from their experiences. You may provide quiet, restful areas where children can go to ponder recent experiences on their own, or you may form groups to encourage children to discuss their views of a shared experience. Through collaboration and conversation, children can see experiences from different points of view, thus opening up new choices and possibilities (Crafton and Burke, 1994).

Children who become reflective thinkers are able to listen to themselves, but they must first be able to listen to each other (Graves, 1994). The reflective learner can listen to others and keep their thoughts in mind while listening to his or her own thoughts. In other words, the reflective learner shifts back and forth among the different points of view being expressed while simultaneously maintaining or modifying his or her own views.

Journals and various types of learning logs offer opportunities for students to think about and comment on their learning (Routman, 1994). At the end of a special event, each day, or a week, children can record reflections in their journals. Writing their thoughts makes them aware of what they learned and, in the case of dialogue journals, enables you to identify any misconceptions they hold and find out what they thought was important from your lesson. You may find, however, as I did with my college students, that some students will simply give you the facts of the lesson or experience, not their reflections. If this happens, you may need to model explicitly what you mean by writing your own reflections of a lesson on a transparency that is projected for the class to see.

Thought-Provoking Idea

Here are some options for reflecting:
1. Have students close their eyes and recall what they learned and what they think about it.
2. Ask students to share the most important thing they learned with a partner.
3. Before they leave school each day, have students record entries in a journal of something new they learned.

In order to help children learn to reflect, you may want to focus on some key questions, both for class discussion and journal writing. Try using the prompts in Figure 11-1.

Figure 11-1. Prompts for Reflection

Ask yourself the following questions:
- What did I learn?
- How can I use what I learned?
- How does what I learned change the way in which I think about things?
- What will I remember for a long time?
- What surprised me?
- How did I learn it?
- What helped me most as I learned?
- What still confuses me?
- What else do I want to find out?

Reflective thinking is particularly valuable in various content areas. As children share their views of books and authors during literature response groups, they gain new insights and discover diverse ways to interpret literature. By sharing thoughts about environmental and multicultural issues, they expand their understanding of worldwide concerns. As they look back on history, they see evidence of great leadership or social injustice. They are likely to remember their reflections and shared observations long after the facts have slipped away.

Thought-Provoking Idea

Occasionally, at the end of an important lesson or after a significant experience, give the children 3 x 5 inch index cards. Ask them to write something specific they learned on one side and something they still need to know on the other side.

If reflection is effective, it results in changed behavior or attitudes. Through reflection, students learn to think critically in order to analyze what they have experienced and to think creatively in order to transfer and apply experiences to new situations. Such thinking, if acted upon, challenges learners to adopt more informed attitudes and modify former behavior patterns. Change may be difficult to implement because it often brings with it uncertainty, risk, and anxiety, but when successful, it results in excitement, approval, and satisfaction (Wilson and Wing Jan, 1993).

Goal setting and monitoring provide opportunities for reflective thinking and taking responsibility for learning. As children establish goals, they need to think about what they already know and still want to learn, as well as what they can do and wish they could do. You can model goal setting at the beginning of the school year by asking the children to brainstorm things they want to learn and do during the year. With the class, monitor progress periodically by referring back to the original set of goals, checking off those that have been achieved, and reconsidering those yet to be completed. Team goals work well in cooperative learning situations.

In a similar way, children can establish personal goals. You can guide them to reflect on what they might realistically accomplish and how they could achieve it. At first, goals may be simple and short-term, such as getting a good score on a spelling test. Later, however, guide children into forming more meaningful, long-term goals, which might include the following:

- Getting along better with classmates
- Completing work on time
- Finding ways to be helpful to others
- Being a good sport, even when losing
- Paying attention in class
- Doing my share of the work in groups

Many of these goals, though worthy, are hard to measure, so they may need to be broken down into specific behaviors.

Students need to reassess their goals periodically, perhaps every six weeks, and reflect on the progress they are making toward reaching them. They may want to keep a separate journal for entering their goals and recording their progress and setbacks. If they discover that some goals are unrealistic, they may wish to modify them or create new goals to replace them. Children can get feedback about their goals from discussions with their peers in small groups or from conferences with you. When children have reached their goals or are making significant progress toward them, give them recognition through praise or by allowing them to share their achievements with the class. Setting and reaching personal goals is an important step toward learning independently and assuming responsibility.

Self-Evaluation

Closely linked to reflection, self-evaluation is the process of objectively analyzing one's own performance, attitudes, and interests for the purposes of self-understanding and self-improvement. Although the teacher usually assigns grades, the students' own perceptions of their strengths and weaknesses are often more revealing. Self-evaluation enables students to make reasoned, supportable judgments about their progress. As they reflect on their work and evaluate its worth, they are taking steps toward becoming independent learners, capable of making decisions and guiding their own activities. Some benefits of self-evaluation are given in Figure 11-2.

Figure 11-2. Benefits of Self-Evaluation

Requires students to take responsibility for their learning
Promotes critical and creative thinking
Makes students aware of their strengths and weaknesses
Increases the likelihood of discovering misconceptions or the use of poor strategies before they become habitual
Causes students to become aware of standards or expectations
Lets students keep personal records of progress based on standards and individual goals
Enables students to participate actively in their education
Helps students realize how they learn best
Gives teachers insights into students' perceptions of themselves
Increases the likelihood of constructive change when students discover their own needs

Fostering Self-Evaluation

Young children intuitively know what they like and what they dislike before they are inhibited by the standards of others. Evaluation comes to them naturally. Before children can become effective self-evaluators, however, they need to understand the criteria for evaluating their work, be familiar with the terminology, and develop confidence in their ability to make judgments. Participating in class discussions and seeing models of exemplary work help them develop proficiency in these areas. For example, a teacher might help students develop self-evaluative skills after a writing lesson by doing the following:

- Using appropriate terminology, such as *first draft, voice, editing, insertion, caret, proofreading* and *revision,* so that students can discuss their work
- Showing and discussing samples of students' work (with student permission, of course)
- Raising questions about their writing to make them aware of their strengths and potential weaknesses
- Guiding students in a discussion of what to look for in good writing

The teacher might then ask each student to select a piece of writing to read to a partner, to evaluate it for the partner, and to ask for the partner's response to the evaluation and for any additional comments. Students can follow this same procedure in small groups until they develop an understanding of what to look for when evaluating their work. In order to give feedback to their peers, students need to give constructive criticism rather than make negative, unkind remarks that only destroy confidence. Students should realize that they are not competing with other students in their self-evaluations but are looking for progress in their own work.

Students can judge their work against a *rubric,* a set of criteria that describes different levels of proficiency in certain areas. Although rubrics can be much more complex, Figure 11-3 gives a simple rubric for evaluating the content of a piece of writing.

Figure 11-3. Rubric for Evaluating Writing Content

Level 3: Well organized, interesting, clear
Level 2: Somewhat disorganized and confusing
Level 1: Poorly organized, unclear, not interesting

Students can help develop the rubrics to be used and can thus become familiar with standards and terminology. Samples of writing might accompany each level so that students can see how to apply the levels to their own work.

Helping children become good self-evaluators takes time and practice. Although children may be able to select the work they like best, they may not be able to tell you *why* this piece is their best. Through conferences, minilessons, and feedback from other children, they can gradually acquire skill and confidence in making evaluations. Evaluation, after all, is the most advanced skill in Bloom's taxonomy; it represents higher-order thinking and may not be developed easily. Here are some guidelines for helping students avoid problems they may encounter as they attempt to evaluate themselves and their work.

- Use self-evaluation sparingly so that it doesn't become tedious and eventually meaningless.
- Provide students with the special vocabulary they need to articulate their feelings about their work.
- Encourage students to recognize their own needs and set their own goals instead of doing these things for them.
- Accept students' evaluations if they are reasonable, even if they don't necessarily agree with yours.

If discrepancies occur regularly between your evaluation and a student's evaluation, you may need to spend some time conferring with that student about criteria for evaluation. Students are basically honest in their self-evaluations, and, for the most part, teacher and student evaluations agree. When disagreement occurs regularly, however, you should confer with the student. Perhaps you are overlooking something that the student is doing that deserves credit, or perhaps the student misunderstands your expectations. In any case, you should both have the opportunity to provide supporting evidence and communicate your reasons.

Types of Self-Evaluation

Self-evaluation takes many forms, ranging from informal to formal. Children make such casual remarks about their work as "This is really sloppy" or "I really like the way this turned out" many times during the day. Self-evaluation also occurs as students establish and review their goals, complete forms, select pieces for their portfolios, lead parent conferences, and evaluate group work. Many of their thoughts grow out of the types of reflective questions suggested in Figure 11-1.

Goals

Goals should be the basis for evaluating progress. Class goals may be negotiated between the teacher and the students on the basis of curriculum mandates, student interests, and observed needs, and student goals reflect what the students want to accomplish for themselves. When students are allowed to set personal goals, they need time and resources to work on them, either in or out of class. Setting their own goals motivates students to reach them because they have a personal investment in them. When evaluating their progress, students consider how far along they are toward achieving their goals. Thus, goals provide purpose and also serve as measuring sticks.

Student-Written Report Cards

Because students are already familiar with the format, filling in their own report cards is an easy way for them to understand how to evaluate themselves. Near the conclusion of each reporting period, give students copies of the report card form and ask them to fill in the grades they think they have earned and to write comments about their overall performance. Encourage them to reflect on their accomplishments, areas that still need improvement, and progress that has been made in each area. Such evaluation works well with students at all grade levels and with those of widely differing abilities (Anthony et al., 1991).

Checklists and Other Forms

Students can evaluate themselves in any subject area, as well as in preferred styles of learning, attitudes, interests, and social interactions. Com-

paring self-evaluations over time enables them to see how they are growing and what they need to improve. Remind them to date each evaluation.
They can use a variety of forms to do this, such as those suggested here.
You may want to distribute forms or let students create their own. Since
young children are unable to read much, you can read statements to them
and ask them to mark the faces that match their responses, as in Figure
11-4.

Figure 11-4. Response Form for Young Children

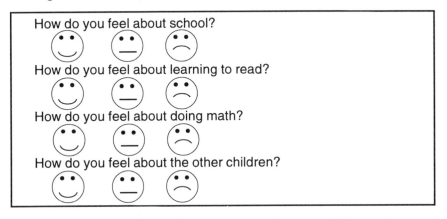

You can ask older children the same types of open-ended questions and
let them respond in writing.

Jill Ramsey asked her third graders to evaluate their work and select
the best piece to share at home. As you can see from the form in Figure
11-5, each child identifies the piece of work and tells why it is the best.
The child takes the work sample and the form home, a parent or caregiver
responds with comments, the child returns the form to the teacher, and
the teacher signs it and may add a comment. This process involves self-
evaluation and results in three-way communication. In this case, Rachel
Fox selected an illustrated report she wrote about Valentina Tereshkova,
the first woman in space. (The form is adapted from one used by Sue
Reynolds, Warrandyte School, Victoria, Australia.)

To make students aware of what they know and can do, Jeni Wilson
and Lesley Wing Jan (1993) suggest using a form that lets students list
their accomplishments. For example, at the top of the paper a student
might write: *Things I Know About Math.* Under this heading the student
identifies those skills already learned. This list can be ongoing, with new
skills being added as students learn them. You can apply this simple form
to any area.

When using checklists, students can respond by writing *yes* or *no*, or
they can use a rating scale such as the one shown in Figure 11-6.

Figure 11-5. Self-Evaluation

Date _Feb, 2_____

Dear _mom é dad_____

Today I am bringing home my best work in ___writing_____

to show you.

I am proud of this work because _I tried my best_
to show that I like doing my
work. Most of my help comes
from my teacher Mrs. Ramsey

Please write a comment here about my work. _I'm proud of_
the effort + pride Rachel puts in her
school work. She really puts her imagination
to work.

Teacher's signature _Jill Ramsey_____

I liked reading Rachel's report. It
was informational as well as imaginative.
She really thought about what she wanted
to say.

Figure 11-6. Self-Evaluation Rating Scale: How I Learn

Mark your responses as follows:

5 = always   4 = usually   3 = sometimes   2 = rarely   1 = never

When I learn something new, it helps me if I can:

a. _____ Picture it in my mind

b. _____ Talk it over with someone

c. _____ Write it down

d. _____ Be alone and think about it

e. _____ Make a chant of key ideas and say them over and over

f. _____ Read about it

g. _____ Draw a diagram of it

h. _____ Go through the motions

What helps you most to learn something? _____

_____

_____

From this information, students can begin to analyze their preferred learning styles and recognize their strengths. They can also find ways to expand the ways they learn by trying some strategies that they use infrequently or not at all.

Portfolios

A *portfolio* is a collection of student work over a period of time, with each piece dated so that changes can be observed through the year. Both teacher and students may select items for inclusion, but students should choose most of the items if they are to feel a sense of ownership. In order for a piece to merit inclusion in a portfolio of limited size, the student must consider it to be outstanding or representative, perhaps in one of the following ways:

- Creativity or originality
- A breakthrough in learning
- Something worth sharing with others
- A well-crafted story
- Something worth keeping and remembering
- A piece of work that shows change in thinking or beliefs

Whatever the reason, the student should be able to justify the inclusion. Many teachers ask the student to attach a short paper stating the reason for selecting a particular piece. Such a request causes the student to evaluate each piece of work carefully in order to decide which selections to include.

Melody Caroline Boze, a second grader, experienced a breakthrough in learning when she wrote a story about a selfish butterfly. She realized for the first time that she was a writer, and she has been writing ever since. In Figure 11-7, Melody explains her awareness of becoming a writer and follows this with her story.

Figure 11-7. Portfolio Selection

This is my portfolio and these paprs are my verey best, best,best. The selifsh buttrfly was my best. When I was doing it I thot abaut how pretty ther colors were pink, purppl, blue, gree, oreng, and gold. I started writing and every thing jest came in my head. I did't know I was a writer untell I wrote this story. Then I new I was.

Melody
Caroline
Boze

figure 11-7 continued on following page

figure 11-7 continued from previous page

The Selfish Butterfly

One day there were hundreds of butterflies, all colors. There were pink, purple, blue, green, orange, red and gold.

The butterfties were so happy they flew around all day for every creature in the forest to see. The animals in the forest were glad to see them. They made everyone feel good about themselves.

Then one day one butterfly decided he wanted to be the prettiest butterfly in the forest. One night he went to every butterfly, and stole their colors for himself.

The next day the butterflies woke up to find they had no color." Everyone in the forest went to find the one selfish butterfly. When they found him they told him " Just because you are pretty on the outside, doesn't make you pretty on the inside."

figure 11-7 continued on following page

figure 11-7 continued from previous page

Pretty is as pretty does. This Made the Selfish butterfly Sad, So he decided to give back the Colors to every butterfly. The animals were glad to See the butter flies and their beautiful Colors again. Even the Selfish butterfly was happy.

So always rember this is the reason there are So many colors of butterflies and why we feel happy When we See them.

Student-Led Conferences

Parent-teacher conferences do not typically include students, who are often the last to know what the teacher thinks about their performance. If students are present, they are often silent witnesses to what the teacher has to say about them. Such conferences fail to consider students' own perceptions of their progress.

In student-led conferences, however, students assume a leadership role and discuss their goals and achievements with their parents. Student-led conferences give students an authentic context for self-evaluation and enable them to assume some of the responsibility for communicating their progress to their parents (Anthony et al., 1991). Many thinking strategies come into play as students prepare for and execute conferences, including reflection, evaluation, organization, and decision making.

In order to take responsibility for the conference, students must prepare carefully by selecting representative samples of their work, perhaps organized in a portfolio, and thoughtfully considering areas of strengths and possible difficulties. Marsha Riss (Lenski et al., 1996) helps her fifth graders learn to evaluate their work and concludes the year with student-led conferences. Periodically during the year, she asks her students to prepare Thinking Sheets that give reflections on their work about what they do well, what they need to improve, how to improve, and what goals they have for the rest of the year. In the spring they summarize the material from the Thinking Sheets and add a space for parents to write comments at the end of the conference.

Students also prepare by planning an agenda and role playing a conference. The agenda keeps students on track during the role playing and the conference, and it consists of the following items:

- Sharing information from the summary sheet
- Sharing projects and portfolio papers
- Having parents write messages
- Looking at room projects together
- Having parents sign the guest book and write remarks

Marsha believes that student-led conferences enable the students to reflect on and assume responsibility for their learning.

Terri Austin (1994) leads her students through a similar process, but she includes practice sessions with education students from a local college, who act as stand-ins for parents prior to the actual conferences. After the college students leave, Terri asks her students to do reflective fast-writes to encourage them to think about what went well and what changes to make. Following the parent conferences, Terri's students think about their successes, compare practice sessions with parent meetings, and consider what surprised them most during the conferences.

Team or Group Evaluation

With much learning occurring in groups these days, children can use the same types of procedures that they use individually to evaluate themselves as team members (Ellis and Whalen, 1990). Of course, the criteria would shift from evaluation of the student's own work to evaluation of the student's contributions to group projects. Sample criteria might look like this:

- I listened attentively to the ideas of others.
- I contributed worthwhile ideas.
- I did my share of the work.
- I was an active part of my group.

In addition, children can evaluate progress for the team as a whole. At the conclusion of some group sessions, give students time to discuss their work as a team. Encourage the students to give reasons to support their evaluative statements. By listening in on these discussions, you will learn a great deal about the group's effectiveness. Also, occasionally ask group members to complete forms with criteria about the group, such as the following:

- We stay on task and are making progress.
- We encourage each other.
- Each person has a chance to contribute.
- We build on each other's ideas.

Thought-Provoking Idea

For a quick check when you have only a little time, ask students to give a "thumbs up" if they're pleased with the group's work that day, "thumbs down" if they're displeased, and "thumbs to the side" if their feelings are mixed (Ellis and Whalen, 1990).

Thinking Beyond the Classroom

Seated at commencement, I heard the speaker emphasize the importance of knowledge. He continued, however, by saying, "Let your mind be a workshop, not a storehouse." By saying this, he brought home the point that our minds are not merely for acquiring and storing information, but they are active, processing, thinking organisms that enable us to grow in understanding and wisdom as we deal with real-world issues.

Although thinking should be valued in the classroom, it is *essential* for intelligent, responsible life in the world beyond the classroom. Children and adults in today's world confront situations that demand critical thinking. It is not enough to make superficial judgments or go along with the crowd; in fact, doing so often results in careless, irresponsible decisions that can destroy lives. Many elementary school students already have to deal with adult-size problems that they are poorly equipped to handle. Already, as noted in the students' comments at the beginning of this section, children recognize the need to think in order to make decisions about the use of drugs and to deal with family problems. Rebecca Boucher expanded on her answer to the question about the need for thinking outside school as shown in Figure 11-8.

Helping Students Acquire Lifelong Thinking Strategies

As students acquire knowledge and skills, the result of each learning experience enhances their ability to approach future learning tasks (Bull, 1989). Education in thinking strategies, beginning early in life, prepares individuals to deal with hard issues later on. Previous chapters have dealt with ways to promote thinking strategies, but here the focus is on those strategies that are particularly useful in adult life. Figure 11-9 identifies some highly useful thinking strategies for consumers and citizens in an adult world.

Figure 11-8. The Need to Think

If you don't think, then you can't work out problems not only in school, but in homelife, too. When you grow up, you need to think out problems because maybe you just got a job at a gas station with the wages $4.25 an hour. You are married with three kids. You are behind in the house payments, you had to sell your car, and you can barely get food on the table. Your wife can't work because she is pregnant with the 4th kid. Not only do you have to work out your financial problems, which require thinking, but you also have to work out your mental problems, which also require thinking.

Figure 11-9. Useful Thinking Strategies for Adults

Analyzing issues from more than one point of view

Separating fact from propaganda, exaggeration, and emotional appeal

Evaluating political candidates and voting for the best

Making decisions that are based on logic and reason (particularly in relation to careers, friends, habits, and finances)

Setting, evaluating, and modifying goals

Finding and solving problems creatively and with ingenuity

Taking risks when viable opportunities arise

Recognizing alternatives and making wise choices

Generating questions that may lead to new ideas

Thought-Provoking Question

What other thinking strategies do adults need to perform as responsible consumers and citizens?

Making the Transition From Teacher-Directed to Student-Centered Learning

How do you take children who have never had opportunities to think for themselves and turn them into independent thinkers? Students who are used to being told what to do and how to do it often find it difficult to make decisions and choices. Teachers will tell you that the transition from traditional teaching to student-centered learning is a matter of gradually relinquishing control and letting students make decisions for themselves. The procedure, though not always easy, is definitely worthwhile.

The following examples show how teachers created situations in which students gradually assumed more control of their learning. Joyce Wiencek and John O'Flahavan (1994) moved from teacher-led to peer discussions of literature. The students learned to choose their own texts, form their own groups, challenge and build on each other's thinking, evaluate themselves, and set new goals. When Marsha Riss (Lenski et al., 1996) began to reduce her leadership and transfer ownership to her fifth graders, she first asked them to think about how they learned and to set goals. They learned to use an appropriate vocabulary for discussing and role playing their progress in their schoolwork, and they were able to conduct student-led parent conferences by the end of the school year. Sixth graders in Catherine Doane's class, who were studying global issues, began to assume greater responsibility for directing their own activities. Catherine said, "My gradual releasing of control to the students resulted in outcomes far surpassing all expectations" (1993, p. 21).

Negotiation is a bridge between teacher-directed and student-centered learning. Students and teachers participate in making decisions about learning by reflecting on their needs and identifying actions that benefit all of them. Negotiation requires active listening, questioning, discussion, and thinking strategies, and it helps students take responsibility for their learning (Wilson and Wing Jan, 1993). It encourages students to consider the pros and cons of different situations and to review their decisions periodically. Negotiation is a real-world skill, particularly in the area of labor-management relations, so its use prepares students for dealing with issues in the outside world.

Not everything in the classroom is negotiable. Some skills and content are mandated, and some behavioral policies are established schoolwide. In the children's literature class I teach at the University, some things are negotiable and others are not. For example, the students will take a final exam, but they can negotiate the time for it. Each group will make a big book, but the students can decide who will work with them in groups, when it is due, and how to design it. They will teach a unit, but they can work out their own time and topic.

Thought-Provoking Question

What is negotiable in your classroom? Is there anything else that could be negotiable?

Pathways to Independent, Responsible Living

Many pathways lead to independent, responsible living, and we will look at some of them here. Where a classroom community of inquiry exists, children are free to listen and speak with open minds, consider various points of view, and sort out their feelings about a variety of beliefs and lifestyles. Although some parents fear indoctrination, just the reverse is true. Children are building foundations for their beliefs through reasoning that can withstand critical appraisal. The capacity to think reflectively and independently ensures that students are committed to supporting their values (Wilks, 1995).

Thought-Provoking Idea

To prevent or respond to criticism, invite parents to join you when you conduct an open discussion.

We follow another pathway when we learn to respect others, regardless of how they differ from us. Individuals from different cultural, ethnic, or religious backgrounds observe various customs and beliefs. We may interpret words, gestures, and facial expressions differently and sometimes misunderstand one another. The move toward inclusion helps students value all learners and realize that we all might need help from one another at times. Understanding and appreciating diversity not only builds respect, but it also broadens our otherwise limited cultural horizons.

Often, linguistic and mathematical prowess is valued above other ways of knowing in the classroom. Being aware that students can demonstrate knowledge and understanding through a variety of intelligences helps us appreciate and respect others who may not learn best in traditional ways.

Literature offers another pathway to creating the character of future citizens (Pradl, 1996). Literature urges us to think openly and reflectively in order to deal with conflicting emotions and interpretations. It helps us understand ways that people think and act in various cultures and in different historical periods. Children discover connections between literature and life and are thus equipped to generalize their understandings of people and issues to the world at large (Tompkins and McGee, 1993).

Authentic Classroom Experiences

Students see little relevance to real life from completing workbook pages and adding up rows of math problems. When such skills are embedded in problem-solving activities, however, their usefulness is readily apparent. New science programs, in order to prepare students for a technological world, are emphasizing student-initiated questions and offering hands-on activities. Sharon Brown-Hall, a sixth-grade teacher, challenged her students to design architecturally sound, freestanding structures. She claims that by working cooperatively and using their knowledge of science and math to solve problems, students are learning the basics of engineering (Ryan, 1997).

Authentic classroom experiences lead to real-world applications. Based on a town council model of subcommittees, middle-school students in Attleboro, Massachusetts, set up committees to meet their needs, thus learning how to control much of their classroom community (Blythe and Bradbury, 1993). Using a variety of thinking strategies, students learn such management techniques as brainstorming, setting and prioritizing goals, analyzing and completing tasks, selecting roles, identifying problems and solutions, and evaluating results. Students agree that such experiences show them that they can make a difference in the world and give them the skills needed to participate in governing their city, state, or country.

Fifth graders in Virginia are on the way to becoming lifelong learners by serving as museum curators for an Egyptian exhibit as part of the Museum-in-Progress program (Koetsch et al., 1994). Students brainstormed what artifacts to include, did library research, and selected sixteen topics they felt were necessary to study a civilization. Because of the variety of resources presented—art, music, hands-on exhibits, and a walk-in pyramid—many students, especially those with learning disabilities and those whose first language was not English, responded more completely than they did to traditional lessons. As museum curators, students became problem solvers and initiators of inquiry-based learning.

In other classrooms students get involved in community, national, and global issues. I watched sixth-grade children in Caroline Hammond's

Future Problem–Solving Program animatedly discussing and working out solutions to hypothetical community problems. Leaders emerged from each group as students brainstormed solutions and voted for the best one. Sixth graders in Glenview, Illinois, conducted in-depth research on such issues as gun control, homelessness, world hunger, and police brutality in connection with their unit on global education (Doane, 1993). Goals were to integrate approaches to learning, apply new knowledge to meaningful tasks, and collaborate with others.

Many students participate in community service projects ranging from making up Thanksgiving baskets and recycling cans to extensive environmental cleanups and tree plantings (Woehrle, 1993). In the school district where I live, schools establish partnerships with stores, businesses, and health care facilities. In a partnership between an elementary school and a nursing home, both children and nursing home residents benefited most from the pleasure of getting to know each other through conversation. In addition, children sang for the residents and made holiday decorations, and the nursing home staff attended academic bowls and provided prizes for the winners. As a result of their interactions, children realized the needs, interests, and worth of the elderly, and the elderly fondly relived their early years.

Partnerships also expose students to a variety of career choices and enable partners to learn from each other about the need for intelligent and creative behavior (Costa, 1991). During career education programs students learn what reasoning, cooperative skills, and creative problem-solving strategies are needed by various occupations.

Transferring Thinking to Home and Beyond

The ultimate goal of teaching students to think is enabling them to apply school-learned strategies to real-life situations, according to Art Costa (1991). Many students proficient in knowledge and skills, however, need help in transferring knowledge learned in school.

When children are encouraged to think in class, parents often report changes in student behaviors at home. They notice that students show increased interest in school, better planning in use of time, and improved organization of their work areas (Costa, 1991). Parents also observe differences in dinner table conversations as children point out contradictions, explore different points of view, and ask for reasons to support statements (Wilks, 1995).

Years from now when elementary-school students prepare to enter the world of work, they will find that business and industry expect them to be able to use their minds (Costa, 1991). Value is being placed on creativity, identifying problems as they arise, collaborative problem solving, processing huge amounts of information, and finding ways to deliver products quickly, efficiently, and economically. Because future workers are likely to change jobs several times during their careers, they need to develop flexibility, the ability to deal with ambiguities, and a willingness to continue learning. Management is stressing environments in which the growth and empowerment of individuals are the keys to success.

In businesses, Total Quality Management (TQM) is a widely accepted concept. It uses teams so that employees can share and build on each other's ideas in order to find the best possible solutions. Collaboration in school projects prepares students to work constructively in later years as team members.

Students preparing for responsible citizenship must be able to think for themselves and act on their decisions. As teachers, we have the opportunity and obligation to infuse young minds with essential thinking strategies.

Summary

Students need to take time to reflect on what they have learned. This reflection may occur as students write entries in journals or logs or as they respond to prompts from the teacher. Reflection also occurs when lessons or thematic units conclude, and students discuss what their new knowledge means to them. By setting goals, students reflect on what they already know and still need to learn.

Instead of teachers assuming total responsibility for evaluating student progress, students should also evaluate their work. They should reflect on what they've done, consider how well they've met their goals, and evaluate their progress. Self-evaluation encourages students to come to know themselves by closely observing their own work.

The world outside school calls for a variety of thinking strategies. Through negotiation and the gradual relinquishing of control, teachers help students acquire strategies they will need later in life. Students in many classrooms are assuming responsibility for their learning as they engage in authentic experiences, and many are beginning to transfer their thinking strategies from school to the world beyond.

References

Anthony, R., Johnson, T., Mickelson, N., and Preece, A. (1991). *Evaluating literacy: A perspective for change.* Portsmouth, NH: Heinemann.

Austin, T. (1994). *Changing the view: Student-led parent conferences.* Portsmouth, NH: Heinemann.

Beyer, B. (1995). *Critical thinking.* Bloomington, IN: Phi Delta Kappa.

Biemiller, A., and Meichenbaum, D. (1992). The nature and nurture of the self-directed learner. *Educational Leadership, 50*(2): 75–80.

Blythe, M., and Bradbury, P. (1993). Classroom by committee. *Educational Leadership, 50*(7):56–58.

Bull, G. (1989). *Reflective teaching*. Carlton South, Victoria: Australian Reading Association.

Burke, K. (1993). *How to assess thoughtful outcomes*. Palatine, IL: IRI/ Skylight.

Church, E.B. (1996). Time for reflection. *Early Childhood Today, 10*(8): 20–21.

Commeyras, M. (1993). Promoting critical thinking through dialogical-thinking reading lessons. *The Reading Teacher, 46*(6): 486–493.

Costa, A. (1991). *The school as a home for the mind*. Palatine, IL: Skylight.

Crafton, L., and Burke, C. (1994). Inquiry-based evaluation: Teachers and students reflecting together. *Primary Voices K–6, 2*(2): 2–7.

Doane, C. (1993). Global issues in 6th grade? Yes! *Educational Leadership, 50*(7): 19–21.

Ellis, S., and Whalen, S. (1990). *Cooperative learning*. New York: Scholastic.

Farr, R., and Tone, B. (1994). *Portfolio and performance assessment*. Fort Worth, TX: Harcourt Brace.

Froese, V. (1996). Assessment: Form and function. In *Whole language* (2nd ed.). Boston: Allyn & Bacon.

Graves, D. (1994). *A fresh look at writing*. Portsmouth, NH: Heinemann.

Gwiazda, C. (1995). *Improving classroom instruction through multiple intelligences*. Presentation at National Council of Teachers of English Annual Convention, San Diego.

Hansen, J. (1994). Literacy portfolios: Windows on potential. In S. Valencia, E. Hiebert, and P. Afflerbach (Eds.), *Authentic reading assessment: Practices and possibilities*. Newark, DE: International Reading Association.

Hill, B., and Ruptic, C. (1994). *Practical aspects of authentic assessment: Putting the pieces together*. Norwood, MA: Christopher-Gordon.

Johnston, P. (1992). *Constructive evaluation of literate activity*. New York: Longman.

Judd, D. (1989). Kids' report. *Teaching K–8, 20*(1): 91.

Koetsch, P., Daniels, M., Goldman, T., and Leahy, C. (1994). Student curators: Becoming lifelong learners. *Educational Leadership, 51*(5): 54–57.

Leland, C., and Harste, J. (1994). Multiple ways of knowing: Curriculum in a new key. *Language Arts, 71*(5): 337–345.

Lenski, S.D., Riss, M., and Flickinger, G. (1996). Honoring self-evaluation in the classroom community. *Primary Voices K–6, 4*(2): 24–32.

Logan, K., Diaz, E., Piperno, M., Rankin, D., MacFarland, A.D., and Bargamian, K. (1994/1995). How inclusion built a community of learners. *Educational Leadership, 52*(4): 42–44.

Pradl, G. (1996). Reading and democracy: The enduring influence of Louise Rosenblatt. *The New Advocate, 9*(1): 9–22.

Routman, R. (1994). *Invitations*, (2nd ed.). Portsmouth, NH: Heinemann.

Ryan, M. (January 19, 1997). Have our schools heard the wake-up call? *Parade.*

Short, K., and Burke, C. (1991). *Creating curriculum.* Portsmouth, NH: Heinemann.

Tompkins, G., and McGee, L. (1993). *Teaching reading with literature.* New York: Merrill.

Wallach, C., and Callahan, S. (1994). The 1st grade plant museum. *Educational Leadership, 52*(3):32–34.

Wiencek, J., and O'Flahavan, J. (1994). From teacher-led to peer discussions about literature: Suggestions for making the shift. *Language Arts, 71*(7):488–498.

Wilks, S. (1995). *Critical & creative thinking.* Portsmouth, NH: Heinemann.

Wilson, J., and Wing Jan, L. (1993). *Thinking for themselves.* Portsmouth, NH: Heinemann.

Woehrle, T. (1993). Growing up responsible. *Educational Leadership, 51*(3):40–43.

Expanded Professional Version

CHAPTER 12

Preparations for Professional Development

Although some teachers may believe that higher-order thinking is an unnecessary frill added to an already crowded curriculum, they should realize the importance of incorporating thinking strategies into their teaching. The need for problem solvers, decision makers, and critical thinkers has never been greater. Giving teachers ways to integrate thinking with content areas and the language arts will help them realize that thinking is not an add-on, but a way of teaching that values student inquiry. Students can learn fundamental facts and skills along with thinking strategies as they investigate authentic questions arising from their natural curiosity.

Many teachers are reluctant to tackle thinking strategies because they feel inadequate. They feel secure as long as they follow a manual, but teaching students to think asks them to move beyond the instructor's guide and respond thoughtfully to students' inquiries. They are uncertain about the vocabulary of thinking and the processes involved. They are hesitant about their ability to ask questions that cause students to think, and they are unsure how to respond to students who raise questions of their own.

Many teachers worry about involving all their students, especially those who seem unable to learn in traditional ways. The discussion in Chapter 2 addresses ways to meet the needs of diverse learners. As schools are adopting a policy of inclusion, teachers need to find ways to get all children to think, including those with various disabilities and nontraditional ways of learning.

Professional development can help teachers gain confidence and skill in their ability to promote thinking strategies. Showing them ways to integrate thinking across the curriculum relieves them of the problem of setting aside a special time to teach thinking in isolation. Demonstrating ways to enable all children to think by recognizing their multiple intelligences and special needs helps teachers realize that there are many ways to involve students in thinking processes.

This chapter contains preparations for providing professional development that will help teachers promote thinking in their classrooms. The focus is on ways to use this book, how to administer a needs assessment, and practical aspects of planning. Chapter 13 presents ideas for implementing professional development, including peer coaching and study groups, as well as evaluation and follow-up. Chapter 14 contains ideas for conducting inservice sessions and chapter-by-chapter suggestions for discussion and activities.

On Using This Book

This text is designed to facilitate the implementation of thinking across the curriculum. It is divided into four sections and eleven chapters. The four sections are Introduction to Thinking in the Classroom, Building Thinking Strategies, Integrating Thinking across the Curriculum, and Creating Independent Learners.

The first two chapters, which make up Section I, should be presented at the beginning in order to lay the foundation for the chapters that follow. The first chapter summarizes some theories about thinking, and the second chapter looks at students' learning preferences, including their multiple intelligences.

Section II, which comprises Chapters 3 through 6, is also basic to the chapters that follow. Chapters 3 and 4 deal with establishing an environment conducive to promoting thinking in the classroom; Chapter 5 presents ideas related to connecting thinking to reading and writing; and Chapter 6 considers questioning strategies.

Chapters 7 through 10, which constitute Section III, are all pathways to thinking and may be presented in any order. Each of these chapters is a way to lead students to think critically and creatively across the curriculum. They cover the following topics: theme studies, children's literature, graphic organizers, and technology. Section IV, consisting of a single chapter, wraps up the book by looking at ways that children can become independent learners and responsible citizens now and in the future.

The Glossary defines many terms related to thinking, so it is a good starting place. If the participants have a common understanding of terms related to thinking, they will be able to communicate more precisely during discussions. The Glossary is also a handy reference as reading and study continue.

Each section begins with children's answers to a question I asked them about thinking. Their ideas show both the diversity and the limitation of their thought. Some answers are right on target, but many of the answers show little thought. Similarly, at the beginning of each chapter are teachers' answers to questions about thinking, followed by the question: "How would you answer this question?" These section and chapter openers may be useful for opening discussion about chapter content. The Thought-Provoking Ideas and Thought-Provoking Questions that appear in the chapters can also lead to viable exchanges of ideas.

The Introduction is actually a metaphor, or an analogy, which compares the text to a journey. The pathways referred to in the title and the Introduction are approaches to creating classrooms of children who can think for themselves. Using the Introduction as an example, you might encourage participants to create their own metaphors about teaching or other phases of their lives.

Each chapter concludes with a list of references that provide supportive information for the chapter content. Appendixes A and B offer a sampling of videotapes to supplement professional development and selected materials for children, including kits and computer software. Be careful about investing in such resources, however, because some of them may be too structured and directive for your purposes. Above all, you want the participants to develop an attitude of inquiry and to make thinking a natural, integral part of their teaching. Work sheets that claim to teach thinking skills or kits with predetermined, single answers may actually be counterproductive.

Needs Assessment

A needs assessment in education is "a broad-based appraisal of objectives and conditions in a particular situation as they interrelate; an attempt to relate goals to existing strengths, weaknesses, and feasible changes" (Harris and Hodges, 1995, p. 163). Since no specific needs assessment suits every situation, procedures vary from one school or school system to another (Oliva and Pawlas, 1997).

One basic purpose of a needs assessment is to determine if a school's or school system's objectives are being met (Oliva and Pawlas, 1997). If there is a gap between objectives and practices, faculty members need to decide if the unmet objectives are still worth pursuing. If they agree that the objectives are still valid, they should prioritize them and begin staff development programs for implementing those considered most important.

Another purpose of needs assessment is to identify needs for which no objectives have been given (Oliva and Pawlas, 1997). If a need is discovered, such as the development of thinking strategies, school personnel may wish to begin inservice training to meet this new objective. The suggestions that follow are based on the assumption that the personnel in a school or school system have expressed interest in infusing the curriculum with thinking strategies. This interest may come from an unfulfilled goal that was previously identified or may arise from a recent awareness of the need to teach students to think for themselves.

Once interest has been expressed in facilitating thinking, a good place to begin is with a needs assessment of knowledge about thinking strategies and the current status of thinking-related practices in classrooms. Knowing what participants already understand about teaching children to think enables leaders to plan a program that fills in the gaps between existing knowledge and new concepts. Figure 12-1 is a survey designed to find out what workshop participants already know. Other items may be added.

Figure 12-1. Survey of Knowledge about Thinking

Name _____   Date _____

Rate yourself on each of the items below according to the following scale:

3 = thorough understanding; 2 = general awareness; 1 = not known

_____ Levels of Bloom's taxonomy

_____ Steps in problem solving

_____ Taba's inductive learning

_____ Graphic organizers

_____ Multiple intelligences

_____ Cambourne's natural conditions for learning

_____ Piaget's theories related to the development of thought

_____ Terminology used to describe thinking strategies

_____ Vygotsky's contributions to how children think and learn

_____ Inquiry curriculum

_____ Computer programs that promote thinking

_____ Think alouds

_____ Reflection

The form in Figure 12-2 can be used to survey how well teachers apply their knowledge of thinking strategies to classroom situations.

Strengths and weaknesses will become apparent when the results of the survey are tabulated. Teachers' perceptions of what they know and can do may differ from reality, however, so some areas may still need to be addressed even if teachers believe themselves to be already proficient.

It is also important to find out what teachers want to know or learn through professional development. You can ask them open-ended questions, such as the following:

• What do you hope to learn from this program?

• What are your greatest strengths in teaching thinking?

• In what areas do you need help?

Figure 12-2. Assessment of Implementation of Thinking Strategies

Name _____   Date _____

Rate yourself on each of the items below according to the following scale:

5 = always; 4 = usually; 3 = sometimes; 2 = rarely; 1 = never

_____ I allow children to work collaboratively.

_____ I give children choices whenever possible.

_____ My students feel free to take risks.

_____ I ask higher-order thinking questions.

_____ I let children show what they can do in a variety of ways.

_____ I give children time to reflect on their work.

_____ I help children make connections between schoolwork and situations outside of school.

_____ I encourage children to find and solve their own problems.

_____ We function as a community.

_____ My students respond to literature thoughtfully and with feeling.

_____ My students understand why it's important to think about things.

_____ I accept more than one answer as correct for thinking questions.

_____ We recognize different points of view.

_____ My students are able to reason and make logical decisions.

_____ My students use higher-order thinking strategies when they work on the computer.

_____ I integrate the curriculum with thematic units.

_____ My students can evaluate their work effectively.

_____ My students accept responsibility for their work.

_____ My students can communicate their ideas in several ways.

- What types of thinking activities would you find most useful in the class(es) you teach?
- How could you be a better teacher of thinking?

Another option is for participants to prioritize the chapters in this book in order to identify the topics they consider most important. From a list of chapters by number and title, they can rank them from 1 to 11. The results can help workshop leaders decide which chapters to emphasize. For a quick and easy assessment, participants can simply circle the numbers of the chapters that interest them most.

Another form of needs assessment is based on the K-W-L (*K*now, *W*ant to know, *L*earn) procedure (Ogle, 1986). In this procedure, teachers identify what they already know about teaching students to think (K) and what they want to know (W). At the conclusion of the workshop, and again a few years later, the teachers write what they learned (L).

Planning for Professional Development

Representatives from all levels of education should be involved in preliminary planning, particularly the teachers themselves and perhaps even parents and interested members of the community. Getting in on the ground floor enables participants to feel a sense of ownership and responsibility for the program.

Deciding who will be on the leadership team is a crucial decision, for team members must generate positive attitudes toward the plan. Obviously, you need administrative support, but you also need teachers who are enthusiastic about implementing the program and those who are opinion leaders within the school (Horsley et al., 1991).

After analyzing the results of the needs assessment(s), the leadership team needs to establish goals, select leaders and participants, determine format, schedule sessions, and identify facilities and resources. The team needs to plan adequately, but a great deal of time can be spent analyzing data and investigating resources. Horsley et al. (1991) warn workshop leaders not to take too long making preparations, or they will lose energy and enthusiasm before the program even starts. A reasonable time line allows for a half to a full year for planning and preparation, one or two years for implementation to take hold, and succeeding years for spreading the practice, analyzing how well teachers are doing, observing changes in student behavior, and modifying and fine-tuning the program. From initiation to full implementation takes about three to five years.

Setting Goals

As you enter into professional development, begin with a *shared vision*, an image of what you hope to accomplish (Horsley et al., 1991). Your vision and subsequent goals should arise from what you consider to be important as you reflect on your beliefs and values. Goals should help you to learn what you need to know and why this knowledge is important. Here are some questions that lead to goal setting:

• What do we hope to achieve?

• What outcomes do we want for our students?

• What changes in teaching do we need to support these outcomes?

• How can we define or measure success?

• What changes, if any, do we need in curriculum and materials?

- What types of professional and administrative support do we need?
- What implications do we see for school, home, and society as a result?

Goals should describe the successful implementation of the program when it is in full operation (Horsley et al., 1991). No one set of goals is appropriate for all situations, and it is important for each group to determine its own goals. In the case of incorporating thinking strategies, goals should relate to students who are learning to think clearly and critically, teachers who are modeling and promoting thinking processes, and ultimately a society composed of thoughtful citizens.

Selecting Leaders and Participants

Because leaders and participants should be involved as soon as possible, it is important to identify them early. The leader may be a local person with expertise in thinking strategies, an outside consultant, or a team of local professionals who have received training in this area. In some cases, school systems send representatives from different schools to professional development institutes. Representatives implement the strategies they learned at the institutes in their own classrooms and share their expertise with other teachers in their school through inservice sessions. You may decide to use a combination of leadership personnel, perhaps relying heavily on local leaders but calling on outside consultants when you need special assistance. In a study by Vynce A. Hines and William M. Alexander (cited in Oliva and Pawlas, 1997), teachers ranked the most influential leaders in curriculum change as follows:

- Administrators in one's own school
- Administrators in the school system
- A regional accrediting agency
- Faculty of the school
- State department of education

Although plans for professional development often look to outside consultants, teachers found them to be less effective for implementing change.

If no one in the local school system has the knowledge to conduct training in thinking strategies, however, you may need to consider inviting an outside consultant. If so, Oliva and Pawlas (1997) suggest following these simple rules:

- Seek faculty input in the selection.
- Choose the most qualified person available.
- Make sure the consultant is oriented to the task and the audience well in advance.
- Expect the consultant to be available for discussion and question periods following each presentation.

Participants are obviously the teachers in a school or school system. If participation is mandatory, all teachers must attend so there will be consistency and a knowledge base shared by all. However, when a program is mandatory, some teachers are likely to resent being forced to attend and may express feelings that negatively influence the willing participants. In a voluntary program, only positive-thinking teachers participate, so there is no attitude problem, but students may have difficulty adjusting to teachers whose teaching styles differ depending on whether or not they were involved in the professional development program. If the program has wide support, most teachers will participate right from the start. If support is divided, some teachers may gradually phase into the program as enthusiasm for it spreads (Horsley et al., 1991).

Some school systems offer incentives to their teachers for participation because many teachers resist giving their time without some form of compensation (Oliva and Pawlas, 1997). Incentives usually take one of the following forms:

- Released time for participation
- Units of credit earned toward salary increments
- Financial support for advanced study at colleges

All these incentives require additional funding for professional development.

In addition to teachers, others who are interested should be involved. The principal is a key participant, because continued support and leadership is essential. You may want to invite teaching assistants, the guidance counselor, the librarian, and other support personnel. Interested parents, especially those who volunteer in the school on a regular basis, may want to participate, as well as those involved in such community activities as scouting and athletic programs. If you decide to include people outside the school, be sure that the group doesn't become too large and diverse, or it may become difficult to keep participants focused on the task.

Whether or not you directly involve individuals outside the school in professional development, you should communicate with them about your program. If parents know that you are encouraging students to think, they may support you by reinforcing thinking strategies at home. Community leaders who work with children may want to adopt and reinforce some of your ideas, so let them know how they can work with you. Thinking strategies should not only permeate the school day, but also the lives of children in and out of school. Communication through newsletters and after-school meetings can help to inform all those who are interested.

Determining the Format

Professional development can take many forms, and giving participants choices allows them to feel a sense of control over what they are learning

(Oliva and Pawlas, 1997). A variety of experiences ensures benefits for different types of teacher-learners. The following list gives some options for professional development (Oliva and Pawlas, 1997).

1. *Formal college or university courses.* Many institutions of higher learning design courses to serve teachers' specific needs if they have the qualified and available staff to do so. They may teach these courses at the schools that express interest when there are enough teachers to make up the course. Participants can apply course credit to advanced degrees.

2. *Locally developed or sponsored professional development modules.* Supervisors and teachers may develop inservice programs that they make available to other teachers. Not only is the resulting product useful for other teachers, but those involved in developing and writing the program also benefit.

3. *Workshops and institutes.* Workshops generally let teachers work together and participate in hands-on activities to find solutions to problems that they have observed themselves. Institutes contribute information and suggestions for solutions to problems, but participants may or may not work together. Workshops and institutes may last from a day or two to two or three weeks.

4. *Conferences.* At conferences, participants attend various types of presentations to get new ideas and information in a short period of time. Much can be learned from major professional conferences, but few school systems have the funds to send teachers to distant locations to attend them.

5. *Visiting days.* Teachers can learn how to apply what they are learning by observing classrooms where other teachers have already implemented new ideas. Watching how successful teachers get their students to think can bring depth of understanding for initiates.

Scheduling Sessions

Many options exist for scheduling professional development activities, and the availability of incentives and the preferences of participants should guide your decisions. Consider also that you may have larger blocks of time in the summer for intensive inservice activities, but sessions held during the school year offer the advantage of letting participants try new procedures in their classrooms as soon as they learn about them. Try to avoid conflicts with regularly scheduled faculty meetings, parent-teacher meetings, or popular outside activities (e.g., ball games or church night). Figure 12-3 shows some possibilities for scheduling professional development activities (Horsley et al., 1991; Oliva and Pawlas, 1997; Wilks, 1995).

Figure 12-3. Scheduling Professional Development Activities

Built-in teacher days when children are not present

Several days at the beginning of the school year

Full-day sessions when teachers are replaced by substitutes

Planning periods during the year

Two- to three-week summer workshops or institutes

Two-hour after-school sessions once a week

Friday night–Saturday morning sessions three times a semester

---

Identifying Facilities and Resources

The location of the professional development program should be convenient for all participants. If only one school is involved, the library, a large meeting room, or even a classroom in the school building is ideal. If the program is districtwide, choose a centrally located school that has a room with a pleasant ambiance. Since many of the activities will center around group work, round tables with movable chairs accommodate needs well. The availability of computers, overhead projectors, and video players is also important for extending ideas.

You may want to collect resources, such as reference books on thinking strategies and multiple intelligences, to expand the knowledge base given in this book. (See chapter references and the appendixes for suggested materials.) Try to locate some of the computer software mentioned in Chapter 10, and have some popular children's books available for carrying out the activities in Chapter 8. You will probably want easels, chart pads, markers, and tape in order to record, display, and refer to ideas throughout the workshop. The learning center should also be equipped with writing supplies to enable participants to experiment with designing thematic units and creating graphic organizers.

If your sessions include refreshments, coffee breaks, or on-site lunches, you will need a room with a refrigerator, sink, and microwave oven. Providing food, or enabling participants to bring their own food, complicates matters, but most of us love to eat and need refreshment breaks from time to time. During these breaks, teachers often share ideas and extend workshop discussions in a comfortable, relaxed setting.

Individual participants may need expandable containers to use as portfolios for keeping handouts, written responses, ideas, notes, and self-evaluations. They may want separate file folders or notebooks for journal writing. So that participants can begin inservice activities with a general awareness of thinking strategies, each person should have a copy of this book in advance.

References

Chuska, K. (1986). *Teaching the process of thinking, K–12*. Bloomington, IN: Phi Delta Kappa.

Harp, B., (Ed.). (1994). *Assessment and evaluation for student centered learning*, (2nd ed.). Norwood, MA: Christopher-Gordon.

Harris, T. and Hodges, R., (Eds.). (1995). *The literacy dictionary.* Newark, DE: International Reading Association.

Horsley, D., Terry, W., Hergert, L, and Loucks-Horsley, S. (1991). *Managing change in rural schools.* Andover, MA: The Regional Laboratory for Educational Improvement of the Northeast & Islands.

Ogle, D. (1986). K-W-L: A teaching model that develops active reading of expository text. *The Reading Teacher, 39*(5): 564–570.

Oliva, P., and Pawlas, G. (1997). *Supervision for today's schools* (5th ed.). New York: Longman.

Villa, R., and Thousand, J., (Eds.). (1995). *Creating an inclusive school.* Alexandria, VA: Association for Supervision and Curriculum Development.

Wilks, S. (1995). *Critical & creative thinking*. Portsmouth, NH: Heinemann.

CHAPTER 13

Strategies for Conducting Professional Development

Four procedures for professional development virtually guarantee success in implementing almost any approach to teaching (Joyce and Showers, 1982). These procedures are as follows:

- Understanding the rationale or theoretical basis of the teaching method
- Observing demonstrations by people who are proficient in using the model
- Practice and feedback in comfortable conditions, such as having participants try out strategies with each other and then with children who are usually easy to teach
- Coaching each other when implementing the new model

The rationale and theoretical basis for incorporating thinking in the curriculum is explained in Chapter 1, a logical place to begin professional development activities. The leader should model ways to promote thinking and provide demonstrations of how thinking can infuse the curriculum, and participants should have opportunities to practice implementing thinking strategies in relatively safe situations. In recent years peer coaching has been recognized as an important aspect of professional development in order to ensure transfer from theory and practice to successful classroom implementation.

Peer Coaching

In a conversation with Ron Brandt, Bruce Joyce explained that most teachers can master almost any approach to teaching with a study of the rationale, demonstrations of how it works, and much practice and feedback. In addition, however, Joyce claimed that teachers need to understand new strategies in terms of their own teaching styles and repertoires. For this, they need the companionship and support of peers that come from learning how to help each other (Brandt, 1987).

"Peer coaching is a confidential arrangement between peers that includes a focused classroom observation and feedback on that observation" (Chase and Wolfe, 1989, p. 37). It is a way of helping teachers work together in order to help each other develop new teaching strategies (Oliva and Pawlas, 1997). It can be viewed as on-site assistance for teachers who are attempting to transfer new teaching strategies into their active teaching repertoires (Neubert, 1988). It is nonevaluative but supportive and positive. These definitions help us understand what peer coaching is, and now we'll look at how it works.

Procedures

In a workshop in Sonoma County, California, Pam Robbins (Raney and Robbins, 1989) began training teachers in peer coaching. She started by asking teachers and principals to envision an ideal peer-coaching situation—what it would look, sound, and feel like. Their responses became the ground rules for the peer-coaching activities that followed and ultimately resulted in changing the name from peer coaching to "Peer Sharing and Caring."

Peer coaching generally follows the steps of *preconferencing, classroom observation* with recorded notes, and *postconferencing*, or debriefing. During the preconference, the teacher may explain the purpose of the lesson and anticipated student outcomes, such as using effective questioning strategies to encourage students to think. The coach observes the lesson and takes notes on specific incidents related to questioning and student response. In postconferencing, the teacher and coach discuss what happened, and the coach asks questions that cause the teacher to reflect on the lesson and recall specific behaviors. Questions might include the following:

- What were you thinking when you . . . ?
- What else could you have said or done?
- What pleased you about this lesson?
- What do you hope to do better next time?

Postconferences also usually include plans for the next lesson. During the debriefing, teachers need to offer constructive criticism, give positive feedback on specific incidents, and be supportive in every way possible. As a result of this shared experience, both coach and teacher learn from different perspectives about teaching and providing support (Raney and Robbins, 1989). You may want to role play peer-coaching procedures with a volunteer from the audience.

To get teachers started with peer coaching, model how it works during the workshop. For instance, begin by modeling a preconference with a volunteer from the workshop. Choose a purpose such as broadening teaching strategies to reach visual/spatial learners (see Chapter 2). Then ask the participants to record relevant information while watching a videotape of a teacher who is doing this. After viewing the tape, model the postconference by asking the volunteer to role play the teacher and reflect on what the teacher on tape did.

Following the modeling of the debriefing (or perhaps before), you might ask either the full audience or groups to discuss how effectively the teacher on tape met the purpose. Of course, you would have to videotape the lesson in advance and secure permission from the teacher to show it.

In order for peer coaching to be effective, teachers must establish an atmosphere of trust and confidentiality. Many teachers are apprehensive as they enter into peer coaching because it is not easy for them to open themselves up to peer review. In many cases teachers work in isolation, greeting each other only as they enter their classrooms or pass in hallways, and interacting briefly during faculty meetings. They communicate only superficially, so analyzing each other's lessons requires a sense of trust and confidence that must build gradually. Teachers must feel that they can take risks, fail, and try again. They need to realize that it's okay to make mistakes and to try new ideas that get better with practice. A sense of humor helps relieve anxiety and enables teachers to laugh at themselves occasionally instead of worrying excessively about something that went wrong.

Coaches can be outside trainers or facilitators with expertise in thinking strategies, in-school colleagues with expertise equal to that of the teachers, or in-school colleagues who are more knowledgeable than other teachers (Neubert, 1988). At the beginning of professional development in thinking strategies, most teachers will have similar understandings, so they will be on a nearly equal basis. As new teachers enter the school system or as teachers who chose not to participate at first join later, teachers experienced in thinking strategies can serve as more knowlegeable in-school coaches. On occasion, they may actually join in the instruction, or team teach, to model for the novice teacher. Knowledgeable teachers can usually help teachers in the shortest amount of time, provide more relevant suggestions because they are familiar with the school, and be more available than outside coaches (Neubert, 1988). Figure 13-1 is a model for peer coaching that helped teachers move from teacher-led to peer discussions about literature (Wiencek and O'Flahavan, 1994).

Benefits and Potential Problems

Both teacher and coach benefit from the shared experience of peer coaching. Teachers are getting into each other's classes and observing different approaches to teaching, some of which they want to adapt to their own

Figure 13-1. One Model for Peer Coaching

Believing that peer coaching should complement or supplant traditional, short-term inservice, staff developers began a school-based initiative with a 90-minute introductory workshop that led to peer coaching. The aim was for teachers to move from leading discussions about literature themselves to enabling students to engage in peer discussions. Participants set dates through the year for individual coaching for those who wished to be involved, as well as for afternoon workshops for all. More experienced teachers acted as coaches to help other teachers coach students in their own classrooms.

Procedures for individual coaching included a coach working with one teacher for about 45 minutes once a week for six to eight weeks. During the 45 minutes, the teacher worked with a group of students for about 30 minutes and then participated in a debriefing session with the coach for about 15 minutes. The debriefing period was especially beneficial because the teacher could ask questions, the teacher and coach could share observations, and both could discuss the evolving role of the teacher. When a substitute teacher accompanied the coach, the teacher could leave the room and concentrate fully on the debriefing session. Several teachers from the same school could participate in this form of coaching in a single day.

In team teaching, the coach worked simultaneously with three or more teachers at the same grade level. One teacher's class became the "home" classroom, and the coach and other teachers visited this class during a designated time. The teacher of the home classroom and the coach proceeded as in individual coaching, while other teachers looked on. All teachers participated in the debriefing by discussing what occurred and what to do during the next peer discussion group.

teaching. Collegiality improves as teachers support each other, feel free to share their ideas, and find in-depth instructional topics to discuss—a far cry from teachers who work in isolation. A spirit of companionship and experimentation emerges as teachers discuss problems, frustrations, doubts, and challenges (Raney and Robbins, 1989). Teachers who might otherwise give up on implementing thinking strategies are prompted by their coaches to continue and rewarded with positive feedback for their efforts.

Peer coaching is not easy, however, and poses a number of problems. Scheduling time for conferences and observations is difficult. Possible solutions are the following:

- Having someone take over the class during the coaching—perhaps the principal, a volunteer, or another teacher with whom team teaching can be arranged

- Asking a parent or community member to teach a craft or serve as a resource person

- Having a certain amount of released time, during which a substitute may teach
- Coaching during planning, library, or music periods
- Partnering with a university faculty member who agrees to teach for you
- Learning from informal encounters

Sometimes peer coaching occurs incidentally as teachers share ideas. When I began teaching first-grade, I had never seen a language experience chart. I noticed that the other first-grade teachers were using these charts, and I found an easel and chart tablets in my classroom. I asked another first-grade teacher what they were for; she explained how to use them and why and I began using them myself. As the children and I wrote our charts, I continued to ask questions of other teachers and was given feedback. I was soon using charts nearly every day. This informal peer coaching was effective and took very little time.

Another problem, especially for experienced teachers, is that they have to modify instructional procedures. Teachers will be trying out new strategies, and they don't know how students will respond, nor do they know how they should react to the ways students respond. Until they fully understand what to do, they are likely to have doubts and concerns.

As I moved from traditional, skill-based reading instruction to a whole language philosophy, I had many concerns. I had used skill-based reading instruction with basal readers and workbooks in elementary schools, and I had taught that approach at the college level as well. First I had to convince myself that I believed in whole language, then unlearn much of what I had known about teaching reading, absorb an entirely new way of thinking about teaching, and finally implement new strategies bit by bit until I felt comfortable using whole language. It took several years!

Any change requires a period of adjustment and time for new ideas to infiltrate teaching practices. Bruce Joyce (Brandt, 1987) says that you need a three-day workshop, or the equivalent, to get started; a couple of days a few weeks later to check on how things are going and to add a little more; another day a few weeks later to polish and share; and later, a day of advanced training. Teachers may need 30 trials, Brandt claims, to get reasonably good at the new model. So much time requires a great deal of patience, perseverence, and commitment.

Another problem with peer coaching occurs if professional development is held during the summer. Peer coaching works best if at least some of the training is held during the school year so that teachers can try out new techniques as they learn them. Of course, you can lay the groundwork during the summer and implement coaching during the year.

Group Work

Working in groups is beneficial for participants for a number of reasons. Participants learn not only from you but also from each other. In groups, they often ask questions or share insights that they would be afraid to do in front of everyone. They build on each other's ideas and adjust the focus of the activity or discussion to their special needs. The same is true for partner work, although interaction is more limited. Partnerships work well, however, if only quick answers are needed or if participants are seated in immovable chairs where group formation is difficult.

Group work is important, so form groups carefully. Study groups may already exist, and participants may want to remain in them, or they may want to sign up for different groups. If assigning group members is up to you, however, consider whether to create them by or across grade levels, by subject areas, by topics of special interest, by teachers within a single school or from different schools, or in some other way. Consider the preferences of the participants when making these decisions.

If possible, include variety among group members, such as experienced and nonexperienced or inner city and rural. Groups should include members who represent strengths in different areas. For example, one teacher might be strong in setting a positive classroom environment but weak in using thinking strategies, whereas the reverse may be true for another teacher. Although group rapport is a reason for a fixed membership in groups, teachers will also benefit from changing groups occasionally to work with other teachers and get fresh ideas.

Group size is a critical factor. Groups should consist of a minimum of three people in order for members to benefit from an exchange of ideas, and six or fewer participants seem to work best (Cramer et al., 1996). When groups are too large, members have fewer opportunities to ask questions and share ideas, and some may feel inhibited in large groups. You may allow individuals to join other groups if personality conflicts or other problems develop.

Teacher study groups function well for focusing on collaborative inquiries (Cramer et al., 1996), and they can work effectively within the framework of a professional development program. These study groups, formed during the inservice sessions but moving beyond them, can meet informally so that members can extend their investigations. On their own, they may take a special idea or topic and pursue it, study related professional materials, or share classroom experiences. Each member should feel a sense of equality and responsibility for contributing to the group. Through these voluntary groups, individuals can pursue their special interests while getting support from others.

Evaluation

Two major focuses for evaluation are the satisfaction of the participants with the professional development program and the ultimate effects of the training on the students (Harp, 1994). To measure the satisfaction of the participants, you can administer a simple, open-ended instrument such as the one in Figure 13-2, or use a checklist such as the one in Figure 13-3. Evaluating the effects on students is much more complex and is sometimes done by an outside evaluator or by quantitative research. In many classrooms today, however, teachers view themselves as researchers, and they informally evaluate changes in students that seem to have occurred as a result of modifying their teaching practices (Harp, 1994). Particularly in the area of teaching thinking, the classroom teacher is the best person to evaluate students' growth, according to Chuska (1986).

Figure 13-2. Evaluation of Professional Development Activities

What are the three most important things you learned?

What changes are you making in your teaching as a result?

What changes, if any, can you observe in your students?

What resources and activities were the most valuable?

What experiences were least helpful?

In what ways could this training have been more beneficial?

How effective was the leader? Why?

What needs and questions do you still have?

Figure 13-3. Checklist for Evaluating Professional Development

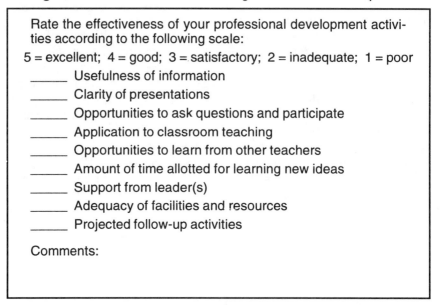

Rate the effectiveness of your professional development activities according to the following scale:

5 = excellent; 4 = good; 3 = satisfactory; 2 = inadequate; 1 = poor

_____ Usefulness of information

_____ Clarity of presentations

_____ Opportunities to ask questions and participate

_____ Application to classroom teaching

_____ Opportunities to learn from other teachers

_____ Amount of time allotted for learning new ideas

_____ Support from leader(s)

_____ Adequacy of facilities and resources

_____ Projected follow-up activities

Comments:

Realistically, you can't expect to see improvements in student learning during the first year of implementation (Horsley et al, 1991). During the first year or two, you can monitor what teachers are doing—what they're doing now that they didn't do before, how they feel about their involvement, the impact on students, and so on. You can find this out through informal follow-up sessions, interviews, and observations. There are likely to be setbacks, for progress is rarely steady. If you plan to do a formal evaluation of the effects on the students, wait until after the new program has gone through its initial growing pains. Evaluating thinking strategies is difficult at best, so make sure that sufficient time has passed for new ways of teaching to begin to take hold.

In order to measure growth in thinking, Chuska (1986) suggests that the teacher establish a baseline of thinking capabilities for each student at the beginning of the school year. Using a checklist similar to the one in Figure 13-4, the teacher can survey each student at the beginning and the end of the year to see if the students have expanded their thinking. In addition, they may evaluate themselves with this checklist.

Individual teachers can be evaluated, and can evaluate themselves, in terms of their ability to integrate thinking into their teaching repertoires. Some teachers may resist change or remain unconvinced of the importance of teaching thinking, or the professional development may have

Figure 13-4. Checklist of Student Thinking Competencies

Student's name _____ Date _____

Check those items that the student usually does.

_____ Supports statements and opinions with valid reasoning

_____ Recognizes gaps in needed information

_____ Asks unusual, thought-provoking questions

_____ Shows awareness of society's problems

_____ Self-evaluates objectively and realistically

_____ Can see things from more than one point of view

_____ Sees connections among subjects and with issues outside school

_____ Exhibits curiosity and a desire to find answers to inquiries

_____ Contributes relevant ideas for problem solving in group situations

_____ Examines various sides of an issue before making decisions

_____ Envisions more than one way to solve a problem

been ineffective. If problems exist, you may need to provide additional training. Figure 13-5 may be used to determine the extent of participation in professional development activities, and Figure 13-6 is designed to show how well teachers are implementing ideas in their classrooms.

Figure 13-5. Participation in Professional Development Activities

Teacher's name_____ Date _____

Place a check beside each true statement.

_____ Attended sessions regularly

_____ Participated in peer coaching

_____ Cooperated well during group work

_____ Read or viewed recommended resource materials

_____ Kept up with journal writing

Figure 13-6. Implementation of Ideas in the Classroom

Teacher's name _____   Date _____

Place a check beside each item that the teacher does.

_____ Communicates effectively with students about thinking
_____ Provides for different learning styles and intelligences
_____ Establishes a risk-free community of learners
_____ Values student-initiated inquiry
_____ Encourages reflection and self-evaluation
_____ Makes clear connections among subjects through themes
_____ Provides authentic experiences that connect with the outside world
_____ Enables students to collaborate

Modifications and refinements are natural outcomes of evaluation, but they should be made only after the program has been tried faithfully (Horsley et al, 1991). From faculty and student responses, you may find that the program as is doesn't fit everyone's needs or that there is insufficient funding to implement it effectively. Refinements often come from the teachers themselves after they have nearly mastered the changes, and they begin to look at the impact on students and seek ways to improve situations. They share ideas about what they're doing, consider additional resources that might be helpful, and develop a true sense of collegiality in the process.

Continuation

Introducing a different philosophy of teaching, such as an inquiry-based, student-centered curriculum, takes a great deal of time. If the concept of getting students to think for themselves is to succeed, teachers must internalize the need to change their approaches to instruction and be willing to turn over some control to the students. For older teachers in particular, whose views are ingrained from years of practice, such changes appear to be radical. The careful preparations and early involvement of key faculty members discussed in the previous chapter are important factors for encouraging teachers to promote the use of thinking strategies.

Professional development works best when it extends beyond the initial presentations. Groups that were formed early should continue to meet, and peer coaching should last as long as it is helpful. Follow-up sessions, and introductory ones for new teachers, should arise from teachers' questions and points of confusion as well as from related topics they wish to discuss. Evaluation of professional development experiences, with an eye to modifying and improving the procedures, should be ongoing. Leaders should be sensitive and responsive to participants' continuing needs, and all should periodically review goals to see if they are being met. As teachers begin to try some of the ideas in their classrooms, they should avoid tackling too much at one time. Selecting and focusing on one method or idea at a time works better than attempting several new strategies at once.

The same kind of atmosphere should exist during inservice activities that teachers create in the risk-free communities of learners described in this book. Teachers need to be comfortable enough to ask questions, build on each other's ideas, and try out and report back on new techniques they've used in their classrooms. They should be able to express ideas and share information through multiple intelligences and have time to reflect on what they are learning. What's true for the students works for the teachers as well.

Professional development costs money, so it's best to find out in advance what resources are available to you. Funding limitations may affect the amount of released time you can offer teachers, the amount you can pay an outside consultant, the types of resources, and the extent of follow-up training. Depending on who is funding your program, amounts may change from year to year according to the interests of politicians, leaders of foundations, or school administrators. If teachers set their own agendas, they may be willing to work out arrangements with fewer costs than if a new program is mandated for them. For instance, if they are committed to improving thinking strategies, they may be willing to learn together without released time or other compensation.

An important aspect of professional development is its ongoing nature. Horsley et al. (1991) identified four important tasks for the continuation of a program:

- Planning ongoing maintenance so that the program becomes a continuing part of school life
- Ensuring administrative support, even when the program no longer retains its high priority
- Renewing staff commitment and skills when enthusiasm and energy begin to fade
- Creating the capacity for ongoing reflection that leads to self-renewal and improvement

If the groundwork has been carefully laid and these sustaining conditions exist, thinking strategies should eventually become an integral part of the curriculum.

References

Brandt, R. (1987). On teachers coaching teachers: A conversation with Bruce Joyce. *Educational Leadership, 44*(5): 12–17.

Chase, A., and Wolfe, P. (1989). Off to a good start in peer coaching. *Educational Leadership, 46*(8): 37.

Chuska, K. (1986). *Teaching the process of thinking, K–12*. Bloomington, IN: Phi Delta Kappa.

Cramer, G., Hurst, B., and Wilson, C. (1996). *Teacher study groups for professional development*. Bloomington, IN: Phi Delta Kappa.

Harp, B., (Ed.). (1994). *Assessment and evaluation for student centered learning*, (2nd ed.). Norwood, MA: Christopher-Gordon.

Horsley, D., Terry, W., Hergert, L., and Loucks-Horsley, S. (1991). *Managing change in rural schools*. Andover, MA: The Regional Laboratory for Educational Improvement of the Northeast & Islands.

Joyce, B., and Showers, B. (1982). The coaching of teachers. *Educational Leadership, 40*(1): 4–8, 10.

Neubert, G. (1988). *Improving teaching through coaching*. Bloomington, IN: Phi Delta Kappa.

Oliva, P., and Pawlas, G. (1997). *Supervision for today's schools*, (5th ed.). New York: Longman.

Radencich, M. (1993). Curiouser and curiouser. . . . *The Reading Teacher, 47*(2): 173–175.

Raney, P., and Robbins, P. (1989). Professional growth and support through peer coaching. *Educational Leadership, 46*(8): 35–38.

Wiencek, J. and O'Flahavan, J. (1994). From teacher-led to peer discussions about literature: Suggestions for making the shift. *Language Arts, 71*(7): 488–497.

Wilks, S. (1995). *Critical & creative thinking*. Portsmouth, NH: Heinemann.

CHAPTER 14

Professional Development Activities

The Role of the Professional Development Leader

Once you have made adequate preparations, activities should quickly get into full swing. You have already met the participants and are familiar with the goals and objectives of the program. You have read this book and have ideas of your own to supplement the content. You will need to adapt inservice activities to the amount of time available and the specific interests and needs of the participants. Be sensitive to the audience's reactions in selecting topics and activities, and keep the format and agenda flexible. Preliminary meetings to form groups and raise specific questions will help sessions get off to a good start. View yourself as an organizer, a facilitator, a timekeeper, and a resource person with readily available materials and an abundance of ideas.

Since modeling is an effective way to teach, be prepared to model any concept or procedure that you present. Talk about what you are doing and explain why you are doing it. Practice what you preach so that teachers can understand and teach through your example.

Keep in mind the following key principles as you work with participants in order to make the most of inservice activities.

- Consider the results of the needs assessments and the interests and needs of the participants, which may change over the course of the program. Listen to what they say and be responsive to them.

- Take time to establish trust, build rapport, and create a risk-free environment so that participants will feel comfortable asking questions and exploring new ideas. A sense of humor helps.

- Keep participants actively involved and avoid too much lecturing or watching videotapes. Active involvement keeps them interested.

- Encourage them to work with partners or in small groups after they have learned something new. Sharing ideas right away helps them to remember and use them.
- Be available for questions and discussion. Encourage them to find their own answers, but be prepared to guide them in their thinking and offer appropriate resources.
- Vary your activities and teaching procedures so that you will address different learning styles over time.
- Be flexible. You may need to change what you had planned to do if participants have something else on their minds.

Working with thinking strategies can be exciting and fun. The type of workshop climate you establish should be a model for what teachers can do in their own classrooms.

Introductory Activities

As you begin, ask the participants, "When did you first learn to think? Who is the first teacher who required you to think and not simply recall? How did this happen? If a teacher helped you to think, could you use the same strategies to help your students? What are your own pathways to thinking?" Share your own experiences with the group.

Then ask, "Why is it important for students to think? What difference does it make if students spend time thinking instead of just memorizing in school? How might learning how to think affect their lives?"

Continue by asking, "Are your students thinking? If so, what are you doing that causes them to think? If not, would you like to discover some strategies that can help create a community of thinkers in your classroom?"

Then refer to the predetermined goals that grew out of the needs assessment, and give an overview of the program. Point out that the purpose is to infuse the curriculum with thinking strategies, not to teach them in isolation. Go over the Contents in this book, pointing out different topics to be covered, and refer to Chapter 1, particularly Figure 1-1, to show the importance of teaching students to think.

Ask teachers what their specific goals are for this workshop and record them on a chart for reference as you progress. As an alternative, you might want to let participants work in groups to identify specific group goals. In this case, you might give each group a page from a chart tablet and a marker. Ask a recorder to list the goals and another group member to share the goals with other groups. Because their goals may differ somewhat from those set by the school system or the planning team, you need to know what they are seeking to accomplish. Refer to the goals from time to time to ensure that they are being met.

You may ask teachers to brainstorm the kinds of thinking that can occur in classrooms. Write their ideas on chart paper and tape the charts on the wall for ready reference.

Activities for Participants

In order for participants to remember how they feel and what questions they have, ask them to keep journals. Give them time to write at the end of each session and take the time to respond to them. Your feedback supports them and helps maintain interest. Their journals may include the following:

- Reflections, which means a personal reaction, not a summary
- Applications of theory or ideas to individual teaching situations
- Questions to raise in future discussions
- Responses to chapters in this book, particularly the Thought-Provoking Questions.

Periodically, ask teachers to write on one side of an index card something they learned and on the other side something they want to know more about. Use these *exit slips* to help you prepare for the next session.

At the beginning of each session, read a children's book that promotes thinking. Encourage teachers to share what they think the author is saying and why they think that. Model efferent and aesthetic responses (see Chapter 8). As you read, model ways to read with children that encourage interactions, predictions, and thoughtful responses. In any college class I teach or any workshop I present, I always read a children's book. I've found that children's books create warm feelings, get us off to a good start, and leave favorable, lasting impressions.

Encourage participants to "show and tell." Give them opportunities, perhaps at the beginning of each session, to share ideas they've tried, articles they've read, books they've discovered, or samples of students' work that reflect their use of thinking strategies. Such sharing often motivates teachers to try new ideas so that they can report their results.

Create graphic aids, such as semantic or concept maps, to illustrate your points. Model procedures with the entire group; then allow small groups to create their own.

Expect participants to read and study before each session so that they will be prepared for discussion. Although you will model and lecture, they will benefit more if they prepare. Depending on the number of sessions, you can make assignments by chapters in this book, perhaps spending two or three weeks on preferred topics and less time on others.

Be sure to follow the lead of Chapter 2 and involve your participants in activities that cover a wide range of intelligences and learning styles.

Try to include at least three different intelligences in each session and give participants time to work alone as well as with others. By modeling the use of different intelligences, you help teachers understand how to use them in their classes.

If possible, arrange for a participant to bring a group of students now and then to demonstrate ways of promoting thinking strategies. Modeling brainstorming or questioning strategies with actual students is more meaningful than discussion. Participants may be eager to demonstrate how well their children can think. If such arrangements are impossible, however, you might videotape lessons to discuss at future sessions.

Teachers learn a great deal from visiting other schools, where they can observe teachers who are already applying many of the techniques they are learning. If possible, arrange school visits so that participants can observe thinking strategies in action. Then ask the participants to discuss their observations at a later session. If such visits cannot be worked out, you might invite a teacher who is experienced in teaching thinking strategies to explain how to encourage children to think. A teacher "who has been there" adds credibility to professional development activities.

Chapter-by-Chapter-Activities

This section provides suggested questions and activities for each of the chapters in this book. Each chapter activity begins with selections from children's literature and continues with discussion questions that encourage participants to think about the chapter contents and, in most cases, find ways to apply ideas to classroom situations. It concludes with additional activities related to the content that you may wish to use during inservice sessions. Of course, you should incorporate as many of your own ideas as possible because you will be comfortable using them, and you will know which types of activities the participants prefer.

Chapter 1: Overview of Thinking Strategies

Suggested Selections from Children's Literature

The Eleventh Hour by Graeme Base (New York: Abrams, 1989). This book challenges the reader to unravel a maze of codes and clues to discover the identity of the animal who stole the feast at Horace's birthday party. The answer is explained in a sealed section at the end of the book.

Counting on Frank by Rod Clement (Auckland, New Zealand: William Collins, 1990). By constantly posing mathematically based problems to himself and discovering the answers, the hero develops his brain so that he easily wins a trip to Hawaii. At the end of the book, readers have a chance to use their brains to find solutions to problems.

Discussion Questions for Participants

1. Do you believe that it is important for children to learn to think? Give reasons to support your answer. Look back at what teachers said about the importance of thinking in the beginning of this chapter. Do you agree with them? Do you have other ideas now?

2. When did you first learn to think in school? What teacher made you actually think? How did it happen? How did you feel about doing your own thinking?

3. Do you cause your students to think? If so, how do you do it? Do you use specific thinking strategies? What are some that you have used or would like to use?

4. How could you combine thinking strategies with lessons and activities? What are some topics that you are teaching or expect to teach, and what thinking strategies could you use with them?

5. Is it more important to cover all the material or to cover less material and make sure that students understand what they are learning? Should you take time for in-depth thinking about some processes and concepts? What difference does your answer make for long-term learning?

6. How do Piaget's and Vygotsky's theories apply to your teaching? You may want to read more about their theories in order to see the applications.

Activities

1. Ask teachers for examples of how they support student thinking. Record ideas on a chart, either as a list or in the form of a graphic organizer. (Begin with their own experiences.)

2. Brainstorm ways for students to think in authentic situations. On the left side of a chart write the situation, and on the other side record the thinking strategy.

3. Review Brian Cambourne's conditions of natural learning. Then demonstrate a lesson that includes most of them.

4. Place teachers in groups. Ask each group to select a topic and create questions about it for the last four levels of Bloom's taxonomy. (You may wish to refer to Fig. 6-2 for question starters.)

5. Six thinking strategies are listed under "Types of Thinking Strategies": decision making, predicting, problem solving, inductive reasoning, comparing and contrasting, and classifying. Place the participants in groups and ask them to work with these strategies and the sample lessons provided in order to do one or more of the following activities:

  a. Role play one of the lessons for the others.

  b. Critique a lesson and suggest improvements.

  c. Create an original lesson for a specific strategy.

6. Set up a debate to take sides on this statement: All students can learn to be better thinkers.

7. Ask participants to brainstorm a list of obstacles to thinking in the classroom. Record answers on a chart and then find ways to overcome as many as you can.

8. Use a children's book as the basis for this activity, perhaps one of those suggested at the beginning of this section. Divide participants into groups of six, and ask each to "wear" one of deBono's six colored hats. Ask them to analyze the main character in terms of the thinking each hat represents.

Chapter 2: Addressing the Needs of Diverse Learners

Suggested Selections From Children's Literature

People by Peter Spier (New York: Doubleday, 1980). This book presents a rich diversity of people from all over the world with rich illustrations of shapes of noses, types of costumes, variations in clothing, ways of communicating, food preferences, and so on. It values the differences among us.

Old Turtle by Douglas Wood (Duluth, MN: Pfeifer-Hamilton, 1992). Because of our own somewhat limited perspectives, each of us tends to view things differently. In *Old Turtle*, we become aware that all views have merit, and we gain a deeper appreciation for the earth and all the creatures that inhabit it.

Discussion Questions for Participants

1. What can you say about your personal strengths in modality, learning style, and intelligences? Have your preferences changed over time? If so, what caused the changes?

2. Identify a few lessons you typically teach or plan to teach. How could you use two or three intelligences other than verbal/linguistic in these lessons?

3. Consider your teaching style and the intelligences of your students. Is there a match, or are there ways that you could expand your strategies so that you will reach more students?

Activities

1. Refer to the section near the end of Chapter 2 that describes each of the multiple intelligences by giving methods and materials for teach-

ing, classroom applications, sample student activities, and career options. By looking at these characteristics, ask participants to think which ones apply to them. What types of intelligences are their strongest, and which ones should they try to develop in order to teach all kinds of learners?

2. Create groups and ask each group to choose a topic or theme. Ask the groups to show how to develop the topic by using as many intelligences as possible. (Refer to Fig. 2-3.)

3. Give case studies of children who do not learn well linguistically or mathematically. Ask teachers (in groups) to plan lessons that would enable students to use other intelligences.

4. Ask each group to consider what special materials enhance learning in multiple intelligences. Brainstorm lists of appropriate materials, discuss cost or availability without cost, storage, and shared use.

5. Ask participants to find ways to represent abstract concepts such as *loyalty, truth, friendship, love,* and *hate* with art. Provide a variety of media (chalk, colored pencils, construction paper, tissue paper, etc.) so that teachers can create their own art.

6. Ask participants to write interpretations of music (play tapes) or art (look at works of art). Discuss what features prompted their interpretations and identify ways to enable students to express such reactions.

7. Encourage participants to act out an episode from history spontaneously, letting them meet only briefly in groups to decide who will play what characters and other significant matters. Give them only about five minutes to prepare so that they will think "on their feet."

8. Ask teachers to meet in groups to create a jingle, rap, or chant related to a curriculum concept. Let them share their creation with the rest of the participants.

Chapter 3: Creating a Supportive Classroom Environment

Suggested Selections From Children's Literature

First Grade Takes a Test by Miriam Cohen (New York: Dell, 1980), *Will I Have a Friend?* by Miriam Cohen (New York: Macmillan, 1967), and other books in this kindergarten–first grade series. Children develop a close relationship as they play and work together so that they become members of a community of learners.

Amazing Grace by Mary Hoffman (New York: Scholastic, 1991). Discouraged at first because she thinks she doesn't qualify to play the part of Peter Pan in the school play, Grace realizes that she can do anything she wants to do if she puts her mind to it.

Discussion Questions for Participants

1. Does your classroom resemble a traditional classroom, or does it reflect current ideas? Which type of classroom feels more comfortable for you?

2. After reading about a stimulating physical environment, would you like to make any changes in your classroom? If so, what might they be?

3. Select a theme for an extended study. What supplies and materials would you make available that would relate to the theme, encourage thinking, and use multiple ways of knowing?

4. Think about your elementary school days. Which teachers provided supportive environments, and how did they do so?

5. How do you feel about sharing control in your classroom? How much control are you willing to relinquish?

6. How could you let children pursue their interests about noncurricular topics such as movie and television personalities or computer games? Can you think of ways to relate these to content you need to cover?

Activities

1. Discuss an inquiry curriculum and how it differs from a traditional curriculum. Model an inquiry lesson (teachers and students seeking answers to real questions).

2. Ask participants to redesign their classrooms to facilitate traffic flow, create centers, and provide areas for individual, partner, small-group, and whole-class activities. Arrangements should be as flexible as possible. Ask teachers to check with their students about ways to improve classroom design.

3. Let participants think of ways to incorporate authors' chairs in their classrooms. Ask them to consider where to find a special chair, how to decorate it, when to use it, and the purposes for using it.

4. Brainstorm ideas for centers that stimulate thinking.

5. Invite participants to share ideas about building self-esteem. Ask each teacher to think of a child who needs help with self-esteem and to suggest ideas for building it.

6. How could you negotiate curriculum? Ask for examples of ways that teachers offer choices, make compromises, and arrive at a curriculum that meshes with students' own purposes.

7. Ask teachers to share ways that they have helped their students accept responsibility for their behavior. What worked and why?

8. Ask teachers to rate their classrooms from 1 (lowest) to 10 (highest) as an environment that supports student thinking. Ask them what they could do to become a 10 if they aren't already there.

9. Brainstorm choices that students can make in their daily work. The teacher must still be in charge, but students also need to feel a sense of ownership. Record answers on a chart.

10. Help participants to understand who they are by asking them to answer the following questions. Once they have done this for themselves, they can do the same things with students in their classes.

   - Who are you?
   - How would you describe yourself?
   - What makes you *you* and not anyone else?
   - Are you the same person you used to be?
   - What causes you to change who you are?
   - How do other living things change? (A seed becomes a flower, a tadpole becomes a frog, etc.)
   - What changes in yourself do you anticipate in years to come?
   - What are your strengths?

11. Ask participants to begin collecting pictures to make a collage of who they are, such as a tennis player (a tennis racket) or someone who likes pizza (slice of pizza). Then suggest that they let their students do this in order to clarify their self-images and build self-esteem.

Chapter 4: Valuing the Social Nature of Learning

Suggested Selections From Children's Literature

Together by George Ella Lyon (New York: Orchard, 1989). In this book two friends share the joys of working and playing together, and they put their heads together to share the same dream.

A House for Hermit Crab by Eric Carle (New York: Scholastic, 1987). Hermit's shell was an adequate house for him, but it took the contributions of other sea creatures to make it complete.

Discussion Questions for Participants

1. Do you trust your children to stay on task when they talk with each other? How can you know if they are talking about the subject or just using the time to socialize? Is it worth the risk to have them wander away from the subject occasionally, or must you always monitor their talk?

2. Tape-record yourself during conferences with students. Who does most of the talking? How might you let students talk more so that you can learn by listening to what they are saying?

3. How do cooperative learning activities affect low-achieving and minority students in your classroom? Compare their responses in these situations with their responses in more traditional settings. How do gifted students feel about cooperative learning?

4. Is there someone with whom you could set up a cross-age class partnership? If so, what would your goals be, and how might students benefit?

Activities

1. Model cooperative learning strategies, particularly jigsaw or expert groups, and show how participants should select significant information and communicate it to others.

2. Ask participants to identify ways that talk has helped them learn and understand ideas in this workshop. Does it clarify thinking, offer new ideas, or give insights? Record ideas on a chart.

3. Discuss and record beneficial and wasteful types of class discussion. *Beneficial talk* relates to the topic, takes advantage of teachable moments, or probes deeply into a topic in order to achieve full understanding. *Wasteful talk* goes too far into personal experiences or may be irrelevant. Consider ways to eliminate wasteful talk without offending students. (Hint: When I was teaching young children, I would say, "Tell me about it later" when they got too long-winded or strayed from the topic too much. This worked. The children understood the need to go on, and they liked being able to tell me later. Often, it was so unimportant that they forgot about it.)

4. Let participants find partners and interview each other. Point out the importance of having some questions in mind before the interview and selecting interesting information. Encourage them to try to find out something new about their partners.

5. Brainstorm ways that talk can encourage thinking. Use formal brainstorming guidelines and piggyback ideas.

6. Start a book discussion group for recreational reading. Encourage participants to respond openly and value diverse reactions. *The Giver* by Lois Lowry (Boston: Houghton Mifflin, 1993) is a good choice for group reading and discussion.

7. Brainstorm some issues that you could use for debate or for the type of point-counterpoint lesson that Jill Ramsey taught. Choose one of the topics for role playing.

Chapter 5: Connecting Thinking to Reading and Writing

Suggested Selections From Children's Literature

From Pictures to Words by Janet Stevens (New York: Holiday House, 1995) and *What Do Authors Do?* by Eileen Christelow (New York: Clarion, 1995). Both books tell how authors get their ideas, how they use their imaginations, what they do when they get stuck, and how they create problems for their characters to solve.

I'm in Charge of Celebrations by Byrd Baylor (New York: Charles Scribner, 1986). Byrd Baylor tells the exciting events that happen in the southwest desert country where she lives. She records these personal celebrations in her notebook.

Discussion Questions for Participants

1. What are some metacognitive strategies you used as you read this chapter? What background experiences did you use to construct meaning for this chapter?

2. Have you seen evidence that some of your students are using metacognition when they read? What are some clues to look for as you observe the students that might indicate that they think about their thinking while reading and studying?

3. Apply metacognitive strategies to a lesson you teach. Are you making plans in terms of students' prior knowledge and experiences, finding ways to help them think about the lesson, and providing opportunities for interaction? During the lesson, are you engaging all of your students, modifying your plans if you see that they are not understanding, adjusting for individual differences, and taking advantage of teachable moments? As you reflect on your lesson, do you need to reteach anything, develop more effective instructional strategies, or find different ways to encourage students to respond?

4. What was your response to the Thought-Provoking Question about your personal meaning for the quotation at the beginning of the reading section? Compare your interpretation with the responses of other participants. Because your experiences differ, you may have different interpretations.

5. In what ways is writing a decision-making process? What kinds of choices and decisions do you need to make as you write something for someone else to read?

Activities

1. To help students understand metacognition, model by thinking aloud how to make sense of a textbook. Talk through a chapter by referring to your own experiences, selecting key points, and commenting on passages that may be difficult. Then let the participants practice modeling this procedure with partners.

2. Ask each participant to select one or two journal entries to share. Discuss how these entries enable writers to recall situations and ask them if they wish to change or add anything.

3. Brainstorm opportunities for writing across the curriculum.

4. Simulate process writing in small groups, with one member being the recorder. Select a topic, discuss it, compose a rough draft, and revise it. Ask each group to identify the types of thinking skills involved in each step. Share the results.

5. Give teachers a written selection that is somewhat ambiguous (e.g., a poem or political piece). Ask each one to write a sentence explaining its meaning. Compare the answers to see how people can interpret printed material differently. Discuss why we have different interpretations (experiences, attitudes).

6. Reading aloud from a children's book, model how listeners (or readers) think before, during, and after reading.

7. Brainstorm ideas for students' authentic writing. The following list provides some examples.

   - Make a "month book" about everything special in that month.
   - Design a greeting card and send it to someone.
   - Create a board game that you can play with others.
   - Interview someone, write up the interview, and publish it.
   - Write new lyrics for a song.
   - Design a brochure about your community, school, or hobby.
   - Write an advertisement using persuasive techniques.
   - Turn a favorite story into a script for a play.
   - Draw or write a story map.
   - Rewrite a story so that you become a character in it.
   - Make a list of things you know or can do well.
   - Write a letter to your parents about what you are learning.
   - Write a report that explains what happened in a science experiment.

- Write a set of goals for what you want to do and learn.
- Create a dictionary page about yourself.
- Make a list of things you know now that you didn't know at the beginning of the year.

9. Ask for two volunteers to read scripts that show differences between two students—one who uses metacognition and one who doesn't. Before the volunteers role play the two students, ask the audience to listen for which student is using metacognition and what strategies are used. Record these strategies on a chart as the audience gives them.

Studying for a Social Studies Test: Larry

Larry: We've got a test in social studies tomorrow, so I'd better study. Mom'll get me if I fail this one. The book is too hard for me—I can't read all the words. Oh well, I guess I'd better get started. I'll read this chapter all the way through two times—that should be enough studying.

(Time passes.)

Larry: I almost went to sleep, but I read each page two times. I don't know whether I know the chapter or not, but that's all I'm going to do.

Studying for a Social Studies Test: Bob

Bob: Another test in social studies! How hard will I need to study so that I will do well on the test tomorrow? I've already read the chapter, and we've been working on it in class for almost two weeks now. I already know it pretty well, but I'll reread it to make sure that I understand everything.

The chapter begins with life on reservations. That should be easy to remember because we acted it out in class, so I can skim over it. I have trouble remembering the names of the different tribes. Maybe it will help if I write them down.

What is the main idea here? I can't figure it out. Oh, I see. The heading is "Regional Cooperation," so it must be talking about how the states work together on saving the grazing lands. What does the word *petrified* mean here? When I'm petrified, I'm scared, but I don't think that's what the book means. Maybe I can figure out the meaning from the rest of the words in the sentence—oh, it must mean to turn into stone.

Why do I have so much trouble understanding this part about mining? Maybe I'll read it again and then try to put it in my own words. Why is this part so confusing? I can skim ahead and see if it's explained more later. If not, I guess I'll just have to slow down and reread until I get it.

(Time passes.)

Bob: I've gone over the whole chapter. I think I understand it pretty well. I'll look at the names of the tribes again before I take the test.

Chapter 6: Questioning Strategies

Suggested Selections From Children's Literature

The Way Things Work by David Macaulay (Boston: Houghton Mifflin, 1988). Here is a book that answers many questions and raises even more. It explains in text and illustration the mechanics of movement, harnessing the elements, working with waves, and electricity and automation.

Stephen Biesty's Incredible Cross-Sections illustrated by Stephen Biesty and written by Richard Platt (New York: Knopf, 1992) and others in this series. This book answers children's questions about how things (a castle, a jumbo jet, an ocean liner, a cathedral, a car, etc.) would look if you could see inside and through them.

Discussion Questions for Participants

1. Construct a factual and a higher-level thinking question about the selection on cave dwellers in Chapter 5. Why does your higher-level question require students to think? What thinking strategies must they use in order to answer it?

2. Record yourself while teaching a lesson and analyze the tape in terms of the types of questions that you and the children ask. Are you asking probing questions, responding thoughtfully to the children's questions, including affective questions, and exploring a variety of thinking strategies with your questioning techniques? What changes might you make to improve your questioning?

3. Think about the last *why* question that a child asked you. How did you answer? Did your answer help extend the child's knowledge or understanding, lead to further investigation, or open dialogue?

4. Listen again to the tape of yourself during a questioning session. How much wait time did you allow after each question you asked? Should you allow more time for all students to consider their answers to the questions?

Activities

1. Ask participants to choose a theme that they normally teach and to construct questions for each level of Krathwohl's Taxonomy of the Affective Domain. Ask them if these are questions that they have typically ask. Would they want to include them in their questioning now?

2. Ask participants to get together in groups by grade levels and for each group to choose a topic normally taught at that grade level. Then ask them to refer to Figure 6-2 and create one or more questions about that topic for each of the strategies given.

3. Review the procedure for Question-Answer Relationships (QARs) (see Fig. 6-5). Then ask participants to find partners and role play this procedure. You may base the activity on any selection from this book, or you may choose a paragraph from a content area textbook.

4. Ask for a volunteer to model Reciprocal Questioning (ReQuest) with you (see Fig. 6-6). You may use the same selection as you used for the QARs activity, or you may prefer to use something different.

5. Role play a lesson that uses probing questions. Introduce a topic, ask a question, and pursue the thought with follow-up questions.

- How do you know?
- What makes you sure?
- Can you explain what you mean?
- Does anyone have another way to think about that?
- Do you agree or disagree? Why?

6. Ask the participants to apply the creative questioning strategies used in SCAMPER (Fig. 6-7) to a story or a product. (*Cinderella* and a bicycle are given as examples in the chapter.) You might choose another commonly known folktale, such as *Goldilocks and the Three Bears* or *Little Red Riding Hood*, or a product, such as television or the automobile. See how many different modifications participants can make.

Chapter 7: Integrated Learning With Themes

Suggested Selections From Children's Literature

Ox-Cart Man by Donald Hall (New York: Viking, 1979). In this book the reader takes a trip back into the early nineteenth century and finds out how families lived and how things were made. This book connects the curriculum through story, history, science, and lifestyles.

A River Ran Wild by Lynne Cherry (New York: Harcourt Brace Jovanovich, 1992). Basically an environmental story, this richly illustrated book traces the history of life along the Nashua River over six centuries and focuses on the reclamation of the river after its ecological death.

Discussion Questions for Participants

1. What kinds of connections do you encourage your students to make? How do you help them become aware of the value of transferring knowledge of content or processes from one area to another? How can you find out if they are making use of school knowledge outside school, and how can you help them do this?

2. What themes does your curriculum guide or reading series suggest for your grade level? What choices can you offer your students within these guidelines? How can you maximize their participation in the development and implementation of the theme?

3. Choose a topic for a theme that is appropriate for your grade. What disciplines would be authentically linked to this topic? How could you use these disciplines as ways of understanding instead of as ends in themselves?

4. This chapter showed connections between math and writing, science and reading, and the language arts and creative arts. Think of another logical connection between two disciplines. In what ways can you promote transfers between the two?

Activities

1. Ask participants to form grade-level groups and choose a few topics for themes that they believe would interest them and their students. Have them identify three or four major understandings for each theme that make the topic worthwhile.

2. Let participants select a topic with a goal (such as trains and their effects on our transportation system) or a children's book (such as *Sarah, Plain and Tall*) and show how it can spread into nearly every area of the curriculum by using a semantic map. Let the teachers construct their own maps as they work in small groups. (They may want to refer to Chapter 9, which deals with mapping.)

3. Ask the participants to select a topic, children's book, or concept and brainstorm ways to incorporate art, drama, and music.

4. Model the K-W-L procedure by selecting a topic, letting participants say what they Know about it, what they Want to learn about it, and what they Learned about it. Choose a narrow topic, such as panthers or honeysuckle, so that they will not already know too much about it. You may want them to create their own K-W-L for topics in small groups.

5. Choose an episode from history or a science concept, have some resource books available, and let groups simulate (act out) what happened or is happening.

6. Let participants work in small groups to find ways to appeal to multiple intelligences as they teach social studies, mathematics, or science. Encourage them to brainstorm materials and methods applicable for diverse learners.

7. Ask small groups to create authentic math problems, act them out, use manipulatives (such as beans, rice, or straws), write them as computations, and describe the types of thinking they used to solve them.

8. Present a three-step math problem to the class. Ask the teachers to work with partners in order to record the thinking processes they used to solve the problem. Ask them to think of different ways to solve it. (Point out how writing out the operations reinforces an understanding of the process.)

9. Demonstrate the use of guided imagery to help students create images to understand scientific phenomena. Then ask each teacher to select a scientific concept and help a partner visualize it.

10. Do a simple science experiment and ask teachers to identify the concept in writing. Let them share and respond to the writing with partners and in small groups. Ask them to list all the thinking strategies that were involved in the science experiment.

11. Give each small group a thinking strategy and ask group members to think of ways to use it in a science activity. Sample strategies include analyzing information, making comparisons, drawing conclusions, developing concepts, and evaluating hypotheses.

Chapter 8: Children's Literature as a Pathway to Thinking

Suggested Selections From Children's Literature

Since there are so many possibilities for this chapter, I suggest that you begin with the selections given in Figure 8-8, "Books That Stimulate Thinking," which are divided into the following categories: mystery, point of view, imagination, values, problem finding and problem solving, and observation and discovery.

Discussion Questions for Participants

1. Ask the participants to choose one or more of the frameworks for thinking strategies described in Chapter 1; for example, Taba's questioning techniques. Apply the framework to a children's book and plan a lesson that would engage children in various types of thinking about it.

2. Review Langer's concept of envisionment explained near the beginning of this chapter. The next time you read a book for pleasure, work through the four stances she proposes (see Fig. 8-2). Can you find ways that these stances support thinking as you read? Based on your own experiences with envisionment, how would you help your students use these stances?

3. Choose a favorite children's book and consider how children could read it for both efferent and aesthetic purposes. How could you encourage children to give both types of responses?

4. How many intelligences or ways of knowing could children choose for responding to literature? What are they?

Activities

1. Ask participants what types of responses to literature they have used or would like to use to promote thinking. Ask them to select one or two responses and explain how they cause children to think about literature. What specific thinking strategies will they need to use?

2. Examine some commercially prepared materials that deal with responses to literature. Evaluate them in terms of their usefulness for stimulating thinking about literature. Which materials ask for single correct answers or literal recall, and which ask for individual interpretations?

3. Give each small group of teachers a children's book. Ask each group to find ways that the book can enhance students' appreciation and understanding of concepts or events in science, math, or social studies.

4. Ask participants to select one page from this chapter and make entries in double-entry journals (see Figure 8.7). They should directly quote a sentence from the text, then write their reflections about the sentence. Ask them to share their entries.

5. Model the Think-Pair-Share activity described in this chapter. Ask a volunteer to role play with you. Then ask participants to find a partner and engage in a Think-Pair-Share activity by reacting to something in this chapter.

6. Model a lesson that encourages listeners to give both aesthetic and efferent responses to a children's book. You may want to draw a continuum and ask participants to mark at what points they would place their responses.

7. Refer to the section in this chapter on visual imagery and observe the recommended procedure for helping readers create visual images. Then invite participants to create visual images with their partners of meaningful scenes from their favorite stories.

Chapter 9: Graphic Organizers

Suggested Selections From Children's Literature

My Map Book by Sara Fanelli (New York: HarperCollins, 1995). Mentioned in this chapter, *My Map Book* shows one child's way of graphically organizing her world through various mapping strategies.

The King's Fountain by Lloyd Alexander (New York: Dutton, 1989). Also referred to in this chapter, this book is the basis for many of the graphic organizers because of its rich vocabulary.

Discussion Questions for Participants

1. Think of a concept you want to teach. How can you represent it with a graphic organizer? How would you present it to your class?

2. Look for graphic organizers in textbooks and reference materials. How are they constructed, and what purposes do they serve? Are there some that you could use with your students?

3. Identify specific children in your class who might especially benefit from graphic organizers, and teach them how to interpret some simple ones. Observe how they react. What do their reactions tell you about your lesson and their interest in using graphics?

Activities

1. Choose a favorite story that lends itself to graphic representation (see Figs. 9-5, 9-17, and 9-25). Model the procedure for constructing a graphic organizer and explain your reasoning. When the participants understand what you are doing, place them in small groups. Ask each group to choose a favorite story and make a graphic organizer for it. Then ask teachers to follow the same procedure with their classes and report the results at the next session.

2. After modeling the formation of a concept map (see Fig. 9-19), ask participants to construct concept maps with their classes about their thematic units. Have each teacher place the main topic in the center of the map. Then the children should contribute related words or phrases, tell where to put them, show how to make connections, and give reasons for what they say.

3. Using the text as a guide, model a variety of graphic aids and then let groups create some of their own that help students to see relationships and develop concepts (pyramids, semantic maps, etc.).

4. After reading *My Map Book* to the participants, ask them to make maps of something important to them—their hearts, the different directions in their lives, their family members, and so on.

5. Brainstorm with the whole group some attributes of a thinking person. Draw a circle in the center of a large piece of paper with lines radiating from it. On each ray write an attribute. Point out that this is a simple form of graphic aid.

6. Ask each participant to choose one form of graphic organizer that relates to sequence—a time line (Fig. 9-4), sequence map (Fig. 9-5), or cycle (Fig. 9-6)—and plot a sequence of events in his or her life. Let each group member share with the others.

7. Ask participants to work in groups to develop a cause-and-effect graphic for this professional development experience. The end result might look like this:

Cause		Effect
If I participate fully in this inservice,	→	my students will become better thinkers.
If my students think better,	→	they will be more responsible citizens.
If we have better citizens,	→	society will improve.
If society improves,	→	we may have world peace.

8. Ask the participants to find ways to use different types of graphic organizers to represent concepts. A concept might be "As the temperatures and length of days and nights change, we have four different seasons." You may wish to let the participants choose their own concepts.

Chapter 10: Using Technology to Stimulate Thinking

Suggested Selection From Children's Literature

Bridge to Terabithia by Katherine Paterson (New York: Crowell, 1977). Reading one or two chapters from this book will provide background for a major activity presented in this chapter.

Discussion Questions for Participants

1. Think about a way that you could make use of a single computer in your classroom to enhance students' thinking strategies. Consider the possibilities of small group work or use of a projection screen to show the material on the computer's monitor.
2. How might you use an Internet search to enhance the study of a specific content unit and encourage higher-order thinking?
3. How can you use television and videocassette recorders to enhance thinking?

Activities

1. Brainstorm ways that computers can stimulate thinking.
2. Have participants who normally teach together consider their computer resources and plan ways to use them most effectively, perhaps through creative scheduling and by exchanging software. Ask them to work out tentative plans.

3. Evaluate available software in terms of its potential for stimulating thinking. Consider what programs to purchase when funds become available. You may want to consult the list of software in Appendix B.

4. Ask participants to reread the vignette at the beginning of this chapter. Suggest that they investigate the possibilities of setting up e-mail exchanges with other groups of school students or with college students. You may encourage some teachers to collaborate during an inservice session.

5. Create a database of materials useful for promoting thinking. You could divide the participants into groups that would seek (1) materials for children to use, (2) resource books for adults, (3) audiovisual materials, and (4) computer programs. You may want to start with the end-of-chapter references and the appendixes.

6. Ask participants to share ideas for using desktop publishing for creating a class newsletter or magazine. Invite participants to distribute copies, if available, of products resulting from student use of desktop publishing. Focus on its function as a problem-solving and decision-making process.

7. Arrange for participants to view one of the CD-ROM or laser disc programs mentioned in this chapter and plan a lesson using it that involves both critical and creative thinking.

8. Ask participants to prepare multimedia presentations to use with their students and analyze the thinking strategies that they used during the creation. Then ask them to decide how they might involve their students with the development of multimedia presentations.

Chapter 11: Developing a Sense of Responsibility

Suggested Selections From Children's Literature

Peace Begins with You by Katherine Scholes (New York: Little, Brown, 1989). Beginning with peace at a personal level, this book moves on to consider our responsibilities for becoming peacemakers on national and international issues. It deals with different ways of living and thinking, becoming involved in decision making, and learning how to solve problems peacefully.

Miss Rumphius by Barbara Cooney (New York: Penguin, 1982). Early in her life, Miss Rumphius sets three goals for herself: to travel to faraway places, to live by the sea, and to make the world more beautiful. She accomplishes all three goals.

Discussion Questions for Participants

1. What are some ways that you can turn over some of the control of your classroom to the students? Remember, they need to have some choices, but you are the key facilitator and are responsible for the learning that occurs in your classroom.

2. Explore the possibility of setting up a partnership with a local business or service agency. Is there someone you know or a parent of one of your students who would work with you? What could be gained from such a relationship?

3. How well equipped are your students for dealing with problems they face outside school? What can you do to help them?

Activities

1. Ask participants to reflect on their teaching by keeping journals. Have them write their thoughts about their lessons, their teaching styles, their relationships with the children, or any topic that evokes feelings about their teaching. They may want to set up partnerships with other teachers so that they can respond to each other periodically.

2. Ask participants to work in groups to create checklists that they would like students to use for evaluating themselves in relation to one of the following topics: self-esteem, cooperative learning, social interactions, or their attitudes and feelings about specific subject areas.

3. Ask teachers to evaluate their own learning and participation from this workshop. (You may want them to do this after each session or only at the end.)

4. Have teachers share their experiences with student self-evaluation. How does it work with their students? What do they do if self-evaluations are unfair? How much consideration should be given to self-evaluation for report card grades?

5. Form groups of teachers at similar grade levels and ask them to design self-evaluation instruments for their classes.

6. Brainstorm ways to teach students to self-evaluate. Make a list of criteria that students should consider in evaluating their work. What makes a piece "good" or "bad"?

7. Discuss the importance of self-selection for portfolio inclusions. Ask teachers to consider what they would include in their portfolios if they had to select only their most significant work. Ask them to write justifications for their inclusions.

8. Brainstorm applications of thinking to life for students outside school. How can students use these thinking strategies as they deal with difficult problems and decisions in their lives?

9. Role play a school incident, such as someone observing a student taking the teacher's pen. Discuss and record ideas for resolving this problem. What should the observer do? Why? What choices are available?

10. Ask the teachers to identify from their experiences some problems that students face and how they are resolved. The solution may not be as important as the process of solving the problem.

Appendix A

Videotapes for Professional Development

Accommodating Individual Learning Styles (Insight Media). Twenty-four-minute videotape.

Active Learning (Insight Media). Thirty-minute videotape.

Asking Questions (Insight Media). Thirty-minute videotape.

The Authoring Cycle (Heinemann). Designed and hosted by Jerome C. Harste. Eight videotapes, each about thirty minutes, and a *Viewing Guide*. Titles are "A Natural Curriculum," "The Authoring Curriculum," "A Classroom for Authors," "Taking Ownership," "The Author's Circle," "The Editor's Table," "Celebrating Authorship," and "Extending the Cycle."

Blueprints for Thinking in the Cooperative Classroom (IRI/Skylight). Eight videotapes, including "A Blueprint for Thinking," "A Blueprint for Problem Solving," and "A Blueprint for Assessing Student Thinking and Cooperation." The entire video package also includes three *Team Study Guides,* three *Blueprints for Thinking in the Cooperative Classroom* texts, and a *Staff Development Guide*. Each video comes with a study guide.

Bringing Integrated Curriculum into the Elementary Classroom (IRI/Skylight). One videotape and a book, *The Mindful School: How to Integrate the Curricula*, by Robin Fogarty.

Classroom Climate (Insight Media). Thirty-minute videotape.

Common Miracles: The New American Revolution in Learning (IRI/Skylight). An ABC news special videotape with Peter Jennings and Bill Blakemore about multiple intelligences.

Constructivism (ASCD). Two thirty-to-forty-minute videos, a *Facilitator's Guide,* and the book *In Search of Understanding: The Case for Constructivist Classrooms*.

Cooperative Learning Series (ASCD). Five videotapes (more than two and a half hours of viewing) with *Facilitator's Manual* and the book *Circles of Learning*.

Creating a Community of Learners (Insight Media). Thirty-minute videotape.

Creating and Managing the Child-Centered Classroom (Rigby). By Janine Batzle et al. Two thirty-minute videos and a *Teacher's Guide* in a storage case.

Creating the Cooperative Classroom (Insight Media). Twenty-five-minute videotape.

Developing Effective Thinking (Insight Media). Thirty-minute videotape.

Developing High-Order Thinking Skills in the Elementary School (Insight Media). Twenty-seven-minute videotape.

Dimensions of Learning (ASCD). Six eight- to twelve-minute videotapes about this learner-centered approach.

Helping Students Acquire and Integrate Knowledge (ASCD). Five twelve- to thirty-minute videotapes, *Facilitator's Guide*, five workshop outlines, handouts, and overheads.

How to Teach Critical Thinking (Insight Media). Two videos: "How To Teach Students to Seek the Logic of Things" and "How To Teach Students to Assess Their Own Work" (total of 111 minutes).

How to Teach through Socratic Questioning (Insight Media). Three volumes, sixty minutes each.

Kentucky Educational Television Integrated Learning Video Series (IRI/Skylight). Eight videos, manuals for lessons, guides for curriculum integration, and the book *The Mindful School: How to Integrate Curricula.*

Learning Styles and the Learning Process (Insight Media). Thirty-two-minute videotape.

Learning to See: Observing Children's Inquiry in Science (Heinemann). Created by Bernie Zubrowski and the Education Development Center, Inc. Four sixty-minute videotapes of children's exploratory behavior. Each video has a *Facilitator's Guide* and *Participant's Guide*.

A Look at Children's Thinking (Dale Seymour). By Kathy Richardson. Video I: K–1 on counting and comparing numbers (twenty-two minutes), and Video II: grades two and three on understanding number combinations, with *Study Guide*.

Making Meaning: Integrated Language Arts Series (ASCD). Five videotapes (nearly two hours of viewing) with *Facilitator's Guide* and the book *When Writers Read* by Jane Hansen.

Manipulatives (Dale Seymour). A series of six twenty-minute videos on math concepts, each with a *Teacher's Guide*.

Motivating Students to Think Critically (Insight Media). Twenty-seven-minute videotape.

Multicultural Education (ASCD). One forty-minute videotape with *Facilitator's Guide* and the book *Teaching with a Multicultural Perspective: A Practical Guide* by Leonard Davidman and Patricia T. Davidman.

Multiple Intelligences (Insight Media). Thirty-minute videotape.

Multiple Intelligences in the Classroom (Insight Media). Teacher's version: thirty-one minute videotape; administrator's version: forty-one-minute videotape.

The Multiple Intelligences Series (ASCD). Three videotapes: "Understanding Multiple Intelligences," thirty-eight minutes; "Classroom Applications," thirty-five minutes; "Creating the School of the Future," twenty-five minutes; a *Facilitator's Guide* for each tape, a book, and an audio program.

Portfolios (Heinemann). Created by Jane Hansen and Kathy Staley. Three videotapes, each about twenty-five minutes. Titles are "Students Find Value in Themselves," "Students Find Value in Each Other," and "Students Find Value in Their Work."

Problem Solving (Insight Media). Thirty-minute videotape.

Questioning (Insight Media). Thirty-minute videotape.

Questioning Strategies for Effective Teaching (Insight Media). Eighteen-minute videotape.

Reading, Thinking, and Concept Development (IRA). Six videotapes (more than four hours of viewing time) and workshop guide with reproducible worksheets.

Science and Technology: The Formative Years (Films for the Humanities and Sciences). Six videotapes: "An Overview," "The Inquiry Process," "Including Technology," "Science and Literature," "Using Kits," and "Child-Centered Science."

Sense Making in Science (Heinemann). Edited by Ann S. Rosebery and Beth Warren. Professional development resource package consisting of three professional development videos, a resource book, and a pamphlet describing how to film in the classroom.

TACTICS for Thinking (ASCD). Five forty- to sixty-minute videotapes, *Trainer's Manual, Teacher's Manual*, and blackline activities.

Talking Mathematics (Heinemann). Created by Rebecca B. Corwin, Judith Storeygard, Sabra L. Price, and David Smith. Resource guide and seven videotapes: an introductory video, four twenty-minute videos on aspects of children's mathematical talk, six unedited classroom episodes, and a twenty-minute summary of a *Talking Mathematics* teacher seminar.

Teachers Teaching Thinking (IRI/Skylight). A series of four sixteen- to eighteen-minute videotapes: "Setting the Climate," "Metacognitive Processing," "Structuring Interaction," and "Explicit Thinking Skills."

Teaching and Learning With Technology (ASCD). One thirty-minute video with a *Facilitator's Guide*.

Teaching and Learning With the Internet (ASCD). Two twenty-two- to twenty-three-minute videos with a *Facilitator's Guide*.

Teaching for Understanding (Dale Seymour). Three twenty-minute videotapes, each with a *Teacher's Guide*.

Teaching Skillful Thinking (ASCD). Produced by Ronald S. Brandt and Lewis Rhodes. Four videotapes: "Issues in Teaching Thinking," thirty minutes; "The Skillful Thinker," twenty-one minutes; "Teaching for Thinking," thirty minutes; "Teaching of and about Thinking," twenty-two minutes; with *User's Guide*.

Teaching Thinking: What Every Teacher Should Know (Insight Media). Twenty-seven-minute videotape.

Teaching to Learning Styles (ASCD). One thirty-minute video or a level one videodisc with *Leader's Guide* and the book *Marching to Different Drummers*.

Thinking in Social Studies (Insight Media). Thirty-minute videotape.

Thinking Mathematically (Films for the Humanities and Sciences). Series of five videotapes: "The Math Factor," "Whole Math," "Outdoor Math," "Math and Literature," and "Family Math."

Thinking Science: Work in Progress (Heinemann). Created by Wendy Saul in collaboration with the Elementary Science Integration Project. A thirty-minute videotape with an accompanying *Viewing Guide*.

Twice Five Plus the Wings of a Bird (Heinemann). Produced by BBC Enterprises. A fifty-minute videotape that recognizes children as mathematical thinkers.

Understanding Our Frames of Mind: Unique Learning Styles (Insight Media). Two sixty-minute videotapes.

Visions of Literacy (Heinemann). Designed and hosted by Jerome C. Harste. Ten videotapes, each about thirty minutes, including such titles as "Alternate Sign Systems," "Voice and Choice," "Multicultural Education," "Literature Circles," "Teachers as Learners," and "Education as Inquiry."

Why Do These Kids Love School? (Insight Media). Sixty-minute videotape.

Appendix B

Kits, Software, and Other Materials for Students

Challenge Boxes (Dale Seymour). Activity book of 50 projects that challenge thinking skills (grades four to eight, gifted).

Creatrivia (Good Apple Fearon Teacher Aids). Activity book providing students with models of how people solve real problems (grades four to eight or higher).

Design and Make Series (Dale Seymour). *Pulley Activities*, a kit with wheels, blocks, mounting plates, nuts, bolts, axle pins, cord, and teacher's booklet (grades three to six). *Challenging Artstraws*, a kit with 250 straws in two thicknesses (grades three to six).

Editor in Chief Software A-1 (Critical Thinking Books & Software). Application of language rules to stories. Windows requires Windows 3.1 or higher, SVGA, 4 MB RAM; Macintosh requires system 7.0.1 or higher, fourteen-inch color monitor, 4 MB RAM (grades four to six).

Figure It Out: Thinking Like a Math Problem Solver (Curriculum Associates). Student books and teacher guides to promote critical thinking. Available in English (grades one to six) or Spanish (grades one to four).

Five in a Row Mental Math Software (Critical Thinking Books & Software). Critical-thinking and problem-solving skills in a mental math game format. Windows requires Windows 3.1 or higher, VGA, 4 MB RAM; Macintosh requires system 7.0 or higher, color monitor, 2 MB RAM (grades two to adult).

Frog Pondering Set (Frog Publications). Kit with cards for developing critical thinking and problem solving (reading level at 2.5 or higher).

Get Me Out of Here! Software A-1 (Critical Thinking Books & Software). Higher-order thinking adventures. Windows requires Windows 3.1 or higher, SVGA, 4 MB RAM; Macintosh requires system 7.0 or higher, fourteen-inch color monitor, 2 MB RAM (grades four to seven).

A Guide to Problem Solving (Dale Seymour). A poster that presents steps in the problem-solving process (grades four to twelve).

Logic Brain Boosters (Good Apple Fearon Teacher Aids). A collection of logic-based puzzles and activities to cause children to think (grades one to four).

Mars City Alpha: A Classroom Simulation (Dale Seymour). Simulation kit with *Teacher's Guide, Mission Manual,* a map of Mars, posters, NASA bulletins, and Mission Log sheets for allowing teams to research, develop, design, and build a habitat for 25 crew members (grades five to eight).

Math Journals (Curriculum Associates). Two-page spreads for students to write or paste the problem in place, rewrite it in their own words, solve the problem, and explain their solution. Available in English or Spanish (grades three to eight).

Math Problem Solver Software (Curriculum Associates). Review and practice in six mathematical strands, including "Create Your Own Problem." For Macintosh and IBM/PC compatibles (grades three to eight).

Memory Challenge! Software (Critical Thinking Books & Software). Activities for strengthening visual-memory skills. DOS requires DOS 3.3 or higher, VGA, 512 K; Windows requires Windows 3.1 or higher, VGA, 4 MB RAM; Macintosh requires system 6.07 or higher, color monitor, 1 MB RAM (kindergarten to adult).

Oregon Trail (Library Video). Learning simulation adventure for learning history, geography, reading comprehension, and writing skills. Windows, IBM and compatibles. MS-DOS 3.1 or higher. VGA graphics adapter, VGA color monitor. Macintosh, 4 MB RAM (ages ten to adult).

Perplexing Puzzlers (Good Apple Fearon Teacher Aids). 80-page book of puzzles for improving thinking skills (grades four to eight).

Problem Solving in Science (Curriculum Associates). Multiple copies of student books on thinking, *Teacher's Guide*, and set of four posters on tips for problem solvers (grades five to eight).

Riddle Mysteries Software (Critical Thinking Books & Software). Solving riddles to find missing objects, then classifying them. Windows requires Windows 3.1 or higher, VGA, 4 MB RAM; Macintosh requires system 6.07 or higher, color monitor, 1 MB RAM (grades two to four).

Solutions (Curriculum Associates). Student books and teacher guides for applying problem-solving skills in math (grades three to eight).

SOLVE (Curriculum Associates). Problem-solving process for students struggling with word problems, using student books and teacher guides (grade four to adult education).

Solving Story Problems (Dale Seymour). A set of 100 cards with multi-step story problems (grades four to six).

Tales for Thinking, Levels 1–4 (Curriculum Associates). Collections of multicultural student books, teacher guides, and take-home books using the Directed Reading, Thinking Activity (DRTA) strategy. High-interest, low-level tales (grade two to eight).

Target Math Software (Critical Thinking Books & Software). Games involving mental math, problem solving, logical thinking, deductive reasoning, and probability. Windows requires Windows 3.1 or higher, VGA, 4 MB RAM; Macintosh requires system 6.07 or higher, color monitor, 2 MB RAM (grade two to adult).

Think (Good Apple Fearon Teacher Aids). Activity sheets for teaching basic thinking skills (pregrade one).

Thinker Task Cards (Good Apple Fearon Teacher Aids). More than 200 multidisciplinary cards beginning with a fact and then posing a question, activity, or motivator to inspire thinking (grades three to eight).

TOPS: Techniques of Problem Solving (Dale Seymour). *TOPS Problem Solving Card Decks* with 200 problem cards and *Teacher's Commentary* (K–8) and *TOPS Communication Card Decks* with 100 cards in each of three decks, grouped by grade levels, with *Teacher's Commentary* (grades one to six).

The Way Things Work (Dale Seymour). Interactive CD-ROM and book about inventions and principles of science. System requirements: Windows, 386 SX MHz or faster IBM PC or compatible (grade five and up).

What's My Logic? Software (Critical Thinking Books & Software). Mind-stretching figural and verbal games to enhance reasoning skills. Windows requires Windows 3.1 or higher, VGA, 4 MB RAM; Macintosh requires system 6.07 or higher, color monitor, 1 MB RAM (grade three to adult).

Appendix C

Publisher Contacts

Association for Supervision and Curriculum Development (ASCD), 1250 Pitt Street, Alexandria, VA 22314-1453. Phone: (703)549-9110; fax: (703)549-3891.

Critical Thinking Books & Software, P.O. Box 448, Pacific Grove, CA 93950-0448. Phone: (408)393-3288; fax: (408)393-3277; e-mail: ct@criticalthinking.com; www.criticalthinking.com.

Curriculum Associates, Inc., 5 Esquire Road, P.O. Box 2001, North Billerica, MA 01862-0901. Phone: (800)225-0248; fax: (508)667-5706.

Dale Seymour Publications, P.O. Box 10888, Palo Alto, CA 94303. Phone: (800)872-1100; Internet http://www.aw.com.dsp/.

Films for the Humanities, P.O. Box 2053, Princeton, NJ 08543-2053. Phone: (800)257-5126.

Frog Publications, P.O. Box 280096, Tampa, FL 33682-0096. Phone: (800)777-FROG.

Good Apple Fearon Teacher Aids, Customer Service Center, Supplemental Education, 4350 Equity Drive, P.O. Box 2649, Columbus, OH 43216. Phone: (800)321-3106.

Heinemann, 361 Hanover Street, Portsmouth, NH 03801-3912. Phone: (800)541-2086; fax: (800)847-0938; Internet http://www.heinemann.com.

Insight Media, 2162 Broadway, New York, NY 10024-6620. Phone: (212)721-6316; fax: (212)799-5309.

International Reading Association (IRA), 800 Barksdale Road, P.O. Box 8139, Newark, DE 19714-8139. Phone: (800)336-READ, ext. 266; fax: (302)731-1057.

IRI/Skylight, 200 East Wood Street, Suite 274, Palatine, IL 60067. Phone: (800)348-4474.

Library Video, P.O. Box 1110, Bala Cynwyd, PA 19004. Phone: (800)843-3620; fax: 610-667-3425.

Rigby, 500 Coventry Lane, Suite 200, Crystal Lake, IL 60014-7539. Phone: (800)822-8661; fax: (800)427-4429; Internet: http://www.rigby.com.

GLOSSARY

A

Abstracting Pulling out the essential ideas or message of a text.

Aesthetic response A type of response in which a reader focuses attention on emotions evoked during the reading (from Rosenblatt's reader response theory).

"Aha" experience Sudden awareness or discovery of something new.

Analogy A partial similarity between things that are otherwise dissimilar. An analogy may be stated as follows: *Hand* is to *glove* as *foot* is to *shoe*.

Analysis Breaking down a whole into its parts and examining the parts in terms of their functions and relationships.

Application Making sense of information and putting it to use.

Assumption Something that is taken for granted without evidence or proof.

B

Brainstorming Unrestrained generating of multiple ideas by group members about a topic, concept, or problem.

C

Cause-and-effect reasoning Association between what makes something happen (cause) and its outcome (effect).

Classifying Arranging items in groups according to common characteristics and labeling each group by its commonalities.

Comparing and contrasting Examining objects or bodies of information to identify similarities and differences among them.

Comprehension The level of understanding information (as in Bloom's taxonomy).

Concentration Focus of attention on the issue at hand.

Constructivism In reading, the interaction between the text and the reader's prior experiences, attitudes, and purposes in order to make meaning.

Convergent thinking The process of analyzing information and arriving at a single correct answer.

Creative thinking A type of thinking that results in the production of original ideas.

Critical thinking The process of analyzing a problem or information and arriving at reasoned conclusions.

D

Decision making The process of identifying and evaluating alternatives to a problem or situation and then selecting the best alternative, based on personal values and probable outcomes.

Deductive reasoning Considering a given generalization or rule and then applying it to specific examples or situations.

Divergent thinking Generating a number of varied responses to an open-ended question.

E

Efferent response A type of response in which a reader gains information from the text (from Rosenblatt's reader response theory).

Elaboration Embellishment or expansion by adding details to an object, a picture, or an idea.

Estimating Predicting an answer based on rough calculations.

Evaluation Making a judgment based on specific criteria.

F

Fact versus opinion Differentiating between substantiated information (facts) and assumptions or beliefs (opinions).

Flexibility The generation of varied responses; the ability to alter thoughts and ideas and to shift categories.

Fluency The generation of a large number of relevant responses without regard to quality.

H

Hypothesizing Constructing a tentative proposition or possible explanation to help understand what might happen.

I

Imagining Visualizing or making a mental image; creating new ideas; fantasizing.

Inductive reasoning Examining specific examples to find a common characteristic that leads to the formation of a generalization or rule.

Inferences Conclusions drawn from partial information.

Inquiry The process of involving students in identifying problems and seeking solutions.

Insight Sudden awareness of the solution to a problem, the existence of a new relationship, or the nature of something.

Interpreting Creating meaning by making inferences from available information.

Invention The process of creating a new product or idea to meet a specific need.

Investigation A thorough, detailed, systematic observation or inquiry.

K

Knowledge The level of recalling information (as in Bloom's taxonomy).

L

Learning how to learn Acquiring general and specific strategies to gain knowledge in a variety of fields.

Logical thinking A process that involves following sequential steps, considering relationships, and solving problems through deductive reasoning.

M

Metacognition Awareness of one's thought processes and the ability to monitor and control them.

Metaphor A figure of speech that contains an implied comparison.

Modality Any of the primary sensory systems (auditory, visual, kinesthetic) for receiving, processing, and responding to sensations.

Multiple intelligences Howard Gardner's theory of several distinct intelligences: verbal/linguistic, logical/mathematical, visual/spatial, bodily/kinesthetic, musical/rythmic, interpersonal, and intrapersonal.

O

Observing Gathering information from what is seen, heard, or noticed.

Originality Generation of creative, inventive, and unique responses.

P

Point of view An individual's perception of things, based primarily on prior experiences, culture, attitudes, and values.

Predicting Anticipating or foretelling possible consequences.

Problem solving The process of analyzing and resolving a problem, often involving a series of prescribed steps, including collecting data, forming a hypothesis, conducting an experiment, and evaluating outcomes.

Process A systematic series of actions or thoughts undertaken to achieve a goal; in education, for example, the writing process that includes several steps leading to a published piece.

Product A tangible creation; the end result of someone's efforts; in education, for example, the correct answer.

R

Reasoning The ability to think logically about cause and effect in order to form conclusions and make judgments.

Recalling Bringing back from memory previous knowledge and experience; remembering.

Reflecting Thoughtfully considering the meaning and implications of one's experiences.

Rehearsal The period of time when a writer contemplates various versions of a composition before deciding which version to pursue.

Relationships Patterns or connections that can be observed.

Remembering Recalling something previously known or experienced.

Research method Systematic inquiry into a field of knowledge to discover or establish facts or principles related to that field.

Risk taking Taking a chance by experimenting, making choices, and proposing or defending ideas.

S

Scaffolding Providing support through modeling, feedback, and questioning and gradually withdrawing the support as the learner demonstrates increased competence in handling learning activities.

Sequencing Arranging items or events in order.

Strategy A plan of action to improve performance or reach a goal.

Summarizing Reducing content to a brief form that includes essential information.

Synthesis Combining elements in a new way to form a whole.

T

Think alouds Verbalizing aloud about one's thought processes while reading.

Transfer of learning Applying what is learned in one subject to another subject.

Z

Zone of proximal development The difference between what a child can do independently and what he or she can do with assistance.

About the Author

Elinor Parry Ross

Elinor Parry Ross is Professor of Curriculum and Instruction at Tennessee Technological University in Cookeville, Tennessee. She was a classroom teacher in Pennsylvania, Delaware, and Maryland before getting her Ed.D. at the University of Tennessee. She currently teaches courses in reading, children's literature, and whole language. She serves as State Coordinator of the Tennessee Reading Association, and she participates in Phi Delta Kappa's author seminar–lecture program. She is the author or coauthor of fifteen textbooks and sixty-five articles, which have appeared in professional journals.

Subject Index

Author Index